WILEY CIAexcel® EXAM REVIEW

FOCUS NOTES 2021

WILEY CIAexcel® EXAM REVIEW

FOCUS NOTES 2021

PART 1

Essentials of Internal Auditing

S. RAO VALLABHANENI

Wiley Efficient Learning™

Cover image: © John Wiley & Sons Inc.
Cover design: © John Wiley & Sons Inc.

This book is printed on acid-free paper.

Published by John Wiley & Sons, Inc., Hoboken, New Jersey.
Published simultaneously in Canada.

For general information about our other products and services, please contact our Customer Care Department within the United States at (800) 762-2974, outside the United States at (317) 572-3993 or fax (317) 572-4002.

Wiley publishes in a variety of print and electronic formats and by print-on-demand. Some material included with standard print versions of this book may not be included in e-books or in print-on-demand. If this book refers to media such as a CD or DVD that is not included in the version you purchased, you may download this material at http://booksupport.wiley.com. For more information about Wiley products, visit www.wiley.com.

Library of Congress Cataloging-in-Publication Data:

ISBN 978-1-119-75338-4 (Paperback); ISBN 978-1-119-75340-7 (ebk); ISBN 978-1-119-75341-4 (ebk); ISBN 978-1-119-75337-7 (Part 2); ISBN 978-1-119-75346-9 (Part 3)

Printed in the United States of America
SKY10023051 120420

Contents

Preface

The Certified Internal Auditor (CIA) Examination is a program of the Institute of Internal Auditors (IIA), Inc. The CIA examination certifies a person as a professional internal auditor and is intended to measure the knowledge, skills, and competency required in the field of internal auditing. The Certified Internal Auditor designation is the hallmark of an expert in internal auditing. Wiley's CIA Exam Review Products are developed to help prepare a CIA Exam candidate for the CIA Exam by reflecting the exam syllabus and to reflect the new International Professional Practices Framework of 2017 (new IPPF of 2017) issued in January 2017 consisting of professional standards.

The CIA Exam syllabus tests a CIA Exam candidate's knowledge at two cognitive levels—proficient level and basic level—as indicated in the IIA's content specifications outlines (www.theiia.org). These cognitive levels suggest allocating more time and effort to prepare for the proficient level topics and comparatively less time and effort to prepare for the basic level topics. The scope of the CIA Exam consists of three parts described as below:

Part 1: Essentials of Internal Auditing

Part 2: Practice of Internal Auditing

Part 3: Business Knowledge for Internal Auditing

For each part of the exam, Wiley has developed a comprehensive suite of review products to study and prepare for the CIA Exam. This suite includes (1) Review Book (Study Guide), (2) Focus Notes, and (3) Web-Based Online Test Bank Software.

This book covers the Focus Notes for Part 1 of the CIA Exam.

The focus notes (index cards or flashcards) provides a quick review of the same subject matter presented in the review book but in a condensed manner to reinforce key concepts. Wiley's theme in the Focus Notes is Remember, Reinforce, and Recall the key concepts.

Wiley's goal is to provide all the required study materials for CIA Exam study and preparation in one place with one source for either a self-study or a group-study effort. Visit www.wileyCIA.com for product details and order placement.

CIA Exam Content Syllabus and Specifications

Part 1 of the CIA Exam syllabus is called Essentials of Internal Auditing and the exam duration for Part 1 is 2.5 hours (150 minutes) with 125 multiple-choice questions. The syllabus indicates the required cognitive levels for each topic denoting as proficient level (P) or basic level (B). The following is a breakdown of topics in that Part.

Domain I: Foundations of Internal Auditing (15%)

A Interpret The IIA's Mission of Internal Audit, Definition of Internal Auditing, and Core Principles for the Professional Practice of Internal Auditing, and the purpose, authority, and responsibility of the internal audit activity. (P)

B Explain the requirements of an internal audit charter (e.g., required components, board approval, and communication of the charter). (B)

C Interpret the difference between assurance and consulting services provided by the internal audit activity. (P)

D Demonstrate conformance with the IIA Code of Ethics. (P)

Domain II: Independence and Objectivity (15%)

A Interpret organizational independence of the internal audit activity (e.g., importance of independence and functional reporting). (B)

B Identify whether the internal audit activity has any impairments to its independence. (B)

C Assess and maintain an individual internal auditor's objectivity, including determining whether an individual internal auditor has any impairments to his/her objectivity. (P)

D Analyze policies that promote objectivity. (P)

Domain III: Proficiency and Due professional Care (18%)

A Recognize the knowledge, skills, and competencies required (i.e., whether developed or procured) to fulfill the responsibilities of the internal audit activity. (B)

B Demonstrate the knowledge and competencies that an internal auditor needs to possess to perform his/her individual responsibilities, including technical skills and soft skills (e.g., communication skills, critical thinking skills, persuasion/negotiation skills, and collaboration skills). (P)

C Demonstrate due professional care. (P)

D Demonstrate an individual internal auditor's competency through continuing professional development. (P)

Domain IV: Quality Assurance and Improvement Program (7%)

A Describe the required elements of the quality assurance and improvement program (e.g., internal assessments and external assessments). (B)

B Describe the requirement of reporting the results of the quality assurance and improvement program to the board or other governing body. (B)

C Identify appropriate disclosure of conformance versus nonconformance with the IIA's *International Standards for the Professional Practice of Internal Auditing*. (B)

Domain V: Governance, Risk Management, and Control (35%)

A Describe the concept of organizational governance. (B)

B Recognize the impact of organizational culture on the overall control environment and individual engagement risks and controls. (B)

C Recognize and interpret the organization's ethics and compliance-related issues, alleged violations, and dispositions. (B)

D Describe corporate social responsibility. (B)

E Interpret fundamental concepts of risk and the risk management process. (P)

F Describe globally accepted risk management frameworks appropriate to the organization (e.g., COSO, ERM, and ISO 31000) (B)

G Examine the effectiveness of risk management within processes and functions. (P)

H Recognize the appropriateness of the internal audit activity's role in the organization's risk management process. (B)

I Interpret internal control concepts and types of controls. (P)

J Apply globally accepted internal control frameworks appropriate to the organization (e.g., COSO). (P)

K Examine the effectiveness and efficiency of internal controls. (P)

Domain VI: Fraud Risks (10%)

A Interpret fraud risks and types of frauds and determine whether fraud risks require special consideration when conducting an engagement. (P)

B Evaluate the potential for occurrence of fraud (e.g., red flags) and how the organization detects and manages fraud risks. (P)

C Recommend controls to prevent and detect fraud and education to improve the organization's fraud awareness. (P)

D Recognize techniques and internal audit roles related to forensic auditing (e.g., interview, investigation, and testing). (B)

CIA Exam-Taking Tips

The types of questions a candidate can expect to see in the CIA Exam are fact-based, concept-based, application-based, objective-based, and scenario-based multiple-choice (M/C) questions with four choices of A, B, C, and D or a, b, c, and d . A systematic method in reading, interpreting, and answering the M/C questions can make a difference between a pass or fail in the exam. Moreover, answering the M/C questions requires a good amount of practice and effort.

These tips and techniques will be helpful in answering the CIA Exam questions:

- Stay with your first impression of the correct choice.
- Know the subject area or topic. Don't read too much into the question.
- Remember that questions are independent of specific country, products, practices, vendors, hardware, software, or industry.
- Read the last sentence of the question first followed by all choices and then the body (stem) of the question paragraph containing the last sentence. This is a reversal of the normal reading to highlight the key points quickly.

- Read the question twice, read the keywords twice, and watch for tip-off words where the latter denote absolute conditions. Examples of keywords are *most, least, major, minor, all, not,* and *except*. Examples of tip-off words are *always, never,* and *every*.
- Do not project the question into your own organizational environment, practices, policies, procedures, standards, and guidelines. The examination is focusing on the IIA's Professional Standards and Publications and on the CIA Exam syllabus (i.e., content specifications). Also, questions require a universal answer and knowledge of best practices.
- Try to eliminate wrong choices as quickly as possible. When you get down to two semifinal choices, take a big-picture approach. For example, if choices A and D are the semifinalists, and choice D could be a part of choice A, then select choice A; or if choice D could be a more complete answer, then select choice D.
- Don't spend too much time on one question. If you are not sure of an answer, move on, and go back to it if time permits. The last resort is to guess the answer. There is no penalty for guessing the wrong answer.

Remember that success in any professional certification examination depends on several factors required of any student such as time management skills, preparation time and effort levels, education and experience levels, memory recall of the subject matter in a timely manner, calm and collected state of mind before or during the exam, and decision-making skills. Good luck on the exam!

Professional *Standards* (100%)

Professional standards for Part 1 of the CIA Exam require the knowledge of both Attribute *Standards* (i.e., *Standards* 1000, 1010, 1100, 1110, 1111, 1112, 1120, 1130, 1200, 1210, 1220, 1230, 1300, 1310, 1311, 1312, 1320, 1321, and 1322) and Performance *Standards* (i.e., *Standards* 2100, 2110, 2120, and 2130).

ATTRIBUTE *STANDARDS*

1000—Purpose, Authority, and Responsibility

The purpose, authority, and responsibility of the internal audit activity must be formally defined in an internal audit charter, consistent with the Mission of Internal Audit and the mandatory elements of the International Professional Practices Framework (the Core Principles for the Professional Practice of Internal Auditing, the Code of Ethics, the *Standards,* and the Definition of Internal Auditing). The chief audit executive (CAE) must periodically review the internal audit charter and present it to senior management and the board for approval.

Interpretation:

The internal audit charter is a formal document that defines the internal audit activity's purpose, authority, and responsibility. The internal audit charter establishes the internal audit activity's position within the organization, including the nature of the chief audit executive's functional reporting relationship with the board; authorizes access to records, personnel, and physical properties relevant to the performance of engagements; and defines the scope of internal audit activities. Final approval of the internal audit charter resides with the board.

1000.A1—The nature of assurance services provided to the organization must be defined in the internal audit charter. If assurances are to be provided to parties outside the organization, the nature of these assurances must also be defined in the internal audit charter.

1000.C1—The nature of consulting services must be defined in the internal audit charter.

1010—Recognizing Mandatory Guidance in the Internal Audit Charter

The mandatory nature of the Core Principles for the Professional Practice of Internal Auditing, the Code of Ethics, the *Standards,* and the Definition of Internal Auditing must be recognized in the internal audit charter. The chief audit executive should discuss the Mission of Internal Audit and the mandatory elements of the International Professional Practices Framework with senior management and the board.

1100—Independence and Objectivity

The internal audit activity must be independent, and internal auditors must be objective in performing their work.

Interpretation:
Independence is the freedom from conditions that threaten the ability of the internal audit activity to carry out internal audit responsibilities in an unbiased manner. To achieve the degree of independence necessary to effectively carry out the responsibilities of the internal audit activity, the chief audit executive has direct and unrestricted access to senior management and the board.

1100—Independence and Objectivity (continued)

This can be achieved through a dual-reporting relationship. Threats to independence must be managed at the individual auditor, engagement, functional, and organizational levels.

Objectivity is an unbiased mental attitude that allows internal auditors to perform engagements in such a manner that they believe in their work product and that no quality compromises are made. Objectivity requires that internal auditors do not subordinate their judgment on audit matters to others. Threats to objectivity must be managed at the individual auditor, engagement, functional, and organizational levels.

1110—Organizational Independence

The chief audit executive must report to a level within the organization that allows the internal audit activity to fulfill its responsibilities. The chief audit executive must confirm to the board, at least annually, the organizational independence of the internal audit activity.

Interpretation:
Organizational independence is effectively achieved when the chief audit executive reports functionally to the board. Examples of functional reporting to the board involve the board:

- Approving the internal audit charter.
- Approving the risk-based internal audit plan.
- Approving the internal audit budget and resource plan.
- Receiving communications from the chief audit executive on the internal audit activity's performance relative to its plan and other matters.
- Approving decisions regarding the appointment and removal of the chief audit executive.
- Approving the remuneration of the chief audit executive.

1110—Organizational Independence (continued)

- Making appropriate inquiries of management and the chief audit executive to determine whether there are inappropriate scope or resource limitations.

> **1110.A1**—The internal audit activity must be free from interference in determining the scope of internal auditing, performing work, and communicating results. The chief audit executive must disclose such interference to the board and discuss the implications.

1111—Direct Interaction with the Board

The chief audit executive must communicate and interact directly with the board.

1112—Chief Audit Executive Roles Beyond Internal Auditing

Where the chief audit executive has or is expected to have roles and/or responsibilities that fall outside of internal auditing, safeguards must be in place to limit impairments to independence or objectivity.

Interpretation:

The chief audit executive may be asked to take on additional roles and responsibilities outside of internal auditing, such as responsibility for compliance or risk management activities. These roles and responsibilities may impair, or appear to impair, the organizational independence of the internal audit activity or the individual objectivity of the internal auditor. Safeguards are those oversight activities, often undertaken by the board, to address these potential impairments, and may include such activities as periodically evaluating reporting lines and responsibilities and developing alternative processes to obtain assurance related to the areas of additional responsibility.

1120—Individual Objectivity

Internal auditors must have an impartial, unbiased attitude and avoid any conflict of interest.

Interpretation:

Conflict of interest is a situation in which an internal auditor, who is in a position of trust, has a competing professional or personal interest. Such competing interests can make it difficult to fulfill his or her duties impartially. A conflict of interest exists even if no unethical or improper act results. A conflict of interest can create an appearance of impropriety that can undermine confidence in the internal auditor, the internal audit activity, and the profession. A conflict of interest could impair an individual's ability to perform his or her duties and responsibilities objectively.

1130—Impairment to Independence or Objectivity

If independence or objectivity is impaired in fact or appearance, the details of the impairment must be disclosed to appropriate parties. The nature of the disclosure will depend upon the impairment.

Interpretation:

Impairment to organizational independence and individual objectivity may include, but is not limited to, personal conflict of interest, scope limitations, restrictions on access to records, personnel, and properties, and resource limitations, such as funding.

1130—Impairment to Independence or Objectivity (continued)

The determination of appropriate parties to whom the details of an impairment to independence or objectivity must be disclosed is dependent upon the expectations of the internal audit activity's and the chief audit executive's responsibilities to senior management and the board as described in the internal audit charter, as well as the nature of the impairment.

1130.A1—Internal auditors must refrain from assessing specific operations for which they were previously responsible. Objectivity is presumed to be impaired if an internal auditor provides assurance services for an activity for which the internal auditor had responsibility within the previous year.

1130.A2—Assurance engagements for functions over which the chief audit executive has responsibility must be overseen by a party outside the internal audit activity.

1130.A3—The internal audit activity may provide assurance services where it had previously performed consulting services, provided the nature of the consulting did not impair objectivity and provided individual objectivity is managed when assigning resources to the engagement.

1130.C1—Internal auditors may provide consulting services relating to operations for which they had previous responsibilities.

1130.C2—If internal auditors have potential impairments to independence or objectivity relating to proposed consulting services, disclosure must be made to the engagement client prior to accepting the engagement.

1200—Proficiency and Due Professional Care

Engagements must be performed with proficiency and due professional care.

1210—Proficiency

Internal auditors must possess the knowledge, skills, and other competencies needed to perform their individual responsibilities. The internal audit activity collectively must possess or obtain the knowledge, skills, and other competencies needed to perform its responsibilities.

Interpretation:
Proficiency is a collective term that refers to the knowledge, skills, and other competencies required of internal auditors to effectively carry out their professional responsibilities. It encompasses consideration of current activities, trends, and emerging issues, to provide relevant advice and recommendations. Internal auditors are encouraged to demonstrate their proficiency by obtaining appropriate professional certifications and qualifications, such as the Certified Internal Auditor designation and other designations offered by The Institute of Internal Auditors and other appropriate professional organizations.

1210—Proficiency (continued)

1210.A1—The chief audit executive must obtain competent advice and assistance if the internal auditors lack the knowledge, skills, or other competencies needed to perform all or part of the engagement.

1210.A2—Internal auditors must have sufficient knowledge to evaluate the risk of fraud and the manner in which it is managed by the organization but are not expected to have the expertise of a person whose primary responsibility is detecting and investigating fraud.

1210.A3—Internal auditors must have sufficient knowledge of key information technology risks and controls and available technology-based audit techniques to perform their assigned work. However, not all internal auditors are expected to have the expertise of an internal auditor whose primary responsibility is information technology auditing.

1210.C1—The chief audit executive must decline the consulting engagement or obtain competent advice and assistance if the internal auditors lack the knowledge, skills, or other competencies needed to perform all or part of the engagement.

1220—Due Professional Care

Internal auditors must apply the care and skill expected of a reasonably prudent and competent internal auditor. Due professional care does not imply infallibility.

1220.A1—Internal auditors must exercise due professional care by considering the:

- Extent of work needed to achieve the engagement's objectives.
- Relative complexity, materiality, or significance of matters to which assurance procedures are applied.
- Adequacy and effectiveness of governance, risk management, and control processes.
- Probability of significant errors, fraud, or noncompliance.
- Cost of assurance in relation to potential benefits.

1220.A2—In exercising due professional care, internal auditors must consider the use of technology-based audit and other data analysis techniques.

1220.A3—Internal auditors must be alert to the significant risks that might affect objectives, operations, or resources. However, assurance procedures alone, even when performed with due professional care, do not guarantee that all significant risks will be identified.

1220—Due Professional Care (continued)

1220.C1—Internal auditors must exercise due professional care during a consulting engagement by considering the:

- Needs and expectations of clients, including the nature, timing, and communication of engagement results.
- Relative complexity and extent of work needed to achieve the engagement's objectives.
- Cost of the consulting engagement in relation to potential benefits.

1230—Continuing Professional Development

Internal auditors must enhance their knowledge, skills, and other competencies through continuing professional development.

1300—Quality Assurance and Improvement Program

The chief audit executive must develop and maintain a quality assurance and improvement program that covers all aspects of the internal audit activity.

Interpretation:
A quality assurance and improvement program is designed to enable an evaluation of the internal audit activity's conformance with the *Standards* and an evaluation of whether internal auditors apply the Code of Ethics. The program also assesses the efficiency and effectiveness of the internal audit activity and identifies opportunities for improvement. The chief audit executive should encourage board oversight in the quality assurance and improvement program.

1310—Requirements of the Quality Assurance and Improvement Program

The quality assurance and improvement program must include both internal and external assessments.

1311—Internal Assessments

Internal assessments must include:

- Ongoing monitoring of the performance of the internal audit activity.
- Periodic self-assessments or assessments by other persons within the organization with sufficient knowledge of internal audit practices.

Interpretation:
Ongoing monitoring is an integral part of the day-to-day supervision, review, and measurement of the internal audit activity. Ongoing monitoring is incorporated into the routine policies and practices used to manage the internal audit activity and uses processes, tools, and information considered necessary to evaluate conformance with the Code of Ethics and the *Standards*.

Periodic assessments are conducted to evaluate conformance with the Code of Ethics and the *Standards*.

Sufficient knowledge of internal audit practices requires at least an understanding of all elements of the International Professional Practices Framework.

1312—External Assessments

External assessments must be conducted at least once every five years by a qualified, independent assessor or assessment team from outside the organization. The chief audit executive must discuss with the board:

- The form and frequency of external assessment.
- The qualifications and independence of the external assessor or assessment team, including any potential conflict of interest.

Interpretation:

External assessments may be accomplished through a full external assessment or a self-assessment with independent external validation. The external assessor must conclude as to conformance with the Code of Ethics and the *Standards*; the external assessment may also include operational or strategic comments.

A qualified assessor or assessment team demonstrates competence in two areas: the professional practice of internal auditing and the external assessment process. Competence can be demonstrated through a mixture of experience and theoretical learning. Experience gained in organizations of similar size, complexity, sector, or industry, and technical issues is more valuable than less relevant

1312—External Assessments (continued)

experience. In the case of an assessment team, not all members of the team need to have all the competencies; it is the team as a whole that is qualified. The chief audit executive uses professional judgment when assessing whether an assessor or assessment team demonstrates sufficient competence to be qualified.

An independent assessor or assessment team means not having either an actual or a perceived conflict of interest and not being a part of, or under the control of, the organization to which the internal audit activity belongs. The chief audit executive should encourage board oversight in the external assessment to reduce perceived or potential conflicts of interest.

1320—Reporting on the Quality Assurance and Improvement Program

The chief audit executive must communicate the results of the quality assurance and improvement program to senior management and the board. Disclosure should include:

- The scope and frequency of both the internal and external assessments.
- The qualifications and independence of the assessor(s) or assessment team, including potential conflicts of interest.
- Conclusions of assessors.
- Corrective action plans.

Interpretation:
The form, content, and frequency of communicating the results of the quality assurance and improvement program is established through discussions with senior management and the board and considers the responsibilities of the internal audit activity and chief audit executive as contained in the internal audit charter. To demonstrate conformance with the Code of Ethics and the *Standards,* the results of external and periodic internal assessments are communicated upon completion of such assessments, and the results of ongoing monitoring are communicated at least annually. The results include the assessor's or assessment team's evaluation with respect to the degree of conformance.

1321—Use of "Conforms with the International *Standards* for the Professional Practice of Internal Auditing"

Indicating that the internal audit activity conforms with the *International Standards for the Professional Practice of Internal Auditing* is appropriate only if supported by the results of the quality assurance and improvement program.

Interpretation:
The internal audit activity conforms with the Code of Ethics and the *Standards* when it achieves the outcomes described therein. The results of the quality assurance and improvement program include the results of both internal and external assessments. All internal audit activities will have the results of internal assessments. Internal audit activities in existence for at least five years will also have the results of external assessments.

1322—Disclosure of Nonconformance

When nonconformance with the Code of Ethics or the *Standards* impacts the overall scope or operation of the internal audit activity, the chief audit executive must disclose the nonconformance and the impact to senior management and the board.

PERFORMANCE *STANDARDS*

2100—Nature of Work

The internal audit activity must evaluate and contribute to the improvement of the organization's governance, risk management, and control processes using a systematic, disciplined, and risk-based approach. Internal audit credibility and value are enhanced when auditors are proactive and their evaluations offer new insights and consider future impact.

2110—Governance

The internal audit activity must assess and make appropriate recommendations to improve the organization's governance processes for:

- Making strategic and operational decisions.
- Overseeing risk management and control.
- Promoting appropriate ethics and values within the organization.
- Ensuring effective organizational performance management and accountability.

2110—Governance (continued)

- Communicating risk and control information to appropriate areas of the organization.
- Coordinating the activities of, and communicating information among, the board, external and internal auditors, other assurance providers, and management.

> **2110.A1**—The internal audit activity must evaluate the design, implementation, and effectiveness of the organization's ethics-related objectives, programs, and activities.
>
> **2110.A2**—The internal audit activity must assess whether the information technology governance of the organization supports the organization's strategies and objectives.

2120—Risk Management

The internal audit activity must evaluate the effectiveness and contribute to the improvement of risk management processes.

Interpretation:
Determining whether risk management processes are effective is a judgment resulting from the internal auditor's assessment that:

- Organizational objectives support and align with the organization's mission.
- Significant risks are identified and assessed.
- Appropriate risk responses are selected that align risks with the organization's risk appetite.
- Relevant risk information is captured and communicated in a timely manner across the organization, enabling staff, management, and the board to carry out their responsibilities.

The internal audit activity may gather the information to support this assessment during multiple engagements. The results of these engagements, when viewed together, provide an understanding of the organization's risk management processes and their effectiveness.

Risk management processes are monitored through ongoing management activities, separate evaluations, or both.

2120—Risk Management (continued)

2120.A1—The internal audit activity must evaluate risk exposures relating to the organization's governance, operations, and information systems regarding the:

- Achievement of the organization's strategic objectives.
- Reliability and integrity of financial and operational information.
- Effectiveness and efficiency of operations and programs.
- Safeguarding of assets.
- Compliance with laws, regulations, policies, procedures, and contracts.

2120.A2—The internal audit activity must evaluate the potential for the occurrence of fraud and how the organization manages fraud risk.

2120.C1—During consulting engagements, internal auditors must address risk consistent with the engagement's objectives and be alert to the existence of other significant risks.

2120—Risk Management (continued)

2120.C2—Internal auditors must incorporate knowledge of risks gained from consulting engagements into their evaluation of the organization's risk management processes.

2120.C3—When assisting management in establishing or improving risk management processes, internal auditors must refrain from assuming any management responsibility by actually managing risks.

2130—Control

The internal audit activity must assist the organization in maintaining effective controls by evaluating their effectiveness and efficiency and by promoting continuous improvement.

2130.A1—The internal audit activity must evaluate the adequacy and effectiveness of controls in responding to risks within the organization's governance, operations, and information systems regarding the:

- Achievement of the organization's strategic objectives.
- Reliability and integrity of financial and operational information.
- Effectiveness and efficiency of operations and programs.
- Safeguarding of assets.
- Compliance with laws, regulations, policies, procedures, and contracts.

2130.C1—Internal auditors must incorporate knowledge of controls gained from consulting engagements into evaluation of the organization's control processes.

MISSION OF INTERNAL AUDIT

The Mission of Internal Audit articulates what internal audit aspires to accomplish within an organization. Its place in the new International Professional Practices Framework – 2017 (new IPPF of 2017) is deliberate, demonstrating how practitioners should leverage the entire framework to facilitate their ability to achieve the mission.

> The mission of internal audit is to enhance and protect organizational value by providing risk-based and objective assurance, advice, and insight.

DEFINITION OF INTERNAL AUDITING

The Definition of Internal Auditing states the fundamental purpose, nature, and scope of internal auditing:

> Internal auditing is an independent, objective assurance and consulting activity designed to add value and improve an organization's operations. It helps an organization accomplish its objectives by bringing a systematic, disciplined approach to evaluate and improve the effectiveness of risk management, control, and governance processes.

Internal audit activity is defined as a department, division, function, team of auditors, team of consultants, or other practitioner(s) that provides independent, objective assurance and consulting services designed to add value and improve an organization's operations. The internal audit activity helps an organization accomplish its objectives by bringing a systematic, disciplined approach to evaluate and improve the effectiveness of governance, risk management, and control (GRC) processes.

Internal audit function is a separate function in an organization similar to other functions, such as manufacturing, marketing, service, procurement, accounting, human resources, information technology, and finance. The internal audit department employs several individuals with different job titles to conduct audits, including staff auditor, engagement auditor, in-charge auditor, lead auditor, senior auditor, supervisor, audit manager, and audit director.

DEFINITION OF INTERNAL AUDITING (CONTINUED)

Add value refers to asking what type of value and how much value an internal audit activity is adding to an organization. The internal audit activity adds value when:

- Its charter aligns with the audit committee's charter.
- Its charter is built around and derived from the audit committee's charter.
- Its charter's alignment with the audit committee's charter demonstrates integrity, objectivity, and independence of the internal audit activity.
- Its internal quality assurance assessments are combined with external quality assurance assessments.
- Its yearly, short-term audit plan (current and future) aligns with its long-term strategic plan for the internal audit activity.
- Its long-term strategic plan aligns and integrates with the organization's long-term strategic plan.
- It provides objective and relevant assurance services and consulting services to all of its stakeholders.
- It contributes to the effectiveness and efficiency of GRC processes.
- It hires, promotes, and retains highly skilled and competent auditors with continuing professional development.

DEFINITION OF INTERNAL AUDITING (CONTINUED)

Simply stated, internal audit adds value to the organization when it makes highly significant, high-impact, and high-quality audit recommendations to audit clients through audit work. Significant recommendations are big in scope (nature and extent), size (magnitude), and strength (impact), which is in line with the Pareto principle of the vital few (20%) and the trivial many (80%), representing Pareto's rule of 20/80 or 80/20.

Moreover, value is added when the audit client's business operations are improved, policies are strengthened, procedures are simplified, processes are streamlined, practices match best practices, costs are decreased, revenues are increased, profits are increased, earnings per share are increased, market price per share is increased, employee morale is increased, customers are satisfied, actual risks are controlled, potential risks are avoided or minimized, supply chains are strengthened, regulations are complied with, and competitors are made jealous. This value is seen either directly or indirectly from internal audits.

Value is not added or enhanced until the audit client's management fully accepts and implements the internal auditors' recommendations. The audit client's acceptance is not guaranteed because it depends on whether the auditors' recommendations will help or hurt the audit client's business function. Value is not added when auditors make nitpicking findings and give token recommendations that waste resources, resulting from surface audits (superficial audits) using a checklist approach.

CORE PRINCIPLES

The **Core Principles** (CPs) of internal auditing, taken as a whole, articulate internal audit effectiveness. For an internal audit function to be considered effective, all Principles should be present and operating effectively. How an internal auditor, as well as an internal audit activity, demonstrates achievement of the Core Principles may be quite different from organization to organization, but failure to achieve any of the Principles would imply that an internal audit activity was not as effective as it could be in achieving internal audit's mission. The Core Principles are the foundation for internal audit's framework and support the internal audit's effectiveness.

A set of 10 Core Principles comprise the fundamentals essential to the effective practice of internal auditing. They are the foundational underpinnings of the Code of Ethics and the *Standards*, reflecting the primary requirements for the professional practice of internal auditing now and in the future. The Core Principles can be used as a benchmark against which to gauge the effectiveness of an internal audit activity. Thus, the Core Principles should be well expressed throughout the Code of Ethics and the *Standards*.

CP1: Demonstrates integrity

CP2: Demonstrates competence and due professional care

CP3: Is objective and free from undue influence (independent)

CP4: Aligns with the strategies, objectives, and risks of the organization

CORE PRINCIPLES (CONTINUED)

CP5: Is appropriately positioned and adequately resourced

CP6: Demonstrates quality and continuous improvement

CP7: Communicates effectively

CP8: Provides risk-based assurance

CP9: Is insightful, proactive, and future-focused

CP10: Promotes organizational improvement

INTERNAL AUDIT CHARTER

Each internal audit function should have an internal audit charter (the charter) that describes the purpose, authority, and responsibility of the internal audit function. An audit charter should include the following critical components:

- The objectives and scope of the internal audit function
- The internal audit function's management reporting (i.e., functional and administrative reporting) position within the organization, as well as its authority and responsibilities
- The responsibility and accountability of the chief audit executive (CAE)
- The internal audit function's responsibility to evaluate the effectiveness of the organization's GRC processes

The charter should be approved by the audit committee of the organization's board of directors. The charter should provide the internal audit function with the authorization to access the organization's records, personnel, and physical properties relevant to the performance of internal audit procedures, including the authority to examine any activities or entities. Periodically, the CAE should evaluate whether the charter continues to be adequate, requesting the approval of the audit committee for any revisions. The charter should define the criteria for when and how the internal audit function may outsource its work to external experts.

INTERNAL AUDIT CHARTER (CONTINUED)

The charter is an internal company document and is not an external legal document. It is a formal and critical document, and it is a blueprint or roadmap for the internal audit activity because it contains the agreed-upon purpose, authority, and responsibility of an internal audit activity. In essence, the charter describes how the internal audit department performs and manages its work activities and how it operates in the short term and the long term. As such, the audit charter must be created with a clear understanding of the internal audit function.

Specifically, the charter document should define these elements:

- Objectives, purpose, scope, position (status), roles, and responsibilities of the internal audit activity, including its expectations by the board and senior management
- Functional and administrative reporting lines within the management's hierarchy, including the level of authority and organizational placement
- Authority and budget are given to access records (physical and electronic), property (tangible and intangible), and personnel (internal and external) in order to perform audit engagements

INTERNAL AUDIT CHARTER (CONTINUED)

Specifically, the charter document should require or describe these elements:

- The scope and nature of the CAE's nonaudit responsibilities, which can be either short term or long term (i.e., ongoing). Short-term nonaudit responsibilities require transition plans and require no changes to the charter. Long-term nonaudit responsibilities require no transition plans and require changes to the charter. In a way, all long-term changes to the CAE's roles and responsibilities are required to be documented in the charter (e.g., from audit work to nonaudit work and vice versa) with safeguards established to protect auditors' independence and objectivity. A **transition plan** states how an internal audit department moves its nonaudit responsibilities back to an organization's functional management.

  Short Term ⟶ Transition Plan Required ⟶ No Change to Audit Charter Required

  Long Term ⟶ No Transition Plan Required ⟶ Change to Audit Charter Required

  with Safeguards Established to Protect Independence and Objectivity

- The charter requires an internal audit plan that includes known audits (based on previous years) as well as unknown audits (unanticipated audits or special request projects), requiring contingency plans, such as enforce Plan B if Plan A does not work.
- The charter requires a financial budget that includes known costs and expenditures as well as unknown costs and expenditures, requiring contingency costs and expenditures.

INTERNAL AUDIT CHARTER (CONTINUED)

- The charter requires a staff budget that includes internal staff (in-source) as well as external staff (co-source or outsource), requiring contingency staffing plans for handling emergencies and unexpected events.
- The charter requires a talent budget that includes the requirement and availability of internal staff's skill sets (e.g., education, knowledge, experience, and hard/soft skills) and external staff's skill sets (e.g., costs, risks, deliverables, expectations, education, knowledge, experience, and hard/soft skills). **Internal staff** includes internal auditors and noninternal auditors working within a company. **External staff** includes audit consultants, audit contractors, and external auditors.
  - **Hard skills** are mostly quantitative in nature and include these:
    - Analytical skills
    - Technical skills
    - Functional skills
    - Problem identification and solving skills
    - Decision-making skills

INTERNAL AUDIT CHARTER (CONTINUED)

  - Managing skills
  - Application skills
  - Integration skills

  Higher-level managers and executives need more depth in soft skills and soft controls and less depth in hard skills and hard controls. Lower-level managers and executives need more depth in hard skills and hard controls and less depth in soft skills and soft controls.

- **Soft skills** are mostly qualitative in nature and include these:
  - People skills (interpersonal skills)
  - Motivation skills
  - Leadership skills
  - Communications skills
  - Presentation skills
  - Coordination skills

INTERNAL AUDIT CHARTER (CONTINUED)

  - Project management skills
  - Implementation skills
  - Time-management skills
  - Creative skills
  - Critical-thinking skills

- The charter describes communications plans and protocols to be used when communicating audit work results (e.g., audit memos, letters, and reports) to the appropriate internal and external parties. These communication plans indicate the media, format, frequency, and recipients of various communications (e.g., what, how, when, and to whom to communicate).
- The charter requires that the CAE discuss the IIA's Mission and adherence to Mandatory Guidance with the board and senior management.

TYPES OF AUDIT SERVICES

The IIA's Implementation *Standards* define two types of audit services and include assurance services and consulting services. Each type of services is described next.

Assurance Services

Assurance services involve the internal auditor's objective assessment of evidence to provide opinions or conclusions regarding an entity, operation, function, process, system, or other subject matters. The nature and scope of an assurance engagement are determined by the internal auditor. Generally, three parties are participants in assurance services:

1. The person or group directly involved with the entity, operation, function, process, system or other subject matter—the process owner and/or the audit client
2. The person or group making the assessment—the internal auditor
3. The person or group using the assessment—the user (e.g., audit client, management, and outside parties)

In summary, assurance services are an objective examination of evidence for the purpose of providing an independent assessment on governance, risk management, and control processes for the organization. Examples of assurance services may include operational audits, financial audits, performance audits, compliance audits, and system security and privacy audits.

Consulting Services

Consulting services are advisory in nature and are generally performed at the specific request of an engagement client. The nature and scope of the consulting engagement are subject to agreement with the engagement client. Consulting services generally involve two parties: the person or group offering the advice—the internal auditor—and the person or group seeking and receiving the advice (the engagement client). When performing consulting services, the internal auditor should maintain objectivity and not assume management responsibility.

In summary, consulting services are advisory in nature and provide great insights to clients. The nature and scope of these services are agreed with the client in advance and are intended to add value and improve an organization's governance, risk management, and control processes without the internal auditor assuming management responsibility. Examples of consulting services may include counsel, advice, facilitation, and training.

IIA'S CODE OF ETHICS

The IIA's Code of Ethics comprises broad principles relevant to the profession and practice of internal auditing and more specific rules of conduct, which describe the behavior expected of both entities and individuals who perform internal audit services in accordance with the Definition of Internal Auditing (including IIA members, recipients of IIA certifications, and certification candidates). The purpose of the Code of Ethics is to promote an ethical culture in the global profession of internal auditing.

Code of Ethics is a statement of the principles and expectations governing the behavior of individuals and organizations in the conduct of internal auditing. It is a description of the minimum requirements for conduct. The Code describes behavioral expectations rather than specific activities.

Introduction to the Code of Ethics

The purpose of the IIA's Code of Ethics is to promote an ethical culture in the profession of internal auditing. A code of ethics is necessary and appropriate for the profession of internal auditing, founded as it is on the trust placed in its objective assurance about governance, risk management, and control.

Introduction to the Code of Ethics (continued)

The Code of Ethics extends beyond the Definition of Internal Auditing to include two essential components:

1. Principles that are relevant to the profession and practice of internal auditing.
2. Rules of Conduct that describe behavior norms expected of internal auditors. These rules are an aid to interpreting the Principles into practical applications and are intended to guide the ethical conduct of internal auditors.

"Internal auditors" refers to IIA members, recipients of or candidates for IIA professional certifications, and those who perform internal audit services within the Definition of Internal Auditing.

Applicability and Enforcement of the Code of Ethics

This Code of Ethics applies to both entities and individuals that perform internal audit services. For IIA members and recipients of or candidates for IIA professional certifications, breaches of the Code of Ethics will be evaluated and administered according to the IIA's Bylaws and Administrative Directives. The fact that a particular conduct is not mentioned in the Rules of Conduct does not prevent it from being unacceptable or discreditable, and therefore, the member, certification holder, or candidate can be liable for disciplinary action.

Applicability and Enforcement of the Code of Ethics (continued)

Principles and Rules of Conduct

1. Integrity
2. Objectivity
3. Confidentiality
4. Competency

ROLES AND RESPONSIBILITIES OF MANAGEMENT

Internal auditors, whether they are staff auditors, senior auditors, audit supervisors, audit managers, or audit directors, need to know the roles and responsibilities of their organization's management hierarchy in order to do their work properly during audit engagements, from audit planning to audit reporting.

When internal auditors conduct their audit work, they (1) deal directly with the functional managers as they are the primary, day-to-day, audit clients (audit customers) and (2) deal indirectly with the senior managers as they are the secondary audit clients. The board can be thought of as the final audit client. Here, management hierarchy is that functional managers report to senior managers (e.g., chief executive officer) who in turn report to the board. The level of audit contact is shown next:

Functional managers = First level of audit contact

Senior managers = Second level of audit contact

Board members = Last level of audit contact

Domain 2: Independence and Objectivity (15%)

This domain defines several major theoretical topics, such as independence and objectivity, including their impairments and threats. It presents the required elements of independence and relationships between independence and objectivity and between independence and ethics. The domain also summarizes various threatening and supporting factors in independence and objectivity and lists policies to promote objectivity.

INDEPENDENCE DEFINED

Independence is defined as the freedom from conditions that threaten the ability of the internal audit activity to carry out internal audit responsibilities in an unbiased manner. Independence allows internal auditors to carry out their work freely and objectively. This concept requires that internal auditors be independent of the activities they audit. Independence is achieved through organizational status and objectivity. It is the freedom from conditions that threaten the ability of the internal audit activity to carry out internal audit responsibilities in an unbiased manner. Simply stated, independence can come across as appearance that can be real or imaginary in the eyes of others.

Two professional attributes of internal auditors and internal audit activity are independence and objectivity, where organizational independence deals with the internal audit activity and individual objectivity deals with the internal auditors.

Independence ⟶ Internal Audit Activity

Objectivity ⟶ Internal Auditors

Internal audit activity is an independent function supporting an organization's business strategies and objectives and evaluating the effectiveness of governance, risk management, and control processes. The structure of an internal audit activity should be organized so that its board of directors (directors) has confidence that the

INDEPENDENCE DEFINED (CONTINUED)

internal audit activity can be impartial and not unduly influenced by senior managers and functional managers in day-to-day operations.

In this regard, the chief audit executive (CAE), internal audit director, or internal audit manager should not have any responsibility for operating the system of internal control and should report functionally to the audit committee.

The CAE is functionally accountable and reports directly to the audit committee on internal audit matters, such as the audit plan, audit findings and recommendations, hiring of the CAE, and the CAE's job performance and compensation.

The CAE reports administratively to the chief executive officer (CEO), who is not responsible for the day-to-day operational activities reviewed by internal audit.

Functional Reporting ⟶ Audit Committee

Administrative Reporting ⟶ Chief Executive Officer

Elements of Independence

Independence comprises two elements:

1. **Independence of mind**—It is the state of mind that permits the conduct of an audit engagement without being affected by influences that compromise professional judgment, thereby allowing an individual auditor to act with integrity and exercise objectivity and professional skepticism.
2. **Independence in appearance**—It is the absence of circumstances that would cause a reasonable and informed third party, having knowledge of the relevant information, including any safeguards applied, to reasonably conclude that the integrity, objectivity, or professional skepticism of an audit organization or member of an audit engagement team had been compromised.

Therefore, it is important for internal auditors and internal audit organizations to maintain their independence so that their opinions, findings, conclusions, judgments, and recommendations will be impartial and reasonable and so that informed third parties will view them as impartial.

Independence and Ethics

Ethical principles provide the foundation, discipline, structure, and the environment necessary to conduct an audit engagement independently. **These ethical principles include integrity, objectivity, resource utilization, and professional behavior.**

Internal audit management sets the tone for ethical behavior by maintaining an ethical culture, clearly communicating acceptable behavior and expectations to each employee, and creating an environment that reinforces and encourages ethical behavior. The ethical tone maintained and demonstrated by audit management and audit staff is an essential element of a positive ethical environment for the audit organization.

Performing audit work in accordance with ethical principles is a matter of personal and organizational responsibility. Ethical principles apply in preserving auditor independence, taking on only work that the audit organization is competent to perform, performing high-quality work, and following the applicable standards cited in the audit report.

FACTORS THREATENING AND SUPPORTING INDEPENDENCE

Factors Threatening Independence

Threats or impairments to organizational independence and individual objectivity may include organizational politics (OP); organizational conflict of interest; personal conflict of interest; audit engagement scope limitations; restrictions on access to records, personnel, and properties; and resource limitations in funding and budgeting.

Specific factors threatening independence are listed next.

- The CAE could report administratively to someone other than the CEO, such as the chief financial officer, general counsel, senior vice president of finance, chief accounting officer, or accounting controller.
- If the internal audit activity is not organizationally independent, it could impact the objectivity of the CAE.
- Conflict-of-interest situations for the CAE and staff could arise when auditing areas with known conflicts.
- OP is a major challenge to independence. Extreme and unnecessary playing of OP can slowly lead to an organization's failure or decline. OP and impression management focus on self-interest in response to opposition at the workplace. OP represents stubborn actions and nepotism shown at all levels of management, which conflicts with the goal-congruence principle. Many employees feel that freedom from office politics is important to their job satisfaction.

Factors Threatening Independence (continued)

- Because independence is an aspect of ethics, a threat to the auditor's independence that cannot be addressed through the application of safeguards is considered a form of **ethical conflict**.
- **Self-interest threat** is the threat that a financial or other interest will inappropriately influence an auditor's judgment or behavior.
- **Bias threat** is the threat that an auditor will, as a result of political, ideological, social, or other convictions, take a position that is not objective.
- **Familiarity threat** is the threat that aspects of the relationship with management or personnel of an audit client's department or office, such as a close or long relationship or that of an immediate or close family member or close friend, will lead an auditor to take a position that is not objective.
- **Undue influence threat** is the threat that influences or pressures from sources external to the internal audit organization will affect an auditor's ability to make objective judgments. (OP can also play a key role here.)
- **Management participation threat** is the threat that results from an auditor taking on the role of management or otherwise performing management functions on behalf of the audit client, which will lead an auditor to take a position that is not objective.

Factors Threatening Independence (continued)

- **Structural threat** is the threat that an internal audit organization's placement within a company, in combination with the structure of the company being audited, will affect the audit organization's ability to perform work and report results objectively. (This means that an employee of a company is auditing his/her own employer.)
- **Previous employment threat** is the threat that a current internal auditor previously worked in a nonaudit department, office, or division that is being audited today and will not appropriately evaluate the results of previous judgments made or services provided as part of the previous work when forming an audit judgment today. (This is called a self-review threat.)

Summary of Factors Threatening an Internal Audit Function's Independence Levels

- Restricted access to records, documents, information, facilities, properties, employees, and management
- Organizational misplacement of the CAE
- Reporting restrictions for the CAE with no autonomy
- Across-the-board budget cuts that can limit the scope of the audit work
- Less confidence in internal controls in the eyes of outside auditors due to compromised independence of the internal audit function

Factors Threatening Independence (continued)

- Less reliance and low assurance on the work of internal auditors by outside auditors and third parties due to compromised independence of internal auditors
- OP played by senior internal management in hiring auditors; limiting the scope of audit work; controlling the timing of the audit work; limiting how much time to spend on the audit work; and deciding what employees to meet and what facilities to visit during the audit work
- Conflicts of interest between the audit staff and audit management
- Ethical conflict due to close relationships between the auditor and his or her family, friends, and colleagues working for the same company as the auditor
- Violating ethical principles such as integrity, objectivity, resource utilization, and professional behavior by internal auditors

Factors Supporting Independence

The next factors support an internal audit function's independence levels:

- Presence of a strong internal audit charter
- Requiring all audit committee members to be fully independent of the company
- Presence of strong governance processes and mechanisms
- Proper organizational placement of the internal audit function
- Strong reporting relationship of the CAE
- Segregation of duties between the audit function and other business functions
- Equitable salaries, bonuses, and profit sharing plans for auditors
- Signed conflict-of-interest statements by auditors
- Ethical training and conflict-of-interest training for internal auditors
- Unlimited access to records, documents, information, facilities, properties, employees, and management
- Effective human resource policies in demoting and terminating internal auditors for violating independence rules
- Auditor professionalism through education and certification
- Outsourcing the internal audit function

OBJECTIVITY DEFINED

Objectivity means independence of mind and appearance when conducting audit engagements, maintaining an attitude of impartiality, having intellectual honesty, and being free of conflicts of interest. Maintaining objectivity includes a continuing assessment of relationships with audit clients and other stakeholders. The concepts of objectivity and independence are closely related in that independence impairments affect auditors' objectivity. Simply stated, objectivity deals with the state of mind of an internal auditor, meaning whether she is objective or subjective when dealing with matters of interest.

An individual internal auditor's objectivity means performing job duties such as audit assignments and engagements free from bias and interference. A major characteristic of objectivity is to avoid any conflict-of-interest situations (situations in which a competing professional or personal interest exists, which can make it difficult for the individual to fulfill job duties impartially).

FACTORS THREATENING AND SUPPORTING OBJECTIVITY

Factors Threatening Objectivity

Threats or impairments to individual objectivity may include personal conflicts of interest; auditor's cognitive biases and traps; organizational cultural traps; audit engagement scope limitations; restrictions on access to records, personnel, and properties; and resource limitations in funding.

In a way, all the threats applicable to independence also apply to objectivity because lack of independence leads to lack of objectivity. These threats include self-interest threat, bias threat, familiarity threat, undue influence threat, management participation threat, structural threat, and self-review threat.

Personal Conflicts of Interest

Conflicts of interest are situations in which an internal auditor, who is in a position of trust, has a competing professional or personal interest. Such competing interests can make it difficult for the individual to fulfill job duties impartially.

Auditor's Cognitive Biases and Traps

Internal auditors should avoid the next six cognitive biases and traps rooted in their own personality zone (area) combined with an organization's culture traps that could affect auditors' objectivity.

1. **Mirror-imaging trap**—An auditor's false assumption that his or her thinking is the same as others' thinking. With this trap, auditors are unwilling to examine or analyze other views, variations, or alternatives of the subject matter at hand. This is similar to saying "My way or the highway." Here, the real issue is that the auditor is blindly committing to a set of common assumptions and not challenging those assumptions. One way to avoid the mirror-imaging trap is to have a peer review by people from different backgrounds, which provides a good safeguard of checks and balances.
2. **Target fixation trap**—Some individuals get fixated on one hypothesis, rely only on evidence that is consistent with their preconceptions, and ignore other relevant views. In a way, they lose sight of the big-picture perspectives and push for a quick closure.

Auditor's Cognitive Biases and Traps (continued)

3. **Analogy trap**—Arises when an auditor is unaware of differences between his or her own context and that of others. This is a case of inappropriate or incorrect use of analogies. The net result is that important knowledge and information is missing because the auditor fails to admit ignorance coming from:

   a. Insufficient study and data/information

   b. Inability to differentiate between old facts and new facts and not integrating them

   c. Inability to accept conflicting facts

4. **Projection trap** (halo and horn error)—Occurs when an auditor is conducting an employee's performance appraisals. The halo error occurs when an auditor projects one positive performance feature or incident onto the rest, resulting in an overall higher rating of that employee's performance. The horn error occurs when an auditor projects one negative performance feature or incident onto the rest, resulting in an overall lower rating of that employee's performance. Both halo and horn errors are based on a recent behavior bias.

5. **Stereotyping trap**—Results from maintaining the status quo (no changes) and discouraging creativity (requiring changes). This trap results from the auditor's personal bias.

6. **Stovepiping trap**—Acknowledging only one source of information or knowledge base as the official source and disregarding the other sources of information or knowledge base as unofficial sources. This trap is similar to a silo trap or legacy trap.

More on Human Behavior

Another aspect of understanding behavior is perception. **Perception** is the cognitive process people use to make sense out of the environment by selecting, organizing, and interpreting information. Perceptual distortions can occur in the workplace. These are perceptual errors in judgment that arise from inaccuracies in any part of the perceptual process. Examples include stereotyping, the halo effect, projection, and perceptual defense.

Stereotyping is placing an employee into a class category based on one or a few traits or characteristics. The **halo effect** is an overall impression of a person based on one characteristic, either favorable or unfavorable. **Projection** is the tendency to see one's own personal traits in other people. **Perceptual defense** is the tendency of perceivers to protect themselves by disregarding ideas, objects, or people that are threatening to them.

Examples of cognitive biases and traps include (1) an internal auditor in the audit engagement team having preconceptions about the operations of a function under audit that are strong enough to affect that auditor's objectivity and (2) an internal auditor in the audit engagement team having biases associated with political, ideological, or social convictions that result from membership or employment in or loyalty to a particular type of policy, group, entity, or level of organization that could affect his or her objectivity.

Organizational Culture Traps

Organizational culture traps can make someone unwilling to challenge the views and perspectives of subject matter experts and senior-level managers. Other examples include:

- Assuming that small things in one culture are small things in every culture, where the opposite can be true. For example, adhering to time schedules and waiting in lines or queues is well accepted in some cultures and is not followed at all in other cultures.
- Assuming that all cultures in all countries follow the same way as one culture in one country.
- American businesspeople may push for quicker decisions during negotiations, whereas Japanese businesspeople may push for building consensus and trust first followed by faster decisions.

One way to avoid the organizational culture trap is to read as many books as possible covering organizational cultures and international cultures in order to gain a good working knowledge of various cultures.

Summary of Factors Threatening an Internal Auditor's Objectivity Levels

- Work pressures to produce major audit findings in volume and quickly
- Pressure from audit clients to ignore suspicious issues and major irregularities
- Groupthink behavior from the audit team (e.g., going along and not rocking the boat)

Organizational Culture Traps (continued)

- Being a friend or relative of an audit client and therefore failing to report major negative audit findings
- Owning financial stock in the company where they are employed
- Bias in prejudging the audit client based on previous familiarity with the client (i.e., this time should be good because the last time was good)
- A former consulting auditor becoming an assurance auditor who must do a self-review of his/her own work and ignoring or overlooking previously known errors, irregularities, or deficiencies in order to make him- or herself look good
- Personal and professional conflict-of-interest situations
- Cognitive biases and traps
- Organizational culture traps

Factors Supporting Objectivity

These factors support an internal auditor's objectivity levels:

- Auditor's unbiased behavior
- Audit supervisory reviews of auditors' work
- Auditor's own self-control, self-discipline, and self-accountability mechanisms
- Equitable salaries, bonuses, and profit-sharing plans for auditors
- Auditor's sound judgment
- Ethical training and conflict-of-interest training for internal auditors
- Auditors working in a team environment
- Rotation of auditors between different audits and locations
- Internal and external quality assurance reviews of audit work to provide credibility, recognition, and validation
- Effective human resource policies in demoting and terminating internal auditors for violating objectivity rules
- Signed conflict-of-interest statements by auditors
- Auditor professionalism through education and certification
- Outsourcing the internal audit function

Comparison between Independence and Objectivity

Independence and objectivity are two different concepts because someone can be independent but not objective and someone can be objective but not independent. In some cases, these two concepts are linked in that lack of independence leads to lack of objectivity. Hence, auditors should avoid situations that could lead reasonable and informed third parties to conclude that the auditors are not independent and thus are not capable of exercising objective and impartial judgment on all issues when conducting audit engagements and reporting on the audit work (i.e., audit results).

Independence originates from the organizational placement and assigned responsibilities as shown in an organization chart. This means the internal audit loses its independence if it is a part of another function (e.g., finance) or if it manages other functions (e.g., risk management, loss prevention, insurance, or regulatory compliance) because these functions are subject to internal audit. This situation could result in a compromise of independence. In summary, independence is achieved through reporting lines, professional and regulatory requirements, benchmarking, and an organization's cultural factors.

Objectivity deals with the mind-set of internal auditors, and it can be understood through an organization's policies, such as employee performance evaluation policies, compensation policies, and conflict-of-interest policies, Here objectivity means the auditor being objective when conducting the audit work, documenting the work, evaluating the work results, developing audit findings, drawing audit conclusions, writing audit reports,

Comparison between Independence and Objectivity (continued)

and making audit recommendations, all based on facts gathered and evidence collected. The auditor is not subjective, when working based on gut feel and insufficient evidence.

A clear comparison between independence and objectivity is shown next.

Independence = Unbiased Business Conditions = Internal Audit as an Activity

Objectivity = Unbiased Mental Attitudes or Mind-sets = Internal Auditor as a Person

POLICIES TO PROMOTE OBJECTIVITY

These policies can help promote an internal auditor's objectivity:

- Establishing a policy on salary, bonuses, profit sharing, and other compensation schemes for internal auditors that does not provide incentives to act contrary to the objectives of the internal audit function.
- Establishing a policy that internal auditors should not be responsible for the design, installation, procedures development, implementation, and operation of internal control systems. However, they are responsible for reviewing and evaluating the adequacy, efficiency, and effectiveness of such internal control systems. This means that consulting auditors and assurance auditors cannot be the same for the same type of consulting work and assurance work.
- Establishing a company's code of ethics that emphasizes the principles of objectivity, competence, confidentiality, and integrity, consistent with the IIA's professional internal audit guidance on codes of ethics.
- Establishing a policy on how to assess the independence of specialists used in audit engagements. Examples of specialists include risk management analysts, information technology auditors, statisticians, engineers, quality control analysts, big data analysts, actuarial scientists, control self-assessment analysts, and audit consultants.
- Establishing a policy on how to handle sensitive and confidential information, including privacy concerns.

POLICIES TO PROMOTE OBJECTIVITY (CONTINUED)

- Establishing a policy that auditors should not use their auditing position for financial gain or other benefits.
- Establishing a policy that internally recruited internal auditors should not audit activities for which they were previously responsible until after one year of employment in the internal audit function.
- Establishing a policy on avoiding conflicts of interest of former employees of the organization performing external quality assessments in the audit department after a certain length of time in the previous employment. This is to avoid real or apparent threat to independence and objectivity.
- Establishing an external assessor policy stating that either individually or a team, assessors must have objective minds. This means they should be free from actual, potential, or perceived conflicts of interest that could impair objectivity.

Domain 3: Proficiency and Due Professional Care (18%)

This domain defines several major theoretical topics, such as proficiency, competency, and due professional care. It discusses the need for internal auditors to improve their competency through continuing professional development and the relationship between professional judgment and competence. It presents competency levels for internal auditors in the form of hard skills and soft skills required to do a professional job.

PROFICIENCY DEFINED

Proficiency is defined as the ability to apply knowledge to situations likely to be faced and to deal with them without extensive recourse to technical research and assistance. There is a built-in and direct relationship between a person's proficiency and competency. A person needs to be fully proficient to become a fully competent person, as there are levels of proficiency and competency. This relationship is shown next.

High-Level Proficiency = High-Level Competency

Low-Level Proficiency = Low-Level Competency

COMPETENCY DEFINED

Competency or **competence** is defined as the combination of knowledge, skills, and abilities (KSAs) obtained from education and experience necessary to conduct audit engagements. Competence enables auditors to make sound professional judgments as it includes possessing the technical knowledge and the hard/soft skills necessary for the assigned role and the type of audit work being done.

Competence is derived from a combination of education and experience (i.e., Competence = Education + Experience).

Education is a systemic and systematic process aimed at developing KSAs. It is a process that is typically, but not exclusively, conducted in traditional academic environments. Several ways of teacherless study methods, done outside of the academic environment, such as self-educating, self-teaching, and self-learning, can be considered education. The major difference is that these teacherless study methods do not go through rigorous testing and validation, as occurs in traditional academic environments. Therefore, what is really learned and retained through teacherless study methods is debatable.

COMPETENCY DEFINED (CONTINUED)

Experience refers to workplace activities that are relevant to developing professional auditors. Experiences such as clerical work, administrative work, or assistant to the audit director positions do not qualify as relevant professional audit work. Competence is not necessarily measured by years of auditing experience because such a quantitative measurement may not accurately reflect the kinds of experience auditors gain in any given time period. Maintaining competence through a commitment to continuous learning and development throughout auditors' professional lives is important for auditors. This means that maintaining competence is not a one-time learning or a series of intermittent learnings.

Core Competencies

Core competencies are the unique and collective capabilities (training and know-how) and specific competencies (skills, experience, and education) that a company has and its competitors do not have. Here the scope of competencies includes competencies of employees, products, and services. The idea is that if employees' competencies are at a higher level, a company's products and services will be at a higher level because it is employees who make products and deliver services. Note that a solid linkage can be established between competency and quality in that highly competent employees can deliver high-quality products and services, and vice versa.

Highly Competent Employees = High-Quality Products and Services = Great Competitive Advantage

Competence is an individual's qualification necessary to carry out assigned job duties and responsibilities. The competence-rich situation creates a competency gap between the company and its competitors; the higher the competency-richness level, the larger the competency gap. Of course, a company's core competencies are a simple summation of all of its employees' competencies. The goal of having all employees acquire the core competencies is to remove their talent gaps and skills gaps. Talent management means implementing and maintaining improvement programs to attract, acquire, develop, train, promote, and retain quality employees.

Competency Gaps = Talent Gaps + Skills Gaps

Core Competencies (continued)

Core competencies are observable, measurable, and a critical set of key knowledge, skills, abilities, and behaviors employees need to have in order to successfully perform their job functions or work efficiently, effectively, and productively. Core competencies can help ensure that a person's performance, acting as an individual or as a member of a team, aligns with the organization's mission and strategy.

DUE PROFESSIONAL CARE DEFINED

Due professional care calls for the application of care and skill expected of a reasonably prudent and competent person in the same or similar circumstances. For example, due professional care is exercised when internal audits are performed in accordance with the IIA *Standards*. The exercise of due professional care requires that:

- Internal auditors be independent of the activities they audit.
- Internal audits be performed by those persons who collectively possess the necessary knowledge, skills, abilities, and disciplines to conduct the audit properly.
- Internal audit work be planned and supervised.
- Internal audit reports be objective, clear, concise, constructive, and timely.
- Internal auditors follow up on reported audit findings to ascertain that appropriate action was taken.

A clear comparison between proficiency and due professional care is presented next:

- **Proficiency** refers to education, experience, professional development opportunities (e.g., seminars, training, and continuing education), and professional certifications (e.g., Institute of Internal Auditors' [IIA's] Certified Internal Auditor [CIA]).
- **Due professional care** refers to understanding the systematic and disciplined approach to internal auditing required by the IIA's International Professional Practices Framework (IPPF) and establishing an internal audit's policies and procedures manual for guidance to auditors.

CONTINUING PROFESSIONAL DEVELOPMENT

Competence includes being knowledgeable about the specific audit requirements and having the skills and abilities to proficiently apply that knowledge on audit engagements. Continuing professional education (CPE) contributes to auditors' competence. The continuing competence of the audit organization's personnel depends in part on an appropriate level of CPE so that auditors maintain the KSAs necessary to conduct the audit engagement.

Determining what subjects are appropriate for individual auditors to satisfy the CPE requirements is a matter of professional judgment to be exercised by auditors and audit managers. When determining what specific subjects qualify for the CPE requirement, auditors may consider the types of KSAs and the level of proficiency necessary in order to be competent for their assigned roles in current audit engagements or future audit engagements. CPE programs are structured educational activities with learning objectives designed to maintain or enhance the auditors' competence to address audit engagement objectives and perform work in accordance with audit standards.

Examples of specific subjects that qualify for the CPE requirements may depend in part on the industry the auditors work for and on the audit profession as a whole. These subjects include audit standards; laws and regulations; analytical techniques such as statistics, data mining, and actuarial science; general ethics; time management, audit reporting, and presentation; communications; project management; economics; information technology; and human resources management.

CONTINUING PROFESSIONAL DEVELOPMENT (CONTINUED)

Examples of CPE's structured educational activities or programs can include internal training programs (e.g., courses, seminars, and workshops); external training programs (e.g., conferences, conventions, meetings, and seminars); web-based seminars; audio and video conferences; university and college courses; correspondence courses; developing CPE courses; and publishing articles and books.

Internal audit staff should have the requisite collective skill levels to audit all areas of the organization. Therefore, auditors should have a wide range of business knowledge, demonstrated through years of audit work and industry-specific experience, educational background, professional certifications, training programs, committee participation, joining professional associations, and job rotational assignments. Internal audit should assign staff to audit assignments based on areas of expertise and should, when feasible, rotate staff within the audit function.

Internal audit management should perform knowledge gap assessments at least annually to evaluate whether current staff members have KSAs commensurate with the organization's strategy and operations. Management feedback surveys, internal quality assurance program findings, and external quality assurance program findings are useful tools to identify and assess knowledge gaps. Any identified knowledge gaps should be filled and may be addressed through targeted staff hires, training, business line rotation programs, and outsourcing arrangements. The internal audit function should have an effective staff training program to advance professional development and a process to evaluate and monitor the quality and appropriateness of training provided to each auditor. Internal auditors generally receive a minimum of 40 hours of training in a given year.

PROFESSIONAL JUDGMENT AND COMPETENCE

Auditors must use professional judgment in planning and conducting the audit engagement and in reporting the audit results. Professional judgment includes exercising reasonable care and professional skepticism. **Reasonable care** includes acting diligently in accordance with applicable professional standards and ethical principles. Attributes of professional skepticism include a questioning mind, awareness of conditions that may indicate possible misstatement owing to error or fraud, and a critical assessment of evidence. **Professional skepticism** includes being alert to, for example, evidence that contradicts other evidence obtained or information that brings into question the reliability of documents or responses to inquiries to be used as evidence. Further, it includes a mind-set in which auditors assume that management is neither dishonest nor of unquestioned honesty. Auditors may accept records and documents as genuine unless they have reason to believe the contrary. Auditors may consider documenting procedures undertaken to support their application of professional skepticism in highly judgmental or subjective areas under audit.

A critical component of the audit engagement is that auditors use their professional knowledge, skills, and experiences, in good faith and with integrity, to diligently gather information and objectively evaluate the sufficiency and appropriateness of evidence. Professional judgment and competence are interrelated because judgments made depend on auditors' competence, as shown next.

Competent Auditors ⟶ Good Judgment

Incompetent Auditors ⟶ Poor Judgment

PROFESSIONAL JUDGMENT AND COMPETENCE (CONTINUED)

Issues or concerns regarding professional judgment are listed next.

- Professional judgment is a collection of experiences of all the audit team members, individual auditors, stakeholders, specialists, and audit management involved in an audit engagement.
- Professional judgment considers adhering to independence standards; maintaining objectivity and credibility; assigning competent audit staff; defining the scope of the audit work; evaluating, documenting, and reporting the results of the audit work; and maintaining appropriate quality control over the audit engagement process.
- Professional judgment considers any threats to the auditor's independence (real or apparent) and related safeguards that may mitigate the identified threats.
- Professional judgment considers whether the audit team's collective experience, training, KSAs, and overall understanding of the engagement's subject matter are sufficient to assess the risks that the engagement's subject matter may contain a significant inaccuracy or could be misinterpreted. An example of misinterpretation is big data collection and data analytics.
- Professional judgment deals with audit risk in arriving at improper audit conclusions. Determining the sufficiency and appropriateness of evidence to be used to support the audit findings and conclusions based on the engagement objectives and any recommendations reported is integral to the engagement process.

PROFESSIONAL JUDGMENT AND COMPETENCE (CONTINUED)

- Professional judgment does not imply infallibility on the part of either the individual auditor or the audit organization. Absolute assurance is not attainable because of factors such as the nature of evidence (i.e., complete/incorrect evidence and complete/incomplete evidence) and characteristics of fraud (e.g., collusion and intentional acts and omissions).
- Professional judgment does not mean eliminating all possible limitations or weaknesses associated with a specific audit engagement but rather identifying, assessing, mitigating, and concluding on them.

COMPETENCY LEVELS FOR INTERNAL AUDITORS

Internal auditors must possess the business-related KSAs required to perform their audit work and to meet their professional responsibilities of the internal audit activity. These KSAs, in addition to the core auditing principles and practices required, can be arranged by topic or subject matter. These KSAs can be acquired or developed over time and are classified as common skills, hard skills, and soft skills (the latter two are called general business skills).

Common Skills

Common skills are a collection of skills from a variety of sources necessary to make an internal auditor more proficient and competent. These skills are in addition to the KSAs required from the core auditing principles and practices. Common skills include:

- Business acumen (e.g., mission, vision, strategy, goals, objectives, and plans)
- Critical thinking and logical reasoning (e.g., reasoning skills and problem-framing skills)
- Communications (verbal and written)
- Basic legal and ethical principles (e.g., due process, due care, due diligence, due professional care, duty of loyalty, duty of care, and duty of obedience)

Common Skills (continued)

- Audit and legal evidence (e.g., direct evidence and documentary evidence)
- Forensics and investigations (e.g., using computers to analyze crimes and fraud)
- Analytical and functional knowledge (e.g., basic ratios, reasonableness analysis, audit metrics, and core business functions)
- Assurance services and consulting services (financial, performance, compliance, and system security reviews and advice, facilitation, and training services)
- Risk management and insurance (e.g., governance, control, risk mitigation strategies, and risk recovery practices)
- Sampling and statistics (e.g., statistical sampling, nonstatistical sampling, and regression analysis)
- Information technology in systems development and systems security (e.g., control evaluation and testing and knowledge of system security principles and practices)
- Big data analytics and data mining (e.g., anomaly detection analysis, fraud analysis, predictive analytics, and descriptive analytics)
- Industry knowledge (e.g., retail and healthcare)

Hard Skills

Hard skills are core KSAs learned and acquired by a person in his or her trade, vocation, and occupation through intensive and extensive education, training, testing, and validation to provide a lifetime career of choice and interest (i.e., job-related technical skills in a plumber, carpenter, electrician, teacher, accountant, engineer, lawyer, doctor, and auditor). Hard skills can be improved and enhanced through continued education, training, testing, and validation in a specific career. Most hard skills can be acquired through education, training, and development courses and work-related experiences. Simply stated, hard skills are career-building and career-enhancing KSAs.

Hard Skills = Analytical and Technical Skills + Functional Skills + Problem-Solving and Decision-Making Skills + Managing and Management Skills + Application Skills + Integration Skills

Specifically, hard skills:

- Deal with knowing specific rules, methods, tools, techniques, procedures, and practices that are constant from job to job regardless of the work environment.
- Describe what a person knows and what a person can do.
- Can be learned, acquired, and perfected over time. They are tangible and much easier to quantify.
- Are often listed as a job applicant's qualifications necessary for an open position (e.g., degrees and certificates).

Hard Skills (continued)

- Help a person to get the job done on time with resources provided.
- Are considered as complements to soft skills.

Examples of hard skills are listed next.

- Quantitative, analytical, and technical skills (e.g., knowledge of basic mathematics, statistics, and probability theories to advanced regression/correlation analysis, and forecasting techniques)
- Qualitative, analytical, and technical skills (e.g., content analysis, factor analysis, cluster analysis, link analysis, canonical analysis, discriminant analysis, causal analysis, causality analysis, cost-benefit analysis, and neural research methods to analyze written words and conversation analysis to analyze spoken words)
- Functional skills (e.g., knowledge of accounting/finance, marketing, and operations)
- Problem-solving skills (e.g., identifying and differentiating between symptoms and real problems and equally solving structured and unstructured problems)
- Decision-making skills (e.g., making routine and nonroutine decisions with too little or too much information and differentiating between perfect and imperfect information)
- Managing skills (e.g., planning, organizing, directing, and controlling skills, which are the basic functions of managers and executives)

Hard Skills (continued)

- Management skills (i.e., containing conceptual, human, and technical skills possessed by supervisors, managers, executives, and leaders, not in equal proportion but in proportion to their job)
- Application skills (e.g., the ability to put theory into practice; the ability to apply functional knowledge, say in marketing and operations)
- Integration skills (i.e., the ability to combine, e.g., marketing's functional knowledge with operations functional knowledge and vice versa)

Soft Skills

Unlike hard skills, soft skills do not represent acquired KSAs. Instead, they represent natural skills (innate skills and born-with skills), such as common sense; the ability to deal with people and handle them in a proper manner; the ability to get along with people in difficult situations; and having a positive and flexible attitude. Soft skills are learned by trial-and-error effort in response to a changing environment.

Because some soft skills—such as interpersonal skills, people skills, leadership skills, creative skills, and entrepreneurial skills—are innate skills, they cannot be learned and acquired through education, training, or development programs. Other soft skills, such as communication skills, presentation skills, comprehension skills, time management skills, implementation skills, and coordination skills, can be learned and improved through education, training, and development programs because they are not fully innate skills.

Soft Skills = People Skills + Social Skills + Critical Thinking Skills + Persuasion Skills + Collaboration Skills + Negotiation Skills + Communication Skills

Specifically:

- Soft skills deal with a person's character traits and interpersonal relationships with other people describing who they are and what their personality is.
- Most soft skills are natural, innate, and instinctive, which are difficult to acquire and change. They are intangible and much harder to quantify than hard skills.

Soft Skills (continued)

- Soft skills are a major differentiator in people because they are a major requirement for employment and key criteria for success in a person's life.
- Soft skills are considered as complements to hard skills.
- Soft skills require teamwork, flexibility, patience, persuasion, time management, empathy, understanding, and listening to others.
- Major soft skills in business include communication skills, interpersonal skills (people skills), collaboration skills, persuasion skills, listening skills, coordination skills, time management skills, and project management skills.

Examples of soft skills are listed next.

- Interpersonal skills (i.e., dealing with an individual's attitudes about and behaviors toward others). Interpersonal skills can be considered the same as people skills.
- People skills (i.e., innate skills, meaning people are born with those skills). People skills can be considered the same as interpersonal skills.
- Communication skills (e.g., analyzing written and oral communications).

Soft Skills (continued)

- Comprehension skills (e.g., understanding complex content in words, tables, charts, graphs, exhibits, and figures).
- Presentation skills (e.g., showing complex results in simple ways using tables, charts, graphs, exhibits, and figures).
- Coordination skills (e.g., working together in collaboration with employees in different departments to achieve common goals and objectives). These skills also are called collaboration skills.
- Implementation skills (i.e., bringing project and program new initiatives to a successful completion).
- Motivational skills (i.e., using hard-sell and/or soft-sell strategies).
- Negotiation skills (i.e., skills that yield a win-win, win-lose, lose-lose, and lose-win outcome between two parties).
- Time management skills (i.e., utilizing time more efficiently and effectively and doing more work with fewer resources).
- Diversity management skills (i.e., defining who is included or excluded from a group or subgroup and receiving sensitivity training [also called T-training]).

Soft Skills (continued)

- Leadership skills (e.g., team-building skills; handling people; possessing interpersonal skills; managing motivation teamwork, conflicts, and crisis situations; and possessing contextual intelligence, emotional intelligence, and cognitive intelligence).
- Listening skills (e.g., asking relevant questions with an inquisitive mind and showing genuine curiosity and interest; requiring much more patience and carefulness than normal).
- Assertion skills (skills that enable people to get their needs met with minimal strife). By being assertive when the need arises, one can prevent the buildup of emotions that so often cause conflict.
- Creative skills (i.e., challenging common thinking and the status quo and coming up with groundbreaking and innovative thinking combined with game-changing ideas).
- Learning skills (i.e., the ability to understand what a person knows about his own learning styles and methods to acquire new knowledge in order to do his job now better than before and more efficiently and effectively). Learning skills include collaboration, communication, critical thinking, and creativity.
- Critical thinking skills (i.e., problem-framing skills requiring redefining a problem and reinventing a matched solution).

Soft Skills (continued)

- Reasoning skills (skills based on logical thinking or logical reasoning and are comprised of deductive, inductive, and abductive reasoning).
- Project management skills (i.e., managing resources to meet project goals and managing costs, schedules, deliverables, people, and quality).
- Social skills (e.g., interpersonal skills, people skills, coordination skills, mentoring, negotiation skills, and persuasion skills).
- Collaborative skills (i.e., a group effort requiring knowledge sharing and tool utilization to improve efficiency and increase output in production).
- Persuasion skills (i.e., ability to convince others to do something or to make others believe in something).

Hard Skills versus Soft Skills

Hard skills represent what a person knows, and soft skills represent who a person is. It is important to note that employers need well-rounded employees with both hard and soft skills. Because hard skills are teachable, employers often look for job applicants with the required soft skills, which are not teachable that easily and quickly. This means that employers want new employees who are already equipped with soft skills to make their job effective and efficient. Note that business skills represent a Pareto principle in that 80% of achievements in a person's career are determined by soft skills and only 20% are determined by hard skills.

Specifically:

- Persons who possess both hard skills and soft skills can obtain and hold jobs very easily and quickly.
- Peoples who possess only hard skills and no soft skills cannot obtain and hold a job.
- A person who has several soft skills and only a few hard skills can obtain a job because hard skills can be taught and learned, whereas some soft skills cannot.

Expanded Hard Skills and Soft Skills

Some major hard skills and soft skills are described next.

Communication skills: Oral communications, listening skills, written communications, presentation skills, report writing skills, memo writing skills, project status report writing skills, contract writing skills, weekly/monthly activity report writing skills, comprehension skills, negotiation skills, interviewing skills, and investigative skills. Communications can flow in four directions in an organization: up, down, horizontally, and diagonally. **Communication skills are ranked as a number 1 requirement for auditors.**

Assertion skills: Assertion (or assertive) skills enable people to get needs met with minimal strife. By asserting when needs arise, people can prevent the buildup of emotions that so often cause conflict. Both assertion skills and listening skills help to clear up two major sources of conflict: errors and lack of information. Internal auditors need many more assertive skills than others because they deal with audit clients and other stakeholders in critical situations during their audit work. Auditors need to assert and summarize their understanding of audit client matters in a concise and succinct manner and should positively confirm with the audit client. In addition to auditors, managers and leaders must possess assertion skills.

Persuasion skills: Persuasion skills are the art of convincing someone to do something or to make someone believe in something. Persuasion deals with facts and actions. Factors such as persistence, perseverance, and determination are prerequisites to persuasion.

Leadership skills: Ability to inspire and lead others; explaining strategic mission and vision to others; possessing drive, integrity, and agility; motivating skills; listening skills; negotiation skills; coordination skills;

Expanded Hard Skills and Soft Skills (continued)

diversity management skills; public servicing skills; organizational skills; ability to understand decision traps and decision biases; people skills (relationship-oriented issues and interpersonal dealings between and among individuals); assertion skills; time management skills; business acumen; creative skills; contextual intelligence; emotional intelligence, cognitive intelligence; problem-solving and decision-making skills; and reasoning skills. Essential skills for leaders include communication skills, listening skills, negotiation skills, and delegating skills. **Leadership skills are ranked as a number 4 requirement for auditors.**

Technical skills: Core business functional knowledge (functional skills); subject matter proficiency; quantitative skills; qualitative analysis; technology-oriented skills (e.g., robots, artificial intelligence, CAD, CAM, and lean Six Sigma skills); project management skills (Program Evaluation Review Technique [PERT]); and big data analytics. **Technical skills are ranked as a number 3 requirement for auditors.**

Social skills: Social skills operate in interactions between people and communication with other people, all within the established social rules, norms, relations, and expectations in a society. Social skills are learned through changes in people's attitude, thinking, and behavior over a period of time. Social skills build character traits like trustworthiness, respectfulness, rapport, responsibility, fairness, and above all an internal moral compass.

Reasoning skills: Reasoning skills are based on logical thinking or logical reasoning, which is comprised of deductive reasoning, inductive reasoning, and abductive (inference) reasoning. In deductive reasoning, conclusions are drawn when moving from general principles to specific cases. In inductive reasoning, conclusions are drawn when moving from specific cases to general principles. In abductive reasoning, conclusions

Expanded Hard Skills and Soft Skills (continued)

lead to premises. Moreover, conclusions are drawn from hypothesis testing and heuristics (rules of thumb, intuition, and trial and error) where outcomes are likely to occur but not with certainty. In abductive reasoning, one moves from outputs to inputs.

Problem-solving skills: Identifying and differentiating between symptoms and real problems and equally solving structured and unstructured problems. Problem-framing skills require reverse engineering a current problem (i.e., deconstructing a current problem) and forward engineering the same problem (i.e., reconstructing the same problem). It also includes redefining an old, unclear problem into a new, clear problem.

Decision-making skills: Making routine and nonroutine decisions with too little or too much information and differentiating between perfect and imperfect information. Note that problem-solving skills and decision-making skills go hand in hand because decisions are made in part to solve problems.

Twenty-first-century learning skills: The P21 Organization conducted a research study that identified four deep learning competencies and skills (called the four *C*s) of twenty-first-century learning: collaboration, communication, critical thinking, and creativity.

Teamwork skills: Ability to follow or take direction from a leader, manager, supervisor, team leader, coach, or mentor; delegation skills; valuing and respecting opinions of others; handling cross-cultural diversity and sensitivity; and adaptability to changes and uncertainties. These skills require collaboration skills. **Teamwork skills are ranked as a number 2 requirement for auditors.**

Expanded Hard Skills and Soft Skills (continued)

Managing skills: Managing human capital (people skills); listening skills; negotiation skills; motivating skills; coordination skills; managing a risk-based environment; assertion skills; and reasoning skills. In addition, managing skills require integration skills, application skills, creative skills, business acumen, managing decision-making and problem-solving processes; managing administrative activities; implementing strategy and innovation projects; handling conflict and change; managing diversity skills; organizational skills; and time management skills. Broadly speaking, managing skills are composed of conceptual, human, and technical skills. **Managing skills are ranked as a number 5 requirement for auditors.**

Critical thinking skills: Ability to think objectively and analyze facts and evidence to form an opinion (judgment) with the ultimate goal of reaching an answer or conclusion. This ability is inwardly directed to maximize the thinker's rationality (rational thinking and logical thinking). It provides a self-regulated judgment and self-directed thinking, and it is not "hard" thinking, as the name suggests or implies. Critical thinking skills do not solve problems. Instead, they improve one's own process of thinking. They are used as a systematic approach to problem solving and decision making. Critical thinking skills include observation, interpretation, analysis, inference, evaluation, and explanation. Critical thinking skills provide the ability: to apply professional standards and industry standards; to differentiate between real problems and symptoms; to identify root causes of problems; to apply reasoning and logical skills such as inductive and deductive reasoning; and to apply professional judgment in collecting audit evidence and reporting audit results. Critical thinking skills also need reasoning skills and problem-framing skills.

Expanded Hard Skills and Soft Skills (continued)

Motivation skills: The ability to inspire others to do good things that are expected. These skills use hard-sell (stick approach with punishments) or soft-sell (carrot approach with incentives) techniques to get the expected results.

Negotiation skills: Skills that produce win-win, win-lose, lose-lose, and lose-win outcomes between two parties to a negotiation process who are trying to reach an agreement. These skills push for what one party wants while knowing what the other party wants. Negotiation skills are the ability to influence others to get what is wanted from them. Negotiating uses a hard approach (threats and insults) and a soft approach (calm and collected). Usually, if one party wins, the other party loses.

Career skills: Skills that help a person's career path with growth and versatility. Key elements include agility (e.g., flexibility and adaptability), accountability, productivity, self-direction, self-control, self-motivation, cross-cultural understanding and interaction, social skills, and self-initiatives.

Collaboration skills: Occurs when two or more employees or departments work together to achieve a common goal. Virtual teams, quality teams, audit teams, project teams, and distributed teams are examples of collaboration because team members work cooperatively and in a coordinated manner. In collaboration, face-to-face interaction is better than person-to-machine interaction. Technological collaboration tools include online calendars, spreadsheets, voicemails, electronic mails, chat systems, videoconferencing, workflow systems, messaging systems, virtual collaboration systems, and web-based software such as wiki. Nontechnical collaboration tools are less efficient and include manual systems such as paper and pencil, flipcharts, sticky notes, whiteboards, or chalkboards. For

Expanded Hard Skills and Soft Skills (continued)

example, internal auditors in one division of a major company can work with auditors in other divisions of the same company when conducting similar audits or related audits to share common business knowledge and audit tools.

Interpersonal skills: Ways to improve interpersonal skills include touring facilities; managing by walking around; arranging brown-bag lunches, fireside chats, and face-to-face meetings; and communicating by phone, fax, text, email, voicemail, and intranet. Interpersonal skills are also called people skills.

People skills: Innate skills (meaning people are born with those skills), although some parts can be learned, developed, and practiced. Research has proved that people who are successful possessed more people skills, despite their lack of technical skills. People skills include conflict management, communication, listening, and interpersonal skills for better relationships and rapport building. People skills focus on getting along with coworkers and handling and treating coworkers with respect and dignity and to establish a mutual trust and comfort levels. People skills can be thought of as interpersonal skills.

Business acumen skills: Knowledge of core business functions, such as operations, marketing, and finance (functional skills); commitment to mission and vision; ability to develop a grand strategy for the entire business and sub-strategies for each business line, to create and sustain value, to understand competitors and their business games, to come up with counterstrategies and counteractions to beat competitors, to treat shareholders and stakeholders equally and properly, to understand how business functions integrate and work with each other to create value; and implementing best practices or meta-practices to create value and to improve business processes and functions in a sustainable manner.

Required Skills for Internal Auditors

A summary of competency levels and business skills required of internal audit staff and management is presented next.

Role	Skills Needed
Staff auditors and senior auditors	Communication, assertion, persuasion, technical, social, reasoning, collaboration, people, teamwork, critical thinking, and business acumen
Audit supervisors and audit managers	Communication, technical, problem solving and decision making, managing, critical thinking, collaboration, people, and business acumen
Chief audit executive and internal audit director	Communication, leadership, problem solving and decision making, critical thinking, motivation, negotiation, creative, people, and business acumen

Business Skills for Directors and Officers

All directors, officers, executives, and senior managers, including chief audit executives, need both hard skills and soft skills to perform their jobs more effectively and efficiently. However, the depth and the type of skills needed for an executive or manager depends on his or her level in the management hierarchy. This means that higher-level managers and senior executives need more depth in soft skills and less depth in hard skills. In contrast, lower-level managers and junior executives need more depth in hard skills and less depth in soft skills.

Domain 4: Quality Assurance and Improvement Program (7%)

This domain contains only a few key theoretical topics. It describes the required elements of the quality assurance and improvement program, including its reporting results. In addition, it discusses conformance or nonconformance with the IIA's *Standards*. It also shows how to apply total quality management (TQM) approaches to improve internal audit operations.

REQUIRED ELEMENTS

A well-designed, comprehensive quality assurance (QA) program should ensure that internal audit activities conform to the Institute of Internal Auditors' professional *Standards* and the organization's internal audit policies and procedures. **The QA program contains two required elements of internal quality assessments and external quality assessments:**

Audit QA = Internal Quality Assessment + External Quality Assessment

The internal audit function should develop and document its internal assessment program to promote and assess the quality and consistency of audit work across all audit groups with respect to policies, procedures, audit performance, and workpapers. The QA review should be performed by someone independent of the audit work being reviewed. Conclusions reached and recommendations for appropriate improvement in internal audit process or staff training should be implemented by the chief audit executive (CAE) through the quality assurance and improvement program (QAIP). Action plan progress should be monitored and subsequently closed after a period of sustainability. Each organization should conduct an internal quality assessment exercise annually, and the CAE should report the results and status of internal assessments to senior management and the audit committee at least annually.

Quality Assurance (QA) + Improvement Programs (IP) = QA + IP = QAIP

REQUIRED ELEMENTS (CONTINUED)

The IIA recommends that an external quality assessment of internal audit be performed by a qualified independent party at least once every five years. The review should address compliance with the IIA's Definition of Internal Auditing, Code of Ethics, Core Principles, and Professional *Standards*. In addition, the review should address the internal audit function's charter, policies, and procedures, and any applicable legislative and regulatory requirements. The CAE should communicate the results, planned actions, and status of remediation efforts to senior management and the audit committee.

In addition, the internal audit function should contain five key characteristics that form the foundation on an effective QAIP:

1. Policy
2. Methodology and process
3. People
4. Systems and information
5. Communication and reporting

REQUIRED ELEMENTS (CONTINUED)

A list of highlights of internal assessment and external assessments follows.

- The goals of internal assessment and external assessment are the same regarding compliance and conformance with the IIA's *Standards* and the Code of Ethics and alignment with the Definition of Internal Auditing and the Core Principles.
- The scope of internal assessments consists of ongoing monitoring and periodic self-assessments, where the ongoing monitoring is conducted first and the periodic self-assessment is performed next. Internal assessments focus on continuous improvement of the audit activity.
- Ongoing monitoring, which takes a narrow scope, is an integral part of the day-to-day supervision and operation of the internal audit as they are blended into the audit policies, practices, tools, processes, and information. Ongoing monitoring focuses on individual audit engagements.
- Periodic self-assessments, which take a broad scope, focus on the entire internal audit activity as a whole.

REQUIRED ELEMENTS (CONTINUED)

- A self-assessment may be performed in lieu of a full external assessment, provided it is validated by a qualified external assessor and that the scope of a self-assessment is the same as that of a full external assessment.
- An external assessment can be done as a stand-alone and full external assessment or a self-assessment with independent external validation and assurance. The scope of external assessment can be expanded to provide comments on operations and strategy.
- Internal assessments are performed first and external assessments are conducted second. Internal assessment supports external assessments.
- Internal assessments are conducted every year. External assessments are conducted every five years.

Manufacturing Quality versus Audit Quality

Manufacturing-oriented companies have long been developing and maintaining comprehensive QA programs and quality control methods to continuously improve the quality of their products. Best practices in TQM are applied to manufacturing processes, primarily at three production stages, such as quality before, during, and after production. TQM is a management philosophy containing quality principles, practices, tools, and techniques to continuously improve the quality of products. Specifically, TQM focuses on QA plans, quality control practices, and continuous improvement programs. Later, TQM was introduced in service-oriented companies. Similarly, an internal audit activity, which is a part of service-oriented organizations, needs a comprehensive quality assurance and improvement program (QAIP) to conduct quality audit work and deliver quality results to its stakeholders. A comparison between manufacturing TQM and audit QAIP follows:

TQM in Manufacturing = QAIP in Internal Audit

Quality before Production = Audit Planning

Quality during Production = Audit Engagement

Quality after Production = Audit Reporting

Potential Risks in Audit Quality Assessments

At least five types of risks exist when conducting internal assessments and external assessments: peer review risk, audit sampling risk, auditor cognitive risk, assessment rating risk, and assurance risk. Note that the last four risk types can be by-products of the peer review or stand-alone risks in internal and external assessments. Each of these risks is briefly discussed next.

Peer review means that one colleague reviews and checks another colleague's work to ensure the work's accuracy, completeness, and quality. Peer reviews are done in a team environment during internal and external assessments to provide additional QA. Peer **review risk** is the risk that the review team:

- Fails to identify significant weaknesses in the reviewed audit organization's system of quality control for its auditing practice, its lack compliance with that system, or a combination thereof
- Issues an inappropriate opinion on the reviewed audit organization's system of quality control for its auditing practice, its compliance with that system, or a combination thereof
- Makes an inappropriate decision about the matters to be included in, or excluded from, the peer review report

In summary, peer review risk deals with not reporting significant weaknesses, issuing an inappropriate opinion, and making an inappropriate decision.

Potential Risks in Audit Quality Assessments (continued)

Audit sampling risk occurs when selecting specific audit engagements for review across many audit divisions of a large audit organization that completes many audit engagements in a year. As the peer review is based on selected tests, it is not designed to test every audit engagement, compliance with every professional standard, or every detailed component of the audit organization's system of quality control. This means that a peer review would not necessarily detect all weaknesses in the system of quality control or all instances of noncompliance with it. Specifically, audit sampling risk can arise based on whether (1) statistical or nonstatistical sampling methods are used when selecting audit tests for review; (2) auditors have sampling experience or not; and (3) auditors have considered sampling and nonsampling risks when selecting audit tests for review.

Auditor cognitive risk occurs from the auditor's own cognitive traps and biases, because these traps and biases are deeply embedded in people's own personality. Cognitive biases are human tendencies that can lead to human biases and that can act as judgment triggers (good or bad). Examples include stereotyping (i.e., maintaining the status quo and failing to invite creativity), target fixation (i.e., evidence is consistent with perceptions and no big-picture views), and projection traps (i.e., a recent behavior bias, resulting in halo errors and horn errors and seeing one's own traits in other people). Projection of current review results to future reviews is an example of a cognitive risk because future conditions can change, thus making the current review results invalid.

Assessment rating risk occurs when the rating system used in a peer review work is unfair and subjective. Possible rating types include pass, fail, or pass with deficiencies needing improvement, requiring ratings to be fair and objective. An auditor's cognitive traps and biases can influence the assessment rating risk.

Potential Risks in Audit Quality Assessments (continued)

Assurance risk means all the internal assessments and external assessments can result only in reasonable, not absolute, assurance. Usually, reasonable assurance is provided in performing and reporting in conformity with applicable professional standards. The real question is whether a reasonable assurance is good enough to accept.

REPORTING REQUIREMENTS

The CAE is required to report to the board and senior management at several critical points, as listed next.

- After internal assessments are completed, a report is issued identifying areas for improvement and showing corrective action plans.
- After external assessments are completed, a report is issued identifying areas for improvement and showing corrective action plans.
- After uncovering any impairments to independence or objectivity, audit scope restrictions or limitations, and resource limitations for auditors and audit clients, a report is issued with documented details and evidence.
- After completing internal assessments and external assessments, a report is issued showing the conformance rating scale, whether it generally conforms, partially conforms, or does not conform.
- After discovering nonconformance outcome, a report is issued showing the impact of nonconformance by quantifying it as much as possible on specific areas, such as:
    - Providing reliable assurance services
    - Providing consulting services
    - Completing the audit plan

REPORTING REQUIREMENTS (CONTINUED)

  - Addressing high-risk audit areas
  - Impact on the overall scope or operation of the internal audit activity
- A report is issued by the external assessor describing observations and recommendations to management in order to improve internal audit quality, efficiency, and effectiveness.
- A benchmarking report is issued showing how the external assessor went through a vetting process (i.e., how he or she was screened, selected, and hired) with a request-for-services document, all demonstrating internal audit's commitment to the due diligence process. Note that the vetting process does not apply to guest auditors.

CONFORMANCE VERSUS NONCONFORMANCE

Whether it is an internal assessment or an external assessment, the QA review should eventually address compliance with the IIA's Definition of Internal Auditing, Code of Ethics, Core Principles, and *Standards*. Two outcomes are possible: conformance or nonconformance.

Conformance means compliance with the Definition of Internal Auditing, Code of Ethics, Core Principles, and *Standards*. Note that the Core Principles are a new requirement starting with the 2017 *Standards*. Conformance means both internal assessments and external assessments are carried out.

Examples of Conformance

- There are no impairments or threats to independence and objectivity.
- There are no audit scope restrictions or limitations.
- There are no resource limitations for auditors and audit clients.
- People performing internal and external assessments possess collective knowledge, skills, and experiences.
- Risk was explicitly considered during the development of annual and individual audit plans.
- There are no peer review risks and audit work sampling risks during internal and external assessments.

CONFORMANCE VERSUS NONCONFORMANCE (CONTINUED)

Nonconformance means noncompliance with the Definition of Internal Auditing, Code of Ethics, Core Principles, and *Standards*. Nonconformance means (1) there is no internal assessment and no external assessment and/or (2) internal assessments without external assessments. Nonconformance can become conformance after full validation by external assessors.

Examples of Nonconformance

- The internal audit activity did not conduct external assessment at least once every five years.
- An internal auditor did not meet individual objectivity requirements during an audit engagement.
- An audit engagement did not have auditors possessing collective knowledge, skills, and experiences.
- The CAE and managers and supervisors failed to consider risk when developing the audit plan.

TQM IN INTERNAL AUDIT OPERATIONS

Many internal audit departments have installed TQM approaches to improve internal audit operations. One such approach is recommended by the U.S. Government Accountability Office (GAO), which outlined eight steps to apply and implement TQM approaches in audit operations.

1. **Initial quality assessment.** This step includes:
   a. Identifying the audit department's customers
   b. Establishing the needs of customers
   c. Setting priorities so as to best meet customers' needs
   d. Assessing the quality of audit products (audit reports) as perceived by audit customers as to timeliness, usefulness, responsiveness, and cost
   e. Interviewing customers so as to reveal pertinent information about the audits, audit staff performance, and the audit department as a whole
2. **Chief audit executive awareness.** Awareness training should stress the importance of TQM as a philosophy or an approach, not a program.

TQM IN INTERNAL AUDIT OPERATIONS (CONTINUED)

3. **Formation of a quality council.** Audit managers, audit supervisors, and audit staff members should be part of the quality council, and they should acquire the knowledge of TQM principles, practices, and tools. This council should report to the CAE. It should coordinate training and participate in prototypes.
4. **Fostering teamwork in audits.** The audit department should establish a participative environment that fosters teamwork and quality work. Audit plans, audit work programs, fieldwork, workpapers, and audit reports all require quality orientation and thinking.
5. **Development of prototypes.** To convince some auditors who are doubtful about the TQM philosophy, the quality council should demonstrate the practical value of new ways of organizing the audit work with highly visible prototype and productivity initiatives. When tested and proven successful, these prototypes can convince or clarify the doubts of the audit staff.
6. **Celebration of success.** The audit department should publicize the achievements of the prototype to encourage the cautious and hesitant audit staff.

TQM IN INTERNAL AUDIT OPERATIONS (CONTINUED)

7. **Organizational implementation.** All units and all locations of the audit department should successfully implement audit quality methods, and appropriate recognition should be given for those units that are most successful. This provides motivation and promotes healthy competition.
8. **Annual audit quality review.** There should be an annual audit quality review for audit departments that are spread throughout the organization. The annual review, together with a rating system, will demonstrate the success of the implementation of quality in the audit department.

Domain 5: Governance, Risk Management, and Control (35%)

This domain is very important for internal auditors due to its core functions of the board and senior management as it covers governance, risk management, and control subjects. Specifically, it addresses:

- Governance principles, components, and problems
- Governance models and frameworks
- Roles of the board of directors
- Characteristics of effective and ineffective boards
- Roles of executives and officers
- Roles of the audit committee
- Roles of internal auditors in governance, risks management, and control processes
- Roles of the board-level committees
- Roles of shareholders and stakeholders
- Scope of board-level audits

- Organizational culture
- Organizational ethics
- Corporate social responsibility, including sustainability
- Risk concepts, risk types, and risk management processes
- Globally accepted risk management frameworks
- Effectiveness of risk management
- Internal audit's role in the risk management processes
- Internal control concepts and types of controls
- Globally accepted internal control frameworks
- Effectiveness and efficiency of internal controls
- Compliance management

CIA Exam candidates should note that this domain is given the largest weight (35%) in Part 1 of the CIA Exam.

GOVERNANCE PRINCIPLES, COMPONENTS, AND PROBLEMS

Corporate Governance Defined

Corporate governance refers to the method by which a firm is being governed, directed, administered, or controlled and to the goals for which it is being governed. It is concerned with the relative roles, rights, and accountability of such stakeholder groups as owners, boards of directors, managers, executives, employees, labor unions, and others who assert to be stakeholders. Note that boards of governors or directors are not the guarantors of the governance process as long as they use good judgment.

What Is Corporate Governance?

Corporate governance sets the right tone and proper stage for the entire corporation. While there is no standard definition of corporate governance, it can broadly be understood to refer to the system by which companies are directed and controlled, including the role of the board of directors, management, shareholders, and other stakeholders. Corporate governance provides the structure through which the objectives of the company are set and the means of attaining those objectives and monitoring performance are determined.

A weak form of corporate governance is one of the root causes of many problems that corporate management is facing today. A weak board means a weak governance and vice versa. Note that corporate governance and corporate ethics should support corporate management.

The issue of corporate governance is a direct outgrowth of the question of legitimacy. For business to be legitimate and to maintain its legitimacy in the eyes of the public, its governance must correspond to the will of the people and interests of stakeholders.

What Is a Corporation?

A **corporation** is a legal entity that is separate from its owners and shareholders, where it is responsible for paying debts it owes and receiving money it is owed, and where its owners and shareholders would not be responsible for the corporation's debts or liabilities.

An exception to this legal entity concept occurs in specific situations where courts are required to pierce (lift or remove) the corporate veil and where the corporation's owners and shareholders would be liable for the corporation's debts or wrongful conduct. Examples of these specific situations include misconduct, dishonest and improper actions, fraud, criminal acts, deceiving third parties, and setting up sham corporations based on "alter ego" theory by owners and shareholders. This means illegal and unethical acts cannot be hidden behind the name of a corporation and owners and shareholders cannot get away with bad acts.

Piercing the corporate veil applies to closely held corporations, single-person corporations, and shell corporations and does not apply to publicly traded corporations because the latter are assumed to have a better and proper corporate structure and organizational controls. Piercing the veil is based on the concept of equitable principle and deep rock doctrine.

What Is a Corporate Constitution?

The essential elements of a corporate constitution include corporate charter (bylaws), director power and accountability (right to manage), and shareholder rights and duties (approve sale and purchase of company assets in a merger and acquisition). The purpose of a corporation may be anything that is lawful.

Corporate Governance Principles

Business Roundtable supports eight guiding principles and standards as part of good corporate governance practices.

1. The board approves corporate strategies that are intended to build sustainable long-term value; selects a chief executive officer (CEO); oversees the CEO and senior management in operating the company's business, including allocating capital for long-term growth and assessing and managing risks; and sets the "tone at the top" for ethical conduct.

2. Management develops and implements corporate strategy and operates the company's business under the board's oversight, with the goal of producing sustainable long-term value creation.

Corporate Governance Principles (continued)

3. Management, under the oversight of the board and its audit committee, produces financial statements that fairly present the company's financial condition and results of operations and makes the timely disclosures investors need to assess the financial and business soundness and risks of the company.

4. The audit committee of the board retains and manages the relationship with the outside auditor, oversees the company's annual financial statement audit and internal controls over financial reporting, and oversees the company's risk management and compliance programs.

5. The nominating/corporate governance committee of the board plays a leadership role in shaping the corporate governance of the company, strives to build an engaged and diverse board whose composition is appropriate in light of the company's needs and strategy, and actively conducts succession planning for the board.

6. The compensation committee of the board develops an executive compensation philosophy, adopts and oversees the implementation of compensation policies that fit within its philosophy, designs compensation packages for the CEO and senior management to incentivize the creation of long-term value, and develops meaningful goals for performance-based compensation that support the company's long-term value creation strategy.

Corporate Governance Principles (continued)

7. The board and management should engage with long-term shareholders on issues and concerns that are of widespread interest to them and that affect the company's long-term value creation. Shareholders that engage with the board and management in a manner that may affect corporate decision-making or strategies are encouraged to disclose appropriate identifying information and to assume some accountability for the long-term interests of the company and its shareholders as a whole. As part of this responsibility, shareholders should recognize that the board must continually weigh both short-term and long-term uses of capital when determining how to allocate it in a way that is most beneficial to shareholders and to building long-term value.

8. In making decisions, the board may consider the interests of all of the company's constituencies, including stakeholders such as employees, customers, suppliers and the community in which the company does business, when doing so contributes in a direct and meaningful way to building long-term value creation.

Corporate Governance Components

To appreciate fully the legitimacy and corporate governance issues, it is important to understand the major groups that make up the corporate form of business organization. Only by so doing can one appreciate how the system has failed to work according to its intended design.

The four major groups needed in setting the stage are (1) shareholders (owners or stakeholders), (2) board of directors, (3) managers, and (4) employees. Overarching these groups is the charter issued by the state, giving the corporation the right to exist and stipulating the basic terms of its existence.

Under the U.S. corporate law, **shareholders** are the owners of a corporation. As owners, they should have ultimate control over the corporation. This control is manifested primarily in the right to select the company's board of directors. Generally, the number of shares of stock owned determines the degree of each shareholder's right.

Because large organizations may have hundreds of thousands of shareholders, they elect a smaller group, known as the **board of directors**, to govern and oversee the management of the business. The board is responsible for ascertaining that managers put the interests of the owners (i.e., shareholders) first. The third major group in the authority hierarchy is **management**—the group of individuals hired by the board to run the company and manage it on a daily basis. Along with the board, top-level managers establish overall policy. Middle- and lower-level managers carry out this policy and conduct the daily supervision of the operative employees. **Employees** are those hired by the company to perform the actual operational work. Managers are employees too, but in this discussion, we use "employees" to refer to nonmanagerial employees.

Corporate Governance Problems

Eleven types of governance problems exist:

1. Separation of ownership from control
2. Lack of board independence
3. Occurrence of insider trading scandals
4. Appearance of conflict-of-interest situations
5. Presence of interlocking boards
6. Presence of shadow directors
7. Presence of activist shareholders and directors
8. Experiencing ethical lapses and dilemmas
9. Failure to recognize cognitive traps and biases
10. Lack of reasoning skills in board members
11. Incomplete proxy materials

Corporate Governance Problems (continued)

Summary of Corporate Governance Problems

- Separation of ownership from control, meaning owners cannot control their business or investment because corporate management (hired talent) exercises control of the business
- Unclear roles of the board of directors
- Lack of board's full independence
- Issues surrounding very high compensation (Major issues include CEO compensation—e.g., salaries, bonuses, incentives, stock options, and perks—and outside director compensation)
- Poor consequences of merger and acquisition projects due to bad decisions made, prevalent takeover waves and ugly antitakeover options, and poorly advised divestiture of assets
- Insider trading scandals
- Board member liability, such as a board member's personal reputation risk
- Lack of strong voice or strong teeth for board of directors who are afraid to ask hard questions due to their submissive behaviors
- Shareholder and director activism that is spreading fast to all companies regardless of their size and structure

GOVERNANCE MODELS AND FRAMEWORKS

Six governance models and frameworks are discussed next.

U.S. NACD's Corporate Governance Guidelines

NACD's Board's Duties and Responsibilities

The board of directors (board) oversees the management of the National Association of Corporate Directors through the CEO and senior management by providing guidance and strategic oversight. The board's duties and responsibilities are set out in the board's bylaws, committee charters, and governance guidelines, and include being responsible for:

- The size and composition of the board
- Selection, compensation, and evaluation of the CEO
- Planning management succession
- Reviewing and approving strategic and business plans, including financial objectives and budgets
- Election of board members

NACD's Board's Duties and Responsibilities (continued)

- Evaluation of the board's performance through metrics and key performance indicators
- Oversight of the financial reporting processes and accounting practices
- Assessment of the adequacy and effectiveness of systems of internal controls regarding finance, accounting, and legal and regulatory compliance
- Assessment and management of major risks
- Development of policies, procedures, and programs to ensure that the activities of the board and all employees are in compliance with legal and ethical conduct standards
- Review of governance policies and practices

NACD's Key Agreed Principles

NACD's 10 Key Agreed Principles are grounded in the common interest of shareholders, boards, and corporate management teams in the corporate objective of long-term value creation (through ethical and legal means), the accountability of management to the board, and ultimately the accountability of the board to shareholders for long-term value creation. These key principles provide a framework for board leadership and oversight in the critical areas of strategic planning, risk oversight, executive compensation, and transparency.

Principle I: Board Responsibility for Governance

Principle II: Corporate Governance Transparency

Principle III: Director Competency and Commitment

Principle IV: Board Accountability and Objectivity

Principle V: Independent Board Leadership

Principle VI: Integrity, Ethics, and Responsibility

Principle VII: Attention to Information, Agenda, and Strategy

Principle VIII: Protection against Board Entrenchment

Principle IX: Shareholder Input in Director Selection

Principle X: Shareholder Communications

NACD's Board's Legal and Ethical Conduct

The board is responsible for establishing policies and programs to ensure that NACD activities are conducted in a legal and ethical manner. Topics such as committee roles, conflict of interest, code of ethics, whistleblower protection policy, record retention, and document destruction policy are discussed in this section.

NACD's Board-Level Committees' Roles

The audit and finance committee and the governance committee have shared responsibility with regard to reviewing and monitoring compliance with laws, regulations, and NACD policies. For example, the audit and finance committee assist the board in fulfilling its oversight responsibility relating to finance, accounting, and legal and regulatory compliance matters.

Governance committee	Recommends for board approval a conflict-of-interest policy and a code of ethics
Audit and finance committee	Recommends for board approval a whistleblower protection policy and a record retention and document destruction policy

NACD's Conflict-of-Interest Policy

All directors must comply with the conflict-of-interest policy. It is the responsibility of each director to advise the chair of the board and the governance committee of any affiliation, relationship, or transaction that may create a conflict of interest with NACD. The board takes appropriate steps to identify any potential conflict-of-interest issues and to ensure that all directors voting on an issue are disinterested with respect to that issue.

NACD's Code of Ethics

The board is responsible for overseeing corporate ethics. Each director and all employees are expected to adhere to the highest ethical standards. All directors are expected to comply with the NACD's Code of Ethics. The Code of Ethics is embodied in the following standards, requiring the commitment of directors, officers, employees, and chapter leaders to:

- Honesty, integrity, and transparency
- Acting responsibly
- Maintaining the public trust through full accountability
- Complying with the spirit and the letter of all applicable laws, regulations, and rules

NACD's Code of Ethics (continued)

- Avoiding conflict of interest, whether actual or apparent
- Responsible stewardship of resources
- Treating directors, officers, employees, and others with respect and fairness
- Reporting violations of this Code of Ethics to the designated third party and/or the chair of the audit and finance committee

NACD's Whistleblower Protection Policy

All directors, officers, and employees are responsible for complying with NACD's Whistleblower Protection Policy and to report violations and suspected violations in accordance with the policy. If anyone reports any activity believed to be illegal or improper, all the reporters will be protected against retaliatory actions and kept confidential during investigation. A company maintains a confidential hotline phone number for people to report.

NACD's Record Retention and Document Destruction Policy

It is the policy of NACD to retain records, including paper records, electronic files, and voicemails for the period of their immediate or current use, unless longer retention is necessary for historical reference or to comply with contractual or legal requirements. It is also the policy of NACD to not knowingly destroy a document, if the destruction would result in a violation of the Sarbanes-Oxley Act of 2002. A formal, written record retention and document destruction policy will be distributed to all directors and employees.

U.K. Cadbury Governance Framework

The Cadbury Report of the Committee on the Financial Aspects of Corporate Governance issued in December 1992 consists of internal controls, fraud, internal audit, external audit, financial reporting practices, audit committees, shareholders, corporate governance, the board of directors, and the code of best practice.

Regarding internal controls, the report says that directors should maintain a system of internal control over the financial management of the company, including procedures designed to minimize the risk of fraud. The directors should make a statement in the report and accounts on the effectiveness of their system of internal control, and the auditors should report thereon.

Regarding fraud, the report says that prime responsibility for the prevention and detection of fraud and other illegal acts is that of the board, as part of its fiduciary responsibility for protecting company assets. The auditor's responsibility is to properly plan, perform, and evaluate audit work so as to have a reasonable expectation of detecting material misstatements in the financial statements.

Regarding the internal audit, the report states that the function of the internal auditors is complementary to, but different from, that of the external (outside) auditors. The committee regards the internal audit as good practice for companies to establish internal audit function to undertake regular monitoring of key controls and procedures. Such regular monitoring is an integral part of a company's system of internal control and helps to ensure its effectiveness. An internal audit function is well placed to undertake investigations on behalf of the audit committee and to follow up any suspicion of fraud. It is essential that heads of internal audit should have unrestricted access to the chairman of the audit committee in order to ensure the independence of their position.

U.K. Cadbury Governance Framework (continued)

Regarding the external audit, the report says that an essential first step is to be clear about the respective responsibilities of directors and external auditors for preparing and reporting on the financial statements of companies, in order to begin to narrow the expectation gap. This gap is due to lack of understanding of the nature and extent of the external auditors' role. The gap is the difference between what audits do achieve and what it is thought they achieve or should achieve. The expectations gap is damaging not only because it reflects unrealistic expectations of audits but also because it has led various interested parties to be disenchanted with the value of audits.

The external auditors' role is to report whether the financial statements give a true and fair view, and the audit is designed to provide a reasonable assurance that the financial statements are free of material misstatements. The auditors' role is not (to cite a few of the misunderstandings) to prepare the financial statements, or to provide absolute assurance that the figures in the financial statements are correct, or to provide a guarantee that the company will continue to exist.

Australian Governance Framework

The Australian Securities Exchange Corporate Governance Council defines governance as "the system by which companies are directed and managed. It influences how the objectives of the company are set and achieved, how risk is monitored and assessed, and how performance is optimized."

Germany's Corporate Governance Framework

In 1998, the German government proposed changes for the reform of corporate governance. The KonTrag model in Germany affects control and transparency in business. Specifically, it impacts the board of directors, supervisory board, corporate capitalization principles, authorization of no-par-value shares, small non-listed stock corporations, banks investing in industrial companies, and the acceptance of internationally recognized accounting standards, such as the U.S. GAAP.

King Model in South Africa's Corporate Governance Framework

The Institute of Directors in South Africa established the King Committee on Corporate Governance that produced the King Report in 1994. The committee has developed a Code of Corporate Practices and Conduct, and compliance with the code is a requirement to be listed in the Johannesburg stock exchange (JSE) Securities Exchange in South Africa.

Comparison of Global Governance Models

Due to its dynamic process, the corporate governance structure in each country should be developed based on the response to country-specific factors and conditions. In each country, the corporate governance structure has seven characteristics or constituent elements, which distinguish it from structures in other countries:

1. Key players in the corporate environment
2. Share ownership pattern in the given country
3. Composition of the board of directors or boards in the German model
4. Regulatory framework
5. Disclosure requirements for publicly listed stock corporations
6. Corporate actions requiring shareholder approval
7. Interaction among key players

Global Practices in Corporate Governance

Corporate governance practices differ considerably around the globe, although there are some common practices. Regardless, most of the problems are rooted in poor governance policies and practices; fraudulent accounting practices; and executives' excessive and abusive behavior. Specific issues deal with ownership, board composition, influence, power, and control, as described next.

- Ownership is heavily dispersed in the United States but is much more concentrated in Canada, Germany, Japan, and China. High levels of influence and control over corporate affairs are associated with high concentration of ownership.
- National and state governments also own major stakes of public companies in Germany, Italy, Japan, and China.
- French and German companies have different types of owners than those found in the United States and United Kingdom. In France, nonfinancial corporations and state government are the largest shareholders. In Germany, both banks and nonfinancial corporations are owners. In addition, German banks own both debt and equity in the same corporation; they have direct voting power and proxy voting positions from bank depositors.

Global Practices in Corporate Governance (continued)

- Most public firm shares in China are controlled by state-owned or state-controlled shareholders; the remaining trading shares are owned by a combination of individual and institutional investors.
- In Brazil, China, France, and Russia, the government owns the largest companies in size.
- Owners and workers sit on boards in France, Germany, Japan, and China; outsiders and managers sit on the board in U.S., U.K., and Canadian companies
- CEOs have considerable power over the selection of board members in many U.S. corporations as well as in Canada and the United Kingdom. In France and Germany, owners nominate and elect the board members.
- In Japan, both supplier and customer organizations acquire financial interests and ownership in Japanese corporations and are represented on the corporate board (*keiretsu*).

Improving Corporate Governance

Efforts to improve corporate governance may be classified into two major categories:

1. Changes could be made in the composition, structure, and functioning of boards of directors.
2. Shareholders—on their own initiative or on the initiative of management or the board—could assume a more active role in governance.

Specifically, improving corporate governance requires increased:

- Change in the composition of the directors between inside directors (one is preferred) and outside directors (more are preferred).
- Role of shareholders with their initiatives to companies.
- Role of company initiatives to shareholders.
- Obligation of companies to fairly and fully disclose vital information to shareholders through proxy statements, management's discussion and analysis, compensation discussion and analysis, and other reporting avenues.

In summary, improving corporate governance requires (1) changes in boards of directors to include more outside directors and (2) increased role of shareholders in the governance process.

ROLES OF THE BOARD OF DIRECTORS

The roles and responsibilities of board of directors of a company are varied and complex due to the board's unique position at the top of a company in guiding the company's direction. Some boards excel in their roles while most do not, due to the composition and qualification of board members.

Specific Roles of the Board of Directors

These complex roles can be subdivided into several roles such as:

- Understanding oversight function (governance duties)
- Understanding fiduciary duties (duty of care, no self-dealing, and corporate opportunities)
- Understanding legal and ethical obligations (basic legal principles, such as due process, due care, duty of care, due diligence, duty of loyalty, duty of obedience; and basic ethical principles, such as the Golden Rule, means – ends cycle, might-equals-right principle, professional principle, goal congruence principle, prudent-person concept, and business judgment rule)
- Managing corporate affairs (crisis and issues management, social media platforms, negative press, natural disasters, cybersecurity, and internal and external affairs doctrine)

Specific Roles of the Board of Directors (continued)

- Managing access to information (unlimited and unrestricted access to people, facilities, assets, and information)
- Handling legal liabilities and legal actions (lawsuits by shareholders and others)
- Acquiring knowledge about core functions of a business they represent (marketing, manufacturing, service, finance, and accounting)

Summary of Ethical and Legal Principles Expected of Corporate Officers and Directors

- Due care (e.g., reasonable care, good faith, and prudent person)
- Duty of due care (e.g., no harm, nor risk, and no breach of duty)
- Due diligence (e.g., honesty in fact and honesty in intent)
- Duty of loyalty (e.g., no self-dealing, no stealing of company opportunities, no competition with the company, and no making of secret profits)
- Duty of obedience (e.g., comply with the state corporation statutes, the articles of incorporation, and the corporate bylaws)

CHARACTERISTICS OF EFFECTIVE AND INEFFECTIVE BOARDS

Hierarchy of Boards

Forward-looking boards consist of individual board members whose business practices are high-performing and value-creating in nature and those individuals whose business practices can achieve their stated mission, vision, core values, goals, and objectives. At any point in time, a company's board can be labeled into one of the four hierarchical levels, where level 1 is ineffective boards, level 2 is complacent boards, level 3 is striving boards, and level 4 is effective boards. This hierarchy of board practices is similar to Maslow's hierarchy of human needs (i.e., the lowest level is basic needs such as food and shelter, and the highest level is self-actualization, such as reaching one's lifelong goals and aspirations), where people move on to the next levels after the basic needs are satisfied until they reach the self-actualization level. Similarly, company directors can be expected to move up the hierarchy from ineffective boards to effective boards as their board's practices get better and better over a period of time. One can think of ineffective boards and effective boards as the two extreme ends of a scale and complacent boards and striving boards falling in between. This four-level board hierarchy of practices is shown below with different impact levels on a company.

Hierarchy of Boards (continued)

Levels	Impacts
4. Effective boards (top of the hierarchy)	Very high positive impact and very low negative impact
3. Striving boards	High positive impact and low negative impact
2. Complacent boards	Moderate positive impact and moderate negative impact
1. Ineffective boards (bottom of the hierarchy)	Low positive impact and high negative impact

Ineffective Boards

Ineffective board members are weak-minded as they turn their heads the other way or close their eyes when the CEO and her management team are involved in illegal, unethical, or otherwise questionable business practices. Moreover, ineffective boards do not challenge the CEO's assumptions and approaches and operate in a suboptimal manner regarding:

- Strategy formulation and implementation
- Resource prioritization, allocation, and utilization
- Problem-solving and decision-making processes
- Risk-versus-return trade-offs
- Performance-versus-incentives conflicts

Ineffective boards either consciously or subconsciously invite activist shareholders and directors due to their bad actions and poor image. These activists can create problems for the entire board with their selfish agenda.

Complacent Boards

Complacent boards are little better than ineffective boards and are at level 2 of the practices hierarchy with moderate positive impact and moderate negative impact. The board's goal is to move up to the next level of striving board.

Striving Boards

Striving or trying boards are significantly better than complacent boards and are at level 3 of the practices hierarchy with high positive impact and low negative impact. These boards are trying very hard to reach the next highest level of effective boards.

Effective Boards

Effective boards are at level 4 of the practices hierarchy with very high positive impact and very low negative impact. Effective boards can be thought of as exemplary, ideal, dream, or excellent boards that every public company director dreams to reach. In order to reach this level, effective boards need to strengthen owners' (investors') trust; gain the confidence of the general public; receive positive goodwill from shareholders and other stakeholders; and send positive signals to capital, financial, and stock markets to thrive.

Effective board members are strong-minded as they open their eyes and look straight into the eyes of the CEO and his management team when they are involved in illegal, unethical, or otherwise questionable business practices. Moreover, effective boards challenge the CEO's assumptions and approaches and operate in an optimal manner regarding strategy formulation and implementation; resource prioritization, allocation, and utilization; problem-solving and decision-making processes; risk-versus-return trade-offs, and performance-versus-incentives conflicts. Simply stated, an effective board is more than the sum of its parts due to greater synergy coming from board members with diverse skill sets, relevant work experience, and earned professional competencies.

ROLES OF EXECUTIVES AND OFFICERS

The board of directors selects and hires the chief executive officer (CEO) or the president of a company. The CEO in turn selects and hires a management team consisting of several C-level (chief level) executives, such as chief marketing officer (CMO) and chief financial officer (CFO). For example, the CEO at the top and the CMO and CFO at the next level down form the management hierarchy or the chain of command. In reality, there could be several C-level executives reporting to the CEO and there could be several next-level-down employees reporting to each of the C-level executives.

Improperly defining and practicing employee reporting relationships is often deeply rooted in corporate governance, control, and ethical problems. Improper reporting relationships between and among the C-level executives create control-related problems and pose ethical dilemmas due to conflict of interest, lack of separation of duties, and lack of independence and objectivity. Incompatible job functions and improper separation of duties can lead to fraud, collusion, and other irregularities. Corporate goal congruence is at risk when individual goals and interests dominate and conflict with the goals of the corporation. Proper organizational structure and reporting relationships can enforce clear lines of responsibility and accountability throughout the organization.

ROLES OF EXECUTIVES AND OFFICERS (CONTINUED)

Most C-level executives are vice presidents or directors of a business division or group. The proper and improper reporting relationships between and among the C-level executives are described next.

- The CEO should report to the board of directors and can assume the role of the president but cannot assume the role of chair of the board or of CFO. A nonexecutive board member should assume the role of board chair.
- The CFO should report to the CEO or to the executive vice president (EVP) of finance. The CFO cannot assume the role of the CEO.

Having so many C-level executives directly reporting to the CEO is a challenging administrative task for the CEO to handle on a daily basis, especially when the CEO's time is a limited and critical resource. Some organizations have established EVP or senior vice president (SVP) positions, and some C-level executives directly report to the EVP or SVP in order to reduce the CEO's workload. For example, the CFO, chief accounting officer (controller), chief treasurer, and chief administrative officer directly report to the EVP of finance.

Both the CEO and senior executive management must ensure that employee reporting relationships in the management hierarchy below that of the C-level executives (e.g., group/division heads, general managers, middle-level managers, and lower-level managers) are structured in such a way as to prevent conflict of interest, goal congruence, control, and ethical problems. Goal congruence, consistency, harmony, and a single and collective voice are the primary benefits accruing to private or public sector organizations resulting from this type of wide span of control (i.e., several lower-level employees are reporting to one higher-level employee).

ROLES OF THE AUDIT COMMITTEE

Audit committee is the most important board-level committee as it deals with development of financial statements (e.g., income statement and balance sheet) and coordination between internal audits and external audits. A board member with formal education in accounting and finance with professional certification in accounting and who previously worked on an audit committee for a previous company is a qualified candidate to assign to the audit committee (i.e., financial expert on the board). A board's standards require that fully independent directors serve on the audit, compensation, nominating, and governance committees. The highest standards of independence apply to the audit committee due to its work with financial statements and internal controls. The audit committee is discussed separately due to its financial importance to stockholders, investors, and owners and audit interest to internal auditors.

The audit committee's key responsibility—overseeing the process that produces reliable and credible financial statements while ensuring the company has effective internal controls—requires it to conduct activities that earlier had been executed mostly by management. Today, audit committees are also expected to retain and compensate the external auditors, grasp all of the key information included in a company's financial reporting, and oversee risk management and compliance with the laws and regulations affecting the company. This change is occurring in an environment that demands transparency.

ROLES OF THE AUDIT COMMITTEE (CONTINUED)

The principal responsibilities of the audit committee and its relationship with corporate management are to:

- Ensure that published financial statements are fair and proper and are not misleading.
- Ensure that internal controls are adequate.
- Follow up on allegations of material, financial, ethical, and legal irregularities in response to whistleblower reports.
- Ratify the selection of the external auditor.
- Hire, retain, and terminate the CAE of the internal audit function.
- Coordinate between the external auditors and internal auditors.
- Ensure the integrity of financial reporting and nonfinancial reporting to shareholders and stakeholders.
- Ensure that related-party transactions are fair and proper.
- Ensure that a record retention policy and a document destruction policy are in place and are effective.
- Press more and trust less with corporate management.

ROLES OF INTERNAL AUDITORS IN CORPORATE GOVERNANCE, RISK MANAGEMENT, AND CONTROL PROCESSES

The internal audit activity should assess and make appropriate recommendations for improving the governance, risk management, and control processes in its accomplishment of these objectives:

- Promoting appropriate ethics and values within the organization
- Ensuring effective organizational performance management and accountability
- Effectively communicating governance, risk, and control information to appropriate areas of the organization
- Effectively coordinating the activities of and communicating information among the board, external auditors, internal auditors, and senior management

The internal audit activity should evaluate the design, implementation, and effectiveness of the organization's ethics-related objectives, programs, and activities. Consulting engagement objectives should be consistent with the overall values and goals of the organization and separate from the objectives of assurance engagements.

In summary, internal auditors must assume the roles of governance promoters, risk controllers, and control facilitators. Above all, they should aim to become effective auditors leading an effective audit function.

Internal Auditors = **Governance Promoters** + **Risk Controllers** + **Control Facilitators**

ROLES OF BOARD-LEVEL COMMITTEES

Board-level committees are an effective way to focus on key issues and problems facing an organization because each issue or problem requires a dedicated approach, resources, and attention to solve it. Individual members of the board of directors of an organization join various board-level committees to address specific tasks, issues, problems, and concerns facing that organization. The rationale behind establishing committees is divide and conquer: It is better and easier to handle several small-size issues separately than to handle one big-size issue. Committee members can spend more time on and pay more attention to a small committee than to a large one.

Committees have high visibility and high impact on organizations due to their strategic-level representation of executive management and the board members as their decisions affect the entire company. The outcome of a committee's work is a new or revised policy, plan, or procedure to make current things better or future things even better. Committees are employed in both private and public organizations, managed by committee chairpersons, and they take big-picture perspectives.

The committee should contain nonexecutive and independent directors with no potential for conflict of interest and who exercise due diligence. Committee members' formal education, skills, and work experience are important factors in assigning them to committees. In addition, each committee should have its own "committee charter" describing primary objectives to be achieved, tasks to be accomplished, and roles and responsibilities to be fulfilled, all approved by the chair of the board.

ROLES OF BOARD-LEVEL COMMITTEES (CONTINUED)

Note that the number of committees depends on the type of a corporation (i.e., U.S. domestic or global) and on the type of industry (i.e., bank or healthcare). Examples include (1) some companies may consolidate several committees into a few; (2) a global corporation may have several more committees than a major domestic corporation (3) banks, healthcare, transportation, and financial industries will establish a regulatory and compliance committee more often than the others because they are heavily regulated; (4) banks will establish an asset and liability committee more often than nonbanks because assets and liabilities are their core business; (5) a software development company will establish an intellectual property (IP) committee to address and protect its IP assets; and (6) a manufacturing company or a retail company will establish a supply-chain committee due to its core business more often than other companies. Every publicly held corporation has a nominating committee, and all companies have a human resource committee.

ROLES AND RIGHTS OF SHAREHOLDERS AND STAKEHOLDERS

Both shareholders and stakeholders have basic roles to perform and rights to achieve in any size and type of organization. In addition to discussing these roles and rights, we present initiatives of shareholders and corporations and laws governing shareholder lawsuits.

Roles of Shareholders Defined

Shareholders are owners of and investors in a corporation. The purpose of the corporation is to enhance shareholder value through effective and efficient management practices. Three types of shareholders exist: majority shareholders, minority shareholders, and activist shareholders. Each has different roles and rights.

Basically, **majority shareholders** are controlling shareholders who owns less than 50% of the equity. **Minority shareholders** are noncontrolling shareholders who own less than 10% of the equity due to the number of shares they own in a company.

Activist shareholders, who can be considered minority shareholders, own less than 10% of outstanding shares and put public pressure on a company's management to:

- Change its major policies, investment and disinvestment practices, or financing structure (debt and equity proportions).

Roles of Shareholders Defined (continued)

- Increase revenues and profits.
- Decrease fixed costs in its cost structure.
- Increase the dividend payout ratio.
- Distribute dividends as stock dividends, not as cash dividends, in order to increase their ownership percentage.

Activist shareholders (once called as corporate raiders) use several forms of activism to express their displeasure with a company's management, including proxy fights, adverse publicity campaigns, and lawsuits. Many corporate boards have developed best practices and trained and educated board members to increase their knowledge and skills to combat activist shareholders' efforts. In other words, the competency of board members is on the rise to fight activist shareholders and other challengers.

Rights of Shareholders Defined

Shareholders have a right to vote and right to file lawsuits. They have voting rights, cumulative voting rights, proxy voting rights, preemptive rights, and take-along rights. They can also file class action lawsuits and derivative lawsuits.

Voting Rights

Every active shareholder has a basic right to vote due to stock ownership and can elect a company's board members; vote on stock splits, spinoffs, mergers, acquisitions, and divestitures plans; and vote in regard to compensation for executives and board members. Shareholders exercise their voting rights with in-person or mail-in ballots.

Cumulative Voting Rights

Shareholders can assign their votes to one or more candidates for board member instead of voting separately for each member. Each shareholder requires a number of votes proportionate to his or her shareholdings (i.e., number of shares [say 50] multiplied by the number of open board positions [say 2] equals 100 votes). Ten to 15% is required to select one board member. This approach allows minority shareholders to select some members of the board.

Proxy Voting Rights

Shareholders are authorized to vote on behalf of other shareholders who cannot attend the scheduled general board meeting. Some counties allow mail-in ballots for proxy voting.

Preemptive Rights

Preemptive rights are the first rights given to existing shareholders to participate in any new capital increase (i.e., can purchase new shares issued by a company). They prevent a company from selling new shares on favorable terms to only some shareholders or to nonshareholders.

Take-along Rights

When a controlling or majority shareholder sells enough equity shares to a new shareholder, the new shareholder will inherit all the rights of the controlling shareholders. This means that the original owner's rights can be transferred to subsequent owners or new owners can take along all the rights of the old owners.

Class-Action Lawsuits

Class-action lawsuits are filed by one or more shareholders of a company on behalf of other shareholders of the same company, all having the same problems, complaints, and grievances with the company's management. These lawsuits can save significant amounts of total legal expenses when each shareholder needs to file a lawsuit. An example is a lawsuit filed against the board for not addressing cyberattacks and data breaches in a timely and proper manner.

Derivative Lawsuits

Derivative lawsuits are filed by shareholders on behalf of a corporation against an offending party for damages caused to the corporation when the corporation itself fails to bring a lawsuit against the offending party. Here the shareholders' goal is to recover damages due the corporation in which the recovered money is deposited into the company's treasury account after paying for the legal expenses. The recovered money does not go into the pockets of any shareholders.

Ownership Pyramid

Some companies have complex legal structures with straight shareholdings in one company or cross-shareholdings in two or more companies so a parent company can exercise control over its subsidiary companies in a pyramid organizational structure.

Company A ⟶ Company B ⟶ Company C ⟶ Company D

Here, straight shareholdings means that Company A is an owner of some shares of Companies B, C, and D. Cross-shareholdings means that Company A is a parent company that owns 10% of Company B (Subsidiary 1), Company B owns 15% of Company C (Subsidiary 2), and Company C owns 5% of Company D (Subsidiary 3).

Roles and Rights of Stakeholders Defined

Stakeholders, other than shareholders, have a right to file lawsuits and grievances, but they have no right to vote. The purpose of a corporation is to serve a wider range of interests of its stakeholders and to solve various issues facing its stakeholders.

Stakeholders is a broad term where it includes shareholders (stockholders) and nonshareholders. Stakeholders have a built-in stake in a corporation, meaning whatever a company's management does or does not do can directly or indirectly affect them both economically and socially. The types of stakeholders include shareholders

Roles and Rights of Stakeholders Defined (continued)

(owners and investors), employees, management, creditors, labor unions, customers, suppliers and vendors, consultants and contractors, regulators, business partners, and citizens and society, each with different and conflicting roles, objectives, and expectations. Note that some stakeholders, such as employees and customers can also become shareholders if they own their company's stocks.

Shareholders are the first stakeholders of a corporation and expect dividends, capital gains, and investment growth.

Employees are the internal prime stakeholders. They expect stable employment and decent wages and benefits to them and to their family.

Management is responsible for running a company and meeting the demands of various stakeholders.

Creditors are not the owners and are protected by contracts, covenants, and collaterals for lending their money to a corporation. They are concerned about the solvency of the corporation in terms of receiving interest payments and the principal amount of loans.

Labor unions protect the rights and obligations of their member employees. At times, they are in conflict with corporate management regarding wages, working conditions, and discrimination lawsuits.

Customers are the external prime stakeholders who purchase a company's goods and services to meet their needs and wants.

Suppliers and vendors provide products and materials to operate a company. They expect to be paid after completing their work.

Roles and Rights of Stakeholders Defined (continued)

Consultants and contractors provide various services and expect to be paid after completing their work.

Regulators issue laws, rules, and regulations to protect the interests of businesses and their customers and expect compliance with such laws.

Business partners (e.g., joint ventures, insurance companies, and outsourcing firms) are external companies who collaborate and coordinate with a company to provide goods and services and expect the company to operate ethically and legally with trust and reputation.

Citizens and society expect charitable contributions; sponsor educational, environmental, and health training programs; and develop and improve local community relations. They expect companies to become a good corporate citizen.

An effective corporate governance model requires that all shareholders and stakeholders will have a common purpose and principles of transparency, accountability, fairness, and responsibility, as described next.

- Transparency—Full disclosure of financial and nonfinancial information
- Accountability—An independent and competent governing body that admits their actions and inactions
- Fairness—Treating investors and noninvestors equally
- Responsibility—Fulfilling its defined roles with duty of care and duty of loyalty combined with exercising due process and due diligence

Initiatives of Shareholders and Corporations

Initiatives are new programs and projects to make current and future things better as they are done on a proactive basis to address current problems and issues. Both shareholders and corporations have their own initiative agendas to improve each other and as a response to each other.

Examples of **shareholder initiatives** include increases in (1) filing of shareholder lawsuits against directors especially with respect to buyout offer prices; (2) shareholder activist groups through organizing and exercising power over company management; and filing of shareholder resolutions at annual meetings through booklets of shareholder questions. A rationale behind the shareholder initiatives is to protect shareholders from courts, applying the legal concept of piercing the corporate veil.

Examples of **corporation initiatives** include: (1) increasing amounts of full disclosure of information to investors that affects their investment decisions; (2) showing full accountability and transparency to shareholders about business activities, financial condition, and tender offers made during mergers and acquisitions; (3) avoiding conflict-of-interest situations by board members and executives; (4) avoiding the use of insider information for personal gain by board members and executives; (5) avoiding personal use of company assets and taking personal loans by directors, officers, and executives; and (6) maintaining arm's-length relationships with related entities and third parties during business transactions.

Laws Governing Shareholder Lawsuits

Shareholder activist groups are increasingly suing companies for major or minor reasons, and most of these suits are settled out of court. Examples of major reasons for these lawsuits include paying a high price for the acquisition of new assets and receiving a low price for the divestiture of existing assets. The U.S. Private Securities Litigation Reform Act of 1995 was issued to curb the filing of frequent and frivolous class action lawsuits in federal courts. A loophole in the act diverted the cases from federal courts, which increased the filings of such lawsuits in state courts. The U.S. Securities Litigation Uniform Standards Act of 1998 was issued to plug that loophole; according to this act, state court filings will be referred to the federal district courts for the district in which the action is pending. This means that all lawsuits must be filed in federal courts, which will come under the provisions of the 1995 act.

SCOPE OF BOARD-LEVEL AUDITS

The chief audit executive or an outside consultant can conduct a board-level audit for publicly held companies periodically to ensure that all board-level activities and programs are functioning effectively and efficiently. This audit work also looks at the effectiveness of the board's oversight responsibilities by reviewing corporate governance, risk management, and control policies, procedures, and activities. The following are the required levels of audit clients when conducting board-level audits and when using 360-degree performance reviews with all of the audit stakeholders together to obtain a well-rounded feedback and big-picture assessment.

First-level audit clients ⟶ Board members and board chairperson

Second-level audit clients ⟶ Executives and officers

Third-level audit clients ⟶ Vice presidents and division heads

Fourth-level audit clients ⟶ General managers and functional managers

Audit Scope

The audit scope depends on the type and size of an organization, meaning that a large organization may need a bigger scope than a small organization, which may need a smaller scope. Due to its relative importance, the governance audit is covered here.

Governance Audit

The corporate governance audit is a systematic and structured review of issues and problems related to disclosure and transparency in the areas of financial condition shown in the balance sheet, performance reporting, ownership, and board responsibilities and recommendations to resolve such issues and problems. The governance audit is the final audit of corporate governance practices. It determines whether a corporation is using the right governance framework for its business (i.e., the framework is current and appropriate).

To this end, the board chair must manage and monitor governance risk indicators (GRIs). These GRIs are warning signs of impairments or threats to governance principles and mechanisms. A corrective action is needed to fix these GRIs. A list of such GRIs is presented next.

- No policy on age limits, term limits, service-year limits, and tenure limits for directors. This means that directors can work for the same company for 10 years or longer, which prevents new blood, new thinking, new insights, new experiences, and diverse perspectives. Board members form a close-knit society similar to

Governance Audit (continued)

a country club or social club of elites. They have long experience, but it is the one-year experience that is repeated many times.

- No policy on director nominations or renominations, especially in regard to underperforming directors.
- No clear criteria on a director's required skill sets, relevant work experience, and professionalism with education and certificates of proficiency and competency, all leading to ineffective boards.
- No percentage limit on a director's equity ownership in the company.
- No dollar limits on a director's commercial relationship (e.g., contracts on selling, buying, trading, brokering, and supplying some products or services) with the company.
- No clear picture on how the size and nature of executive compensation, incentives, and perquisites are designed and how it is linked to targeted and actual performance.
- No time limits on a director's previous management job in the company until after a reasonable time has elapsed. (Such limits ensure the director's independence and objectivity.)
- No new director hired in the last 5 or 10 years (shows stagnation at the board level).
- Board composed of a few independent directors and many non-independent directors.

Governance Audit (continued)

- Same board chair and CEO (no separation exists between the chair's role and the CEO's role). The goal is to keep these roles separate to avoid conflicts of interest and to place a cross-check on each person's work. Also, when the CEO retires, he or she should not be appointed as a board member or board chair (because he or she could influence the board's function).
- No executive sessions between independent directors and outside directors for a long time without the CEO. (Excluding the CEO would allow board members to measure the CEO's performance.)
- No executive sessions between the board and the CEO for a long time without the presence of other senior managers, officers, and executives. (Excluding them would enable the board to measure the performance of other senior managers, officers, and executives.)
- Leaderless board. There is no full-time and permanent position as board chair. Instead, board members take on the chair's job on a part-time and rotating basis (such as monthly, quarterly, yearly, per meeting, as needed or ad hoc, crisis, or per request). In the absence of a full-time board chair, individual responsibilities cannot be assigned fully and individual accountabilities cannot be exacted correctly, thus leading to a chaotic and finger-pointing environment. This means the chair is not in the same job long enough to be held accountable and to determine his or her real contribution because the board member is working on borrowed time.

Governance Audit (continued)

- Incomplete and noncurrent succession planning for key management positions. The board stops the succession planning at the CEO level and does not extend it down three or four levels below the CEO level. This means that no backup management is available to continue the business after the CEO level.
- Minimal participation of women and minorities on the board. Boards should conduct benchmark studies with best-in-class companies to find out the optimal level of participation (a 50 – 50 rate is ideal) after considering diversity goals in gender, minority, and ethnicity.
- Use of immature and outdated frameworks for governance, risk management, and control processes, resulting in a greater exposure to new threats and vulnerabilities and missed opportunities, all resulting in unpreparedness.
- Failure of board members to put hard questions to the CEO and senior management in order to maintain good rapport with them. Instead, board members are using box-ticking, box-checking, rubber-stamp approaches and not exercising strong teeth, thus becoming a weak board. Under these conditions, it is hard to make the CEO and senior management accountable for their actions and inactions.
- Table testing documents (i.e., simply reading at a table) instead of stress testing or deep testing to prove that the strategy works in real life.

Governance Audit (continued)

- Shortage of directors due to a personal reputation risk, resulting from legal liabilities and bad propaganda in the media. Hence, many good executives avoid sitting on company boards, thinking that becoming a director is not worth the risk.
- Recycled directors (the same director serves on multiple company boards). Because of this, directors are stretched too thin to attend board meetings and have no time to prepare in advance of the meetings in order to ask hard questions. As a result, some directors are merely token directors who appear just to collect fees, perks, and bonuses.
- Inadequate company-sponsored D&O insurance, so directors and officers are not fully protected against lawsuits by shareholders, stakeholders, competitors, and the government and from personal reputation risk. High deductible amounts and large monthly premium payments for these insurance policies make them cost prohibitive for many directors and officers working in small and mid-cap companies. (A mid-cap company is a company listed on the over-the-counter stock market exchange.)
- Board chair who fails to identify underperforming directors and continues to renominate or reappoint them, thus perpetuating incompetent and ineffective boards.

ORGANIZATIONAL CULTURE

Organizational culture is a set of shared values and norms guiding both employees' and managers' behavior. **Organizational culture** refers to a system of shared meaning held by employees that distinguishes their organization from other organizations. It provides direction to employees and helps them understand how things are done in the organization. In other words, organizational culture defines the rules of the game, which are very difficult to understand.

A strong culture provides stability (asset) to an organization; at the same time, it can become a major barrier to change (liability). Every organization has a culture, and that culture can have a significant influence on employees' attitudes and behaviors. Organizational culture influences many areas, such as organizational ethics, behavior, development, and change.

Summary of Organizational Culture

Corporate management is the major culprit behind corporate failures and management's misdeeds, misconduct, and misbehaviors—all of which point to an organization's culture and its personality. A list of important topics, issues, concerns, and dimensions about organizational culture is presented next.

- Organizational culture can be good or bad, an asset or a liability, soft or hard, fixed or variable, healthy or unhealthy, low risk or high risk, strong or weak, positive or negative, toxic or nontoxic, right actions or wrong actions, and effective or ineffective.

Summary of Organizational Culture (continued)

- Culture is doing the right things at the right times and in the right ways.
- Engaged and empowered employees will always have good things to say and positive comments to make about their organization's cultural accomplishments and improvements, which reflects their job satisfaction and work performance. The reverse is also true.
- Individual audit engagements are positively affected by a positive organizational culture and negatively affected by a negative organizational culture. This means that negative culture creates mistrust toward internal auditors and their work, leading to roadblocks and impairments due to organizational culture traps.
- Organizational culture is conveyed from top-level managers to lower-level managers to frontline employees through reports, memorandums, meetings, letters, face-to-face communications, policies, the intranet, procedures, and dealings with outsiders such as customers, suppliers, and regulators.
- Culture is like oxygen holding the entire organization together to operate, survive, and sustain. It is invisible, powerful, and silent.
- Culture is like a strong glue that holds an organization's employees and management together.

Summary of Organizational Culture (continued)

- Culture can be compared to an onion. Its layers can be peeled away to understand the real culture at the top-level management, middle-level management, lower-level management, and frontline employees (entry-level employees) in that order (i.e., from top to bottom). The culture from the top to bottom management may be consistent or inconsistent from one layer of the onion to an other.
- Culture is reflected and embedded in an organization's mission/vision, strategy, policies, procedures, programs, plans, and business practices.
- Culture is either directly or indirectly related to **ethics and compliance** in that a healthy culture can lead to ethical practices and compliance with laws and regulations; unhealthy culture can lead to unethical practices and noncompliance to laws and regulations. Usually, toxic managers and leaders practice toxic cultures such as unethical and illegal behaviors and actions. They practice such behaviors because they are known as rule-breakers.
- Culture is related to **risk** in that risk culture reflects and represents risk appetite and mind-set of a person facing a risk, which leads to the question whether that person is risk-aware or risk-unaware. Risk culture means whether an organization's culture is risk resistant or risk prone. For example, in a risk-prone culture, innovation is invited; in a risk-resistant culture, innovation is not invited (i.e., the culture expresses the not-invented-here syndrome). Risk culture is rooted in people's beliefs, values, customs, and traditions, which

Summary of Organizational Culture (continued)

are hard to change. In a risk-aware culture, risk thinking is integrated into job descriptions of all employees and managers so that it becomes a part of daily routine work instead of a separate way of working.

Risk culture also asks whether a person is proactive or reactive in risk situations. Proactive persons invite innovation, change, risk, and improvements; reactive ones disinvite innovation, change, risk, and improvements. Reactive persons believe in the not-invented-here syndrome; proactive persons welcome or attempt innovations. Other reactive examples include "We have been doing things the same way all along" or "It is the way we do things around here."

According to the Financial Stability Board, four major areas that can influence in assessing an organization's risk culture include tone at the top, accountability, effective communication and challenge, and incentives. Culture begins with the tone at the top.

- Culture is related to **workplace behavior,** whether it is exhibiting dysfunctional or disorderly behavior. Toxic leaders can exert their office (position) power over subordinate employees by doing and saying certain unwanted things to employees (e.g., sexual harassment and racial slurs).
- Culture is related to **discrimination** at workplace. Management's attitudes toward employee hiring and firing policies, promotion and travel policies, and work assignments based on certain criteria (e.g., age, sexual orientation, race, and ethnicity) can lead to allegations of discrimination, which poses potential legal liabilities to an employer.

Summary of Organizational Culture (continued)

- Culture is related to **strategy** whether it is a mild strategy or an aggressive one. A mild strategy reflects and supports status quo thinking with little or no innovation in introducing new products and services into current and new markets. An aggressive strategy is the opposite of a mild strategy.
- Culture is related to **control environment** where design, implementation, and operation of business controls depend on management's attitudes toward controls. Managers with an indifferent or careless culture would not pay proper attention to implementation of controls. They may even bypass or circumvent the operational controls to conduct their misdeeds. In an indifferent culture, managers can sabotage or override controls or be involved in collusion with insiders and/or outsiders.
- Culture does not provide a simple view with homogeneous entity. Instead, it is a complex view with heterogeneous entity in terms of micro-culture and macro-culture. For example, someone can look at culture from two views, such as micro-culture and macro-culture. A micro-culture is small, contained behavior of individuals or teams and has an internal focus. A macro-culture is large in size, exhibits uncontrolled behavior, and has an external focus.
- A strong culture tends to rely on two-way conversations between parties, including:
  - A collaborative approach in decision making between management and employees.

Summary of Organizational Culture (continued)

- A team-based effort to get things done.
- Employees' positive or negative attitude toward the organization's governance.
- Management's relationships with customers, employees, public community, and other stakeholders.
- How management handles crisis situations and negative events.
- How management behaves toward competitors.

  Communications from the top-management (tone at the top) is one-way conversation, which represents a weak culture.

- Simple and clear communications within an organization can include using newsletters, fireside chats, group meetings, one-on-one meetings, interviews, and the intranet to bring cultural awareness regarding policies on workplace violence, business conduct, harassment, and discrimination.

Auditing Organizational Culture

World-class internal audit functions incorporate the review of their corporate culture into every audit engagement, not as a stand-alone audit or an ad hoc audit when needed or requested. Some special issues arise in reviewing corporate culture due to its sensitive nature and because no concrete evidence is available, unlike traditional assurance reviews.

The next audit procedures can help in reviewing or assessing the corporate culture.

- Determine whether an organization's culture maturity model is stone-age culture or modern-age culture or in between.

  Characteristics of **stone-age culture** are described next.

  - A closed shop for limited members only
  - Mistrust
  - Insensitivity to cultural norms and deviations (e.g., corruption, bribes, and fraud are accepted)
  - Rigid organizational structure (i.e., tall structures with several management hierarchical levels and formal and strict job titles with threats, insults, and punishments)
  - Class discrimination (i.e., rich or poor, educated or uneducated)

Auditing Organizational Culture (continued)

- All exclusiveness (i.e., no outsiders)
- Low expectations from employees
- Innovation discouraged
- Intuition-based risk taking discouraged
- Weak leadership

Characteristics of **modern-age** culture are described next.

- Open shop for all members
- Trust
- Sensitivity to cultural norms and deviations (e.g., ethical actions and good behavior)
- Flexible organizational structure (i.e., flat structure with few management hierarchical levels and loose job titles with no threats, insults, and punishments)

Auditing Organizational Culture (continued)

- No class discrimination (i.e., rich or poor, educated or uneducated)
- All inclusiveness (both insiders and outsiders)
- High expectations from employees by raising the bar
- Innovation encouraged
- Calculated risk taking encouraged
- Strong leadership

- The CAE first should inform the CEO about the assessment of culture (culture audit) in all audit engagements prior to talking to the board and audit committee to gain initial support from the CEO and later from the senior management. Ideally, the CEO, board, and audit committee are champions of the continuous assessment of culture. Next, the CAE should seek the support of senior management and operational management because they are the key managers that make the culture audit happen. Senior management in turn must inform the functional managers in their chain of command. Any resistance to the culture audit at any management level is a red flag indicating cultural problems.

Auditing Organizational Culture (continued)

- The CAE should ensure that soft culture audit findings, which are based on subjective matters, are treated delicately and differently from the hard findings based on hard evidence found in traditional compliance audits. All assumptions and timelines must be verified so as not to reach false conclusions and wrong allegations that can create ill will between the audit function and audit clients.
- Because there is no hard proof and there is no concrete evidence (solid evidence) available in the culture-related audit findings, internal auditors can use surveys (employees and customers), interviews (employee exit interviews and management interviews), customer complaints (wrong prices, poor quality, shipping delays and problems, and product returns), and metrics (culture indicators and scorecards) to increase the concreteness of evidence. In some cases, seeing is *not* believing.
- The CAE should ensure that internal auditors assigned to culture-related audit projects have business acumen and receive sensitivity training.

Auditing Organizational Culture (continued)

A relationship between the three lines of defense and auditing culture is presented next.

First line of defense	Business line management (business unit or division management, functional or departmental management, and frontline supervisors and managers) is responsible for establishing and communicating expected outcomes, value in adhering to code-of-conduct, and promoting good cultural behaviors.
Second line of defense	Oversight function provides advice and support to the first line of defense. These oversight functions include the ethics, compliance, legal, and regulatory offices. The oversight function develops policies, procedures, and programs for adherence in order to minimize culture-related risks and for compliance purposes.
Third line of defense	Internal audit function: Evaluates adherence to the organization's culture-related standards. Evaluates whether the corporate culture supports the organization's mission, vision, and strategy. Assesses the overall organization's culture personality. Identifies areas with weak culture and turns them into areas with strong culture.

First LOD: Business line management (business unit or division management, functional or departmental

ORGANIZATIONAL ETHICS

Organizational or corporate ethics play an important role in ensuring good corporate governance and better corporate management. Corporate ethics and corporate governance support corporate management. Ethical lapses and dilemmas are root causes of many problems that corporate management faces today.

Ethics can be defined broadly as the study of what is right or good for human beings. It attempts to determine what people ought to do or what goals they should pursue. Business ethics, as a branch of applied ethics, is the study and determination of what is right and good in business settings. Unlike legal analyses, analyses of ethics have no central authority, such as courts or legislatures, upon which to rely; nor do they follow clear-cut, universal standards. Nonetheless, despite these inherent limitations, it is still possible to make meaningful ethical judgments.

Personal Ethics and Business Ethics

Broadly speaking, ethics can be divided into personal ethics and business ethics. Personal ethics deal with how an individual conducts his or her own life on a day-to-day basis. Business ethics deal with how a business organization conducts its own business, whether it is a proprietorship, partnership, or corporation. Personal ethics affects business ethics because it is the same individual working for the same business organization. This individual brings his or her own beliefs, attitudes, behaviors, and values (moral compass) to the workplace. Hence, personal ethics are integrated with business ethics.

Interactions between Law, Ethics, and Economics

Law

Law reflects society's codified ethics and is generally regarded as a minimum standard of behavior for individuals and organizations. It is good to respond to the spirit as well as letter of law, assuming law is the floor and ethics are the ceiling on behavior and operating above minimum required between the floor (lower limit) and the ceiling (upper limit). Illegal acts are by definition violations of laws, rules, or regulations. They are failures to follow requirements of laws or implementing regulations, including intentional acts (e.g., fraud, irregularities, and not fully disclosing in financial statements), unintentional noncompliance acts (e.g., errors), and criminal acts. Abuse occurs when the conduct of an activity or function falls short of expectations for prudent behavior. Abuse is distinguished from noncompliance in that abusive conditions may not directly violate laws or regulations. Abusive activities may be within the letter of the laws and regulations but violate their spirit or the more general standards of impartial behavior and, more specifically, the ethical behavior. This means that abusive acts can be legal but unethical.

Some corporate executives are under the false impression that their actions are above the legal and ethical principles and that they will not get caught for their bad behavior. Instead, they should realize that nobody is above the law. Honesty and integrity should be the hallmark of the management profession for business managers and executives.

Law (continued)

It is illegal for corporate management to create complicated and convoluted business divisions and ventures to simply divert the law, thus creating illusory profits and deceiving stakeholders. The underlying, implicit intent could be to increase the company's stock price and to receive higher compensation for executives because compensation levels are tied to performance levels (i.e., profits, stock prices, and earnings per share). If caught, these executives can be fined, punished, and imprisoned for conducting illegal activities and for their bad behavior. Human greed, at its maximum, is at play here.

Ethics

Ethics deal with deciding and acting on what is right or wrong in a particular situation. Basically, ethics is concerned with knowing what is good and bad and separating them. The next guidelines can assist business managers and executives to be ethical in business settings.

Most ethical dilemmas involve a conflict between the needs of the part and those of the whole—the individual versus the organization or the organization versus society as a whole. Managers faced with tough ethical choices often benefit from a normative approach—one based on norms and values—to guide their decision making.

Four normative approaches are the utilitarian approach, the individualism approach, the moral-rights approach, and the justice approach. The utilitarian approach is based on the ethical concept that moral behaviors produce the greatest good for the greatest number. The individualism approach is based on the ethical concept that acts are moral when they promote the individual's best long-term interests, which ultimately leads to the greater good. The moral-rights approach is based on the ethical concept that moral decisions are those that best maintain the rights of those people affected by them. The justice approach is based on the ethical concept that moral decisions must be based on standards of equity, fairness, and impartiality.

Three types of justice are of concern to business managers: distributive, procedural, and compensatory justice. Distributive justice requires that different treatment of people not be based on arbitrary characteristics. Procedural justice emerges from the concept that rules should be clearly stated and consistently and impartially enforced. Compensatory justice requires that individuals should be compensated for the cost of their injuries by the party responsible and that individuals should not be held responsible for matters over which they have no control.

Ethics (continued)

It is unethical for corporate management to create illusory profits and manipulate profits to increase their company's stock price using creative accounting practices, thus deceiving stakeholders. The underlying, implicit intent could be to increase the company's stock price and to receive higher compensation for executives because compensation levels are tied to performance levels (i.e., profits, stock prices, and earnings per share). If caught, these executives can be fined, punished, and imprisoned for conducting unethical activities. Note that illegal activities and unethical activities go hand in hand sometimes but not always.

Economics

Economics deals with effective and efficient allocation and utilization of scarce resources to produce goods and to provide services to citizens of a country or a nation. These scarce resources are money, men, machinery, and materials, often called the 4*M*s.

Types of Ethics

Basically, ethics can be of two types: the normative approach and the descriptive approach. Managers faced with tough ethical choices often benefit from taking a **normative approach**—one based on norms and values—to guide their decision making. Normative ethics are concerned with supplying and justifying a coherent moral system of thinking and judgment. They ask: "What ought to be?" The normative approach includes utilitarian, individualism, moral rights, and justice approaches. An application of the normative approach can occur when a decision is made to recruit, hire, train, and promote both men and women equally.

The **descriptive ethics** approach is concerned with describing, characterizing, and studying the morality of a people, culture, or society. It also compares and contrasts different moral codes, systems, practices, beliefs,

Types of Ethics (continued)

and values. This approach asks a basic question: "What is?" The business judgment rule is a legal presumption that directors and officers of a corporation have exercised due care by acting on an informed basis, in good faith, and in the honest belief that their actions are in the best interests of the corporation. Unless a plaintiff can give persuasive evidence against at least one of the criteria, corporate directors and officers are insulated from liability for breach of the duty of care. A downside is that some people may adopt the view that "if everyone is doing it, it must be acceptable," which is not right. Examples include discrimination, speeding while driving a car, padding expense accounts, and deceptive advertising.

Models of Management Ethics

The three models of management ethics include immoral management, moral management, and amoral management.

The **immoral management** model holds that management's motives are selfish and greedy and that management cares only about its own or its company's gains. For example, if Company A knowingly commits a wrongful act that is detrimental to Company B, Company A has exhibited an immoral type of management ethics. Immoral management decisions, behaviors, actions, and practices are discordant with ethical principles. This model represents unethical behavior and follows an exploitative strategy.

Moral management, as expected, exhibits ethical behavior and follows an integrity strategy. It conforms to the highest standards of ethical behavior or professional standards of conduct.

Amoral management can be intentionally amoral or unintentionally amoral. Intentionally amoral managers do not factor ethical considerations into their decisions, actions, and behaviors because they believe business activity resides outside the sphere to which moral judgments apply. They think that different rules apply in business than in other areas of life. Unintentionally amoral managers do not think about business activity in ethical terms. These managers are simply casual about the negative effects of their decisions on others. They lack ethical perception and moral awareness and do not stop to consider that their actions have ethical dimensions or consequences. Amoral management contains both intentional behavior and unintentional behavior, and follows compliance strategy.

Elements of Making Moral Judgments

The six major elements or capacities that are essential to making moral judgments include: (1) moral imagination, (2) moral identification and ordering, (3) moral evaluation, (4) tolerance of moral disagreement and ambiguity, (5) integration of managerial and moral competence, and (6) a sense of moral obligation and integrity.

Moral imagination refers to the ability to perceive that a web of competing economic relationships is, at the same time, a web of moral or ethical relationships. Developing moral imagination means not only becoming sensitive to ethical issues in business decision making but also developing the perspective of searching out subtle places where people are likely to be detrimentally affected by managers' decision making or behaviors.

Moral identification and ordering refers to the ability to discern the relevance or nonrelevance of moral factors that are introduced into a decision-making situation. The goal of **moral evaluation** is to integrate the concern for others into organizational goals, purposes, and legitimacy. In the final analysis, though, the manager may not know the "right" answer or solution, although moral sensitivity has been introduced into the decision-making process. The important point is that amorality has not prevailed or driven the decision process.

Tolerance of moral disagreement and ambiguity is an extension of a managerial talent or facility that is present in all decision-making situations managers face. **Integration of management and moral competence** combines management's knowledge, skills, and abilities with moral values that provide a future-looking perspective. **A sense of moral obligation and integrity** requires the intuitive or learned understanding that moral fibers—a concern for fairness, justice, and due process to people, groups, and communities—are woven into the fabric of managerial decision making and are integral components that hold systems together.

Code of Ethics and the Internal Auditor

After the board and senior management approves the written code of ethics or code of conduct document, it should encourage the timely and confidential communication of suspected fraud, misconduct, or abuse to a higher-level person, for example, within the bank. Such a code is intended to foster a culture of integrity and accountability. An ethics officer or chief legal counsel can provide advice to all employees regarding ethics-related questions. The ethics officer performs annual reviews of the ethics policy and discusses ethics at all levels of the bank. Internal auditors monitor the effectiveness of the ethics program and whistleblower policy. Internal auditors should assess the corporate culture and ethics processes to identify any governance-related weaknesses. Internal auditors should assure the board that suspected fraud and misconduct are promptly reported, investigated, and addressed.

A comprehensive policy on code of ethics for a bank follows; it can be applied to any organization because it represents a model policy document consisting of nine essential elements.

1. **Conflicts of interest,** A conflict of interest occurs when an individual's private interests conflict with the bank's interests.

2. **Insider activities.** Directors, executives, and officers should refrain from financial relationships that are or could be viewed as abusive, imprudent, or preferential. In addition, laws and regulations (e.g., the SEC Rules and the bank's Regulation O) prohibit certain insider activities.

Code of Ethics and the Internal Auditor (continued)

3. **Self-dealing and corporate opportunity.** Employees, officers, executives, and directors are prohibited from using corporate property, information, or their positions for personal gain. Usurpation of a corporate opportunity is a breach of fiduciary duty.
4. **Confidentiality.** All bank employees and directors must maintain the confidentiality of bank, customer, and personnel information.
5. **Fair dealing.** Employees, officers, and directors should not conceal information, abuse privileged information, misrepresent material facts, or engage in any other unfair dealing practice.
6. **Protection and use of bank assets.** Company assets should be used for legitimate business purposes.
7. **Compliance.** All bank employees, officers, and directors must comply with applicable laws and regulations.

Code of Ethics and the Internal Auditor (continued)

8. **Whistleblower policy.** The board and senior management of an organization should ensure that there is a process for employees to report legitimate concerns about suspected illegal, unethical, or questionable practices taking place within the organization with protection from reprisal. This process includes the ability to escalate operational problems, inappropriate conduct, policy violations, or other risks to the organization for investigation. The suspected individuals can be internal to the organizations (e.g., employees, supervisors, managers, executives, and the board members) and external to the organization (e.g., contractors, consultants, suppliers, and vendors).
9. **Consequences.** Employees, officers, and directors should have a clear understanding of the consequences of unethical, illegal, or other behaviors that do not align with the bank's Code of Ethics. Consequences can include fines, penalties, imprisonment, demotions, or terminations.

In summary, an ethics officer develops, reviews, updates, and communicates the code of ethics to all employees. Internal auditors monitor the effectiveness of the ethics program and whistleblower policy.

Ethics Audit

Specifically, the chief ethics officer or designee should perform an ethics audit by:

- Working with the internal audit department in developing audit plans and identifying areas of audit addressing ethical violations.
- Working with the legal department in pursuing cases that violated ethical principles either inside the company (e.g., employees and management) or outside (e.g., customers, suppliers, vendors, and contractors).
- Conducting ethics audits, special management reviews, and self-assessment reviews periodically and proactively to ensure continuous improvement in ethical matters.
- Encouraging employees and others to report ethical violations through a whistleblower telephone hotline, email, or other means that will be kept confidential.
- Conducting training classes for managers and nonmanagers about ethical principles that include actions and consequences and referencing all applicable laws and regulations.
- Analyzing outside-in views (i.e., views of stakeholders about company management) and inside-out views (i.e., views of company management about stakeholders) to identify disconnections between these views and to integrate them in a coherent manner.
- Issuing an audit report describing significant findings and recommendations to management for corrective actions to take.

Definition of Corporate Social Responsibility

Corporations have obligations to be good citizens of the local, national, and international communities in which they do business. Failure to meet these obligations can result in damage to the cooperation, both in immediate economic terms and in longer-term reputational value. Sustainability of a corporation is a major part of its social responsibility.

A corporation should be a good citizen and contribute to the communities in which it operates by making charitable contributions and encouraging its directors, manager, and employees to form relationships with those communities. A corporation also should be active in promoting awareness of health, safety, and environmental issues, including any issues that relate to the specific types of business in which the corporation is engaged. Organizations must comply with the ISO 26000 Standard regarding social responsibility. The social responsibility of business encompasses the economic, legal, ethical, discretionary (philanthropic), and sustainability expectations that society has of organizations at a given point in time.

Economic Responsibilities

The **economic responsibility** required of business by the U.S. society includes things such as (1) be profitable, (2) maximize sales, (3) minimize costs, (4) make sound strategic decisions, and (5) be attentive to dividend policy.

Legal Responsibilities

The **legal responsibility** required of business by the U.S. society includes things such as (1) obey all laws and adhere to all regulations, (2) obey the Foreign Corrupt Practices Act, (3) fulfill all contractual obligations, and (4) honor all warranties and guarantees.

Ethical Responsibilities

The **ethical responsibility** expected of business by the U.S. society includes things such as (1) avoid questionable practices; (2) respond to spirit as well as letter of law; (3) assume law is a floor on behavior; (4) operate above minimum required; (5) do what is right, fair, and just; and (6) assert ethical leadership.

Philanthropic Responsibilities

The **philanthropic responsibility** desired of business by the U.S. society includes things such as (1) be a good corporate citizen, (2) make corporate contributions, (3) provide programs supporting community (e.g., education, health and human services, culture, arts, and civic duties), and (4) provide for community development and betterment on a voluntary basis.

Sustainability Responsibilities

The **sustainability responsibility** desired of business by the U.S. society includes things such as (1) environmental issues, (2) social issues, (3) governance issues, and (4) health and safety of employees and customers. The goal is to ensure that the corporation survives, thrives, and sustains over long periods of time after considering both financial and nonfinancial performance measures.

Pyramid Layers of Corporate Social Responsibility

A socially responsible firm should strive to:

- Be a good corporate citizen (top).
- Be ethical.
- Obey the law.
- Make a profit (base).

In summary, the total social responsibility of business entails the concurrent fulfillment of the firm's economic, legal, ethical, philanthropic, and sustainability responsibilities. In equation form, this might be expressed as follows.

Total corporate social responsibility = Economic responsibilities + Legal responsibilities
+ Ethical responsibilities + Philanthropic responsibilities
+ Sustainability responsibilities

Social Audit

Social audit is a systematic analysis and testing of an organization's success in achieving its social responsibility. It is a systematic attempt to identify, measure, monitor, and evaluate an organization's performance with respect to its social efforts, goals, and programs. The social audit is a systematic and structured review of identifying issues and problems in the understanding and fulfilling of economic, legal, ethical, and philanthropic responsibilities, and making recommendations to resolve such issues and problems.

Corporate Sustainability Audit

A corporation's sustainability policy addresses developing strategies to enhance environmental management, to reduce negative social outcomes from discrimination and injustice, and to improve corporate governance. This policy deals with environmental, social, and governance (ESG) issues, as shown in the following table.

Environmental issues	Greenhouse gas emissions Pollution from factories and automobiles Climate change matters (e.g., cyclones, tornadoes, hurricanes, mudslides, and wildfires) Water, air, and food quality problems Disposing and recycling of factory and household waste
Social issues	Racial and gender diversity problems at the level of the board and executive and frontline employees Community relations and services Community event sponsorships
Governance issues	Corporate tax strategies Tax havens to hide profits and evade taxes in offshore banks Off-balance-sheet activities to misreport assets and liabilities Supply-chain management issues (e.g., transporting toxic chemicals, inserting fake and dangerous parts and components into finished goods during product assembly and transportation; and experiencing unexpected supplier-labor strikes and supplier-plant shutdowns) Political and lobbying spending data

Corporate Sustainability Audit (continued)

Recently, more and more shareholders and investors are demanding that boards of directors of public companies provide them with sustainable investment strategies and associated disclosures on the ESG matters. Shareholders and investors use this information during proxy voting decisions. Therefore, corporations should provide a management's discussion and analysis (MD&A) of how their ESG strategy and performance relates to overall business strategy and performance.

RISK CONCEPTS, RISK TYPES, AND RISK MANAGEMENT PROCESSES

In this section, we present four important and related topics—risk concepts; risk types; risk vocabulary; and risk management tools and managing corporate risks.

Risk Concepts

Risk concepts include three major terms: vulnerabilities, threats, and risks. Risks are precursors to vulnerabilities and threats. Threats are further divided into threat sources and threat events.

A **vulnerability** is a flaw, loophole, or weakness in a business function, operation, system, plan, policy, procedure, or practice, and design and implementation of internal controls that could be exploited or triggered by a threat source. Vulnerabilities are susceptible to risk sources that can lead to undesirable events with negative consequences. For example,

- A computer system may be flawed due to its poor design of functions and features and insufficient security controls.
- A plan, policy, procedure, or practice may have loopholes that employees and others can use to circumvent a company's intentions and controls.
- Employees may exhibit their weaknesses such as incompetency, dishonesty, bad attitude, and unethical and illegal behavior.

Risk Concepts (continued)

Threat is any circumstance or event with a potential to negatively impact an organization's operations (e.g., mission, function, image, or reputation), assets, information, or individuals on a daily basis. This event is carried out with a computer system or a manual system via unauthorized access, destruction, disclosure, modification of information, and customer service denial. Threats exploit vulnerabilities, resulting in risks.

Threat sources or risk sources are the places where potential risks can originate. These places consist of people, systems, facilities, equipment, machines and devices, processes, operations, functions, tasks and activities, plans, policies, procedures, and practices. Each business initiative or project is a candidate for introducing or creating risks. Threat sources can be found when new products are developed and when new markets are entered with current and new products. Note that a threat source can exploit a particular system's or operation's vulnerability.

Threat events or risk events are tasks and activities taking place every day in an organization. Examples of threat events include when:

- A customer places an order to purchase goods and services.
- Customers are paying for goods and services that they purchased.
- A retailer is shipping a product that a customer ordered and paid for.
- A marketing department introduces a new advertising campaign.
- A new computer system is just put into operation.
- A new employee is hired.

Risk Concepts (continued)

The presence of a threat event does not mean that it will necessarily cause actual harm or loss. To become a risk, a threat must take advantage of vulnerabilities in systems, functions, and operations.

Risk is defined as the probability or possibility of an undesirable event occurring that will have a negative impact on the achievement of objectives, including damage to property and/or loss of: revenues and profits, market share, competitive advantage, goodwill, rights to intellectual property, talented employees, strategic suppliers, loyal customers, life, and property. Risk is measured in terms of consequence (impact) and likelihood (probability).

Risk = Impact × Likelihood

Controls reduce or eliminate risks. A relationship exists between vulnerabilities, threats, risks, and controls, as follows:

Vulnerabilities ⟶ Threats ⟶ Risks ⟶ Controls

Lack of adequate and/or inappropriate controls often increase the vulnerabilities in a system. One needs to focus on vulnerabilities first, threats next, before managing the risks with appropriate controls later. Moreover, when vulnerabilities are eliminated, risks are eliminated too.

Risk Types

The chief risk officer (CRO) must identify as many risk types as possible—both current and future (potential) risks as well as known and unknown risks. Each risk alternative for satisfying the business requirements must be evaluated for each risk type. A risk evaluator reviews each of these risks to determine the overall impact of significant variations from the original assumptions on which the expected success of the alternative is based.

Examples of risk types include human capital risk, managing risk, strategic and business risks, financial and economic risks, product and service quality risks, production and process risks, and many more. Most of these risk types are interrelated and interconnected with a magnifying effect. For example, legal risk and regulatory risk would magnify the reputation (image) risk of an organization. Some risks have a cascading effect; for example, noncompliance with contractual terms and conditions can lead to financial risk (i.e., loss of money due to payment of penalties) and legal risk (lawsuits resulting from violation of contractual rights). Therefore, all the risk types should be viewed from a total business context, instead of on a piecemeal basis.

Four common **best practices** are applicable to each type of risk:

1. Acquire traditional and nontraditional insurance coverage to protect tangible and intangible assets.
2. Conduct surveys of employees, customers, suppliers, and the industry.
3. Perform benchmarking studies to understand existing and new risks better.
4. Keep the chain of knowledge strong and current through continuously acquiring knowledge, skills, and abilities (KSAs) for all employees.

Risk Vocabulary

This section presents from a conceptual viewpoint risk vocabulary as it relates to general risk management program and enterprise risk management (ERM) framework. A number of risk-related terms are discussed.

Risk

Risk is defined as the probability or possibility of an undesirable event occurring that will have a negative impact on the achievement of objectives, including damage to property and/or loss of: revenues and profits, market share, competitive advantage, goodwill, rights to intellectual property, talented employees, strategic suppliers, loyal customers, life, and property. Risk also is uncertainty about loss. it should be avoided where possible; if not, it should be managed well. Risk is the possibility of a loss by a peril for which an insurance policy is purchased to protect from the loss (i.e., pure risk). Risk also is the effect of uncertainty on achieving objectives and the amount of time and effort needed to recover from a loss, damage, disaster, or destruction.

Risk is quantitatively measured in terms of impact (i.e., consequence) and likelihood (i.e., probability) of an undesirable event happening. The relationship between vulnerabilities, threats, risks, and controls can be seen next.

Risk = Impact × Likelihood

Vulnerabilities ⟶ Threats ⟶ Risks ⟶ Controls

Risk (continued)

Risks can be classified or categorized into three types: static versus dynamic, subjective versus objective, and pure versus speculative. There are at least six types of risks, including pure, strategic, operational, financial, hazard, and speculative. One way to avoid risks is by not being exposed to major risks in the first place. However, avoiding risks means missing out on opportunities and ignoring risk – return trade-offs, which is not a good practice. For example, introducing a new product or service into an existing market or a new market is a risk-taking project because the actual outcome could be a success or failure.

Risk Management

Risk management is the total process of identifying, assessing, controlling, and mitigating risks as the risk deals with uncertainty. Risk management includes risk assessment (risk analysis); cost-benefit analysis; the selection, implementation, test, and evaluation of safeguards (risk mitigation); risk financing (risk funding); and risk monitoring (reporting, feedback, and evaluation). It is expressed as:

Risk management = Risk assessment + Risk mitigation + Risk financing + Risk monitoring

The ultimate goal of risk management is to minimize the adverse effects of losses and uncertainty connected with pure risks. Pure risks are those in which there is a chance only of loss or no loss (e.g., default of a debtor or disability). Pure risks are of several types, including personal, property, liability, and performance risks. Risk management is broken down into two major categories: risk control and risk financing.

Audit Risk

Audit risk is the risk that the auditor may unknowingly fail to appropriately modify his or her opinion on financial statements that are materially misstated. It is also defined as the risk that an auditor may fail to detect a significant error or weakness during an examination.

Audit risk = Inherent risk × Control risk × Detection risk

Inherent risk is the susceptibility of a management assertion to a material misstatement, assuming that there are no related internal control structure policies or procedures. Control risk is the risk that a material misstatement in a management assertion will not be prevented or detected on a timely basis by the entity's internal control structure policies or procedures. Detection risk is the risk that the auditor will not detect a material misstatement present in a management assertion.

Heat Maps

A heat map is a visual map highlighting a major activity of interest, using a data visualization technology. It can be applied to several situations, such as (1) a risk heat map, (2) an attacker's heat map, (2) a website's heat map, and (3) an organization's governance, risk, and compliance (GRC) heat map showing data outliers and problem areas. A *risk heat map* can show the impact (consequences) and probability (likelihoods) on a matrix. The impact can be labeled as very low, low, medium, high, and very high impact on a scale of 1 to 5. Similarly,

Heat Maps (continued)

the likelihood (riskiness) can be labeled as very low, low, medium, high, and very high probability between 0% and 100%. Color-coded heat maps highlight a major risk element or component to draw attention.

An *attacker's heat map* shows an attacker's activity as an output from threat intelligence efforts. This map can help victim organizations build a profile of past and current attacker's activity, helping the organizations better understand when, where, and how they will be attacked again in the future.

A *website's heat map* tracks website visitors' click behavior and browsing habits. These maps help a web administrator visualize how visitors are interacting with the website.

An *organization's GRC heat map* can show a quick comprehension of data when its reports are blended into its dashboards. These maps improve the efficiency and effectiveness of risk and compliance staff because they can highlight outliers or other problem areas quickly for their attention.

Probability of Ruin

The probability of ruin is the likelihood of liabilities exceeding assets for a given time period. As the probability of ruin increases, an asset's value decreases and the value-at-risk (VaR) increases.

Residual Risk

Residual risk is the risk remaining after management takes action to reduce the impact and likelihood of an adverse event, including control activities in responding to a risk. Residual risk is current risk; it is also called unmanaged risk, leftover risk, or net risk after existing controls are applied. Residual risk is the portion of inherent risk that remains open after management executes its risk responses. Note that de-risking has an inverse (indirect and opposite) relationship with the residual risk in that while de-risking efforts reduce the overall risk, residual risk decisions result in adding risk to the overall risk. It is true that risk appetite and residual risk are inversely related to each other.

Several equations are available to express the difficult concept of residual risks:

Residual risks = Total risks – Mitigated risks = Unmitigated risks

Residual risks = Unmitigated risks = Unmanaged risks

Residual risks = Accepted risks = Retained risks = Admitted risks

Residual risks = Potential risks – Covered risks = Uncovered risks

Residual risks = Total risks – Control measures (controls) applied

Residual risks = Total risks – Transferred risks or Shared risks

Residual risks = Potential risks – Countermeasures (controls) applied

Residual risks = Uncontrolled risks = Unaddressed risks = Unresolved risks = Uncommitted risks

Risk Acceptance

Risk acceptance means accepting a potential risk and continuing with operating a process or system. It is like accepting risks as part of doing business (a kind of self-insurance). Risk acceptance is also called risk tolerance and risk appetite in order to achieve a desired result.

Risk Retention

Risk retention means some low-level risks are retained on a temporary basis until further study and analysis. Risk retention is most appropriate for situations in which there is a low probability of occurrence (frequency) with a low potential severity. Such risks seldom occur, and, when they do happen, the financial impact is small or negligible. Severity dictates whether a risk should be retained. If the potential severity is more than the organization can afford, retention is not recommended. Frequency determines whether the risk is economically insurable. The higher the probabilities of loss, the higher the expected value of loss and the higher the cost of transfer.

Risk Culture

Risk culture, which is a part of an organization's culture, primarily deals with tone at the top and voice of the top. Risk culture is often the root cause of an organization's scandals, rumors, and downfalls, all leading to reputation risk and corporate failures such as tarnished image and financial damage such as bankruptcy.

In general, strong incentives for management encourage a greater chance of manipulation of business transactions, such as increases in revenues and decreases in costs. Strong incentives also encourage misreporting of business results (e.g., earnings per share and returns on investment, equity, capital, and assets) to earn greater rewards and returns, such as bonuses and promotions.

Risk culture has two basic components: risk behaviors and risk attitudes. Risk behaviors indicate why and how individuals behave or act on things the way they do and how that behavior or those actions affect the overall risk of their organizations. In other words, risk behaviors reflect risk-taking and risk-inhibiting approaches. Risk attitudes reflect a person's risk perceptions and predispositions about risk that can be labeled as risk taker, risk neutral, and risk averter.

Risk Appetite

Risk appetite is the level of risk that an organization is willing to accept. It documents the overall principles that an organization follows with respect to risk taking, given its business strategy, financial objectives, and capital resources. Often stated in qualitative terms, a risk appetite defines how an organization weighs strategic decisions and communicates its strategy to key stakeholders with respect to risk taking. It is designed to enhance management's ability to make informed and effective business decisions while keeping risk exposures within acceptable boundaries. Note that risk appetite is inversely related to residual risk and directly related to value-at-risk (VaR).

An organization's risk appetite statement must be matched with its risk policy; otherwise, a risk policy gap can exist. A risk policy gap is the difference between the risk policy and risk appetite. Note that risk policy is derived from risk strategy. The relationship between risk appetite, risk tolerance, and risk universe is shown next.

Risk appetite $<$ Risk tolerance $<$ Risk universe

Risk Pursuance

Risk pursuance means acknowledging the increased risks and analyzing or exploring different approaches and methods to fully understand the size, scope, and severity of those risks for increased performance. The organization adopts aggressive growth strategies such as introducing new products and services and expanding facilities and operations. It sends a positive signal to further study and exploit risks that can result in either risk acceptance or risk rejection, not to exceed the target residual risk. This increased performance can result from a greater change in organizational strategies, policies, procedures, practices, and programs.

Risk Assessment

Risk assessment includes identification, analysis, measurement, and prioritization of risks. Risk assessment (risk analysis) is the process of identifying the risks and determining the probability of occurrence, the resulting impact, and additional safeguards that would mitigate this impact. It includes risk measurement and prioritization.

Risk Assignment

Risk assignment consists of transferring or assigning risk to a third party by using other options to compensate for the loss, such as insurance company or outsourcing firm.

Risk Avoidance

Risk avoidance eliminates the risk causes and/or consequences (e.g., add controls that prevent the risk from occurring, remove certain functions of the system, or shut down the system when risks are identified). It is like reducing, avoiding, or eliminating risks by implementing cost-effective safeguards and controls. Risk situations that have high severity and high frequency of loss should be either avoided or reduced. Risk reduction is appropriate when it is possible to reduce either the severity or the frequency. Otherwise, the risk should be avoided or transferred. Examples of risk avoidance controls include separating threats from assets or assets from threats to minimize risks and separating resource allocation from resource use to prevent resource misuse.

Risk Control

Risk control identifies the presence or lack of effective controls in the form of prevention, detection, and correction of risks. Risk control focuses on minimizing the risk of loss to which an organization is exposed. The situation of high frequency and low severity should be managed with additional controls (loss control). Risk control includes risk avoidance and risk reduction.

Risk Financing

Risk financing concentrates on arranging the availability of internal funds to meet ongoing financial losses. It also involves external transfer of risk. Risk financing includes risk retention and risk transfer, a tool used by captive insurers. Risk retention applies to risks that have a low expected frequency and a low potential severity. Risk transfer (e.g., buying insurance) applies to risks that have a low expected frequency and a high potential severity. Insurance should be purchased for losses in excess of a firm's risk retention level.

When losses have both high expected frequency and high potential severity, it is likely that risk retention, risk transfer, and loss control all will need to be used in varying degrees. Common methods of loss control include reducing the probability of losses (i.e., frequency and severity reduction) and decreasing the cost of losses that do occur (i.e., cost reduction). Note that "high" and "low" loss frequency and severity rates are defined differently for different firms.

Risk financing includes internal funding for risks (self-insurance and residual risk) and external transfer of risks, such as insurance and hedging. Funding retention can be unfunded or funded. Unfunded retention is treated as part of the overall cost of doing business. A firm may decide to practice funded retention by making various preloss arrangements to ensure that money is readily available to pay for losses that occur. Examples of funded retention include use of credit, reserve funds, self-insurance, and captive insurers.

Risk Limitation

Risk limitation means limiting or containing risks by implementing controls (e.g., supporting, preventive, and detective controls) that minimize the adverse impact of a threat's exercising a vulnerability or by authorizing operation for a limited time during which additional risk mitigation efforts by other means are installed.

Risk Mapping

Risk mapping involves profiling risk events to their sources (i.e., threats and vulnerabilities), determining their impact levels (i.e., low, medium, or high), and evaluating the presence of or lack of effective controls to mitigate risks.

Risk Mitigation

Risk mitigation involves implementation of preventive, detective, and corrective controls along with management, operational, and technical controls to reduce the effects of risks. Risk mitigation includes designing and implementing controls and control-related procedures to minimize risks.

Risk Monitoring

Risk monitoring addresses internal and external reporting and provides feedback into the risk assessment process, continuing the loop.

Risk Transfer

Risk transfer involves payment by one party (the transferor) to another party (the transferee, or risk bearer). Five forms of risk transfer are (1) hold-harmless agreements, (2) incorporation, (3) diversification, (4) hedging, and (5) insurance. Risk transfer is most likely ideal for a risk with a low expected frequency and a high potential severity.

Risk Registers

Risk registers document the risks below the strategic level and include current risks and unchanged residual risks, lack of effective key internal controls, and lack of mitigating factors (e.g., contingency plans and monitoring activities). Risk registers provide direct links among risk categories, risk aspects, audit universe, and internal controls.

Risk Spreading or Sharing

Risk spreading and sharing involves spreading and sharing risks with other divisions or business units of the same organization. Risk sharing is viewed as a special case of risk transfer, in which the risk is transferred from an individual to a group, from one division to another, or from one business unit to another. Risk sharing is a form of risk retention, depending on the success of the risk-sharing arrangement.

Risk Shifting

Risk shifting is transferring risk from one party to another party; it is not risk sharing. Often, companies that are facing financial distress use risk-shifting methods. For example, a company that takes large amounts of debt is shifting its risk from shareholders to debt holders; a company that changes its defined benefit plan to a defined contribution plan for employee pensions is shifting the risk from the company to the employees. The best way to handle financial distress situations is risk management because it can balance risks and returns and generate enough cash flows to meet financial obligations.

Risk Governance

Risk governance, which is part of a corporate governance framework, is the organization's approach to risk management. Risk governance applies the principles of sound corporate governance to the identification, measurement, monitoring, and controlling of risks. Risk governance helps ensure that risk-taking activities are in line with the organization's strategy and risk appetite. Key components of risk governance include risk culture, risk appetite, and the organization's risk management system consisting of its risk governance framework.

Risk Governance Framework

A risk governance framework is part of a corporate governance framework through which the board and senior management establish and make risk-based decisions about the risk culture (top of the framework), the risk appetite (middle of the framework), and the risk management system consisting of three lines of defense (bottom of the framework).

Risk culture, as a subset of corporate culture, is the shared values, attitudes, competencies, and behaviors that shape and influence governance practices and risk decisions. *Risk appetite*, which reinforces the risk culture, is the aggregate level and the types of risk that the board and senior management are willing to assume to achieve the organization's goals, objectives, and operating plans. The development of a risk appetite should be driven by both top-down board leadership and involvement of bottom-up senior management, functional management, and operational management style.

Risk Governance Framework (continued)

The *three lines of defense* are defined as follows. The first line of defense consists of business operating functions, such as frontline business units, business divisions, or business functions that create risk because they are (1) the primary risk takers, (2) responsible for implementing effective internal controls, and (3) responsible for identifying and mitigating risks consistent with risk appetite and risk limits. The second line of defense consists of business support functions, such as risk officers, compliance, officers, ethics officers, legal counsel, credit officers, and loan officers, who oversee risk-taking activities and assess risks independent of and separate from the business operating functions. The third line of defense consists of the internal audit function providing independent assurance services to the board and senior management. The internal audit function can operate as in-sourced (fully inside), co-sourced (inside auditors plus inside nonauditors; inside auditors plus outside auditors; or inside auditors plus outside auditors plus outside nonauditors), outsourced (full or partial), or a combination.

Risk Resilience

A business activity or function is said to be risk resilient or possess risk agility when it survives and sustains despite facing growing risks. Risk resilience means an activity is risk aware and risk prepared. Because of its proactive nature and offensive behavior, an activity or function can withstand potential threats and vulnerabilities and can bounce back to its normal position due to built-in compensating controls. A risk-resilient activity possesses current capabilities and inherent strengths to withstand crisis situations and deflect back all risk attacks and still provide value to stakeholders. Purchasing an insurance policy that gives comprehensive coverage of potential losses helps a corporation to be risk resilient. Also, assuming self-insurance and coinsurance policies can help here. Note that strong and effective controls can reduce vulnerabilities, which in turn reduces threats. Risks come from threats, and controls reduce risks, which means that risks are under control. Risk resilience means having risk agility.

Risk Pyramid

The chief risk officer should develop a risk pyramid for a specific asset or group of assets within his or her own organization. These assets include financial assets (stocks, bonds, marketable securities, and cash), physical assets (buildings, equipment, plants, warehouses, offices, and inventory), technology assets (computer hardware and software, servers, networks, and peripheral devices), information assets (data, information, and data analytics), intellectual property (IP) assets (copyrights, trademarks, service marks, patents, and trade secrets), and management assets (overall quality of managers and executives who are managing their assets, including

Risk Pyramid (continued)

their management style, integrity, honesty, objectivity, culture, and ethics). The goals in building a risk pyramid are to (1) identify any assets with high-risk concentrations, (2) assess whether assets are static or dynamic (i.e., growing or not growing), and (3) determine whether controls are adequate to protect these assets from potential risks.

A three-section risk pyramid can be developed as shown below.

Bottom	Should represent assets that are low risk, offer low returns, are highly safe, and have low disposability (permanent assets) in order to provide a strong foundation for the rest of the assets. This section should consist of large-asset portfolios with the strongest assets (e.g., may be 60% of all the assets). Low-risk and highly safe assets require low-size controls.
Middle	Should contain assets that are medium risk, have stable returns, are medium safe, and have medium-size assets with average strength (e.g., may be 30% of all the assets).
Top	Should be the opposite of the bottom section and represents assets that are high risk, offer high returns, are less safe, and have high disposability (temporary assets). This section should consist of small-asset portfolios with the weakest assets (e.g., may be 10% of all the assets). High-risk and less-safe assets require high-size controls.

Once a risk pyramid has developed, the CRO should monitor its composition in terms of asset movement between and among pyramid sections and the overall adequacy of controls in each section.

Risk – Return Concept

Simply stated, the risk – return concept states that high-risk investments should receive high returns. Here, returns are the compensating factor for the risks taken. Similarly, low-risk investments should receive low returns.

High Risk ⟶ High Return

Low Risk ⟶ Low Return

Risk-on and Risk-off Concepts

Risk-on and risk-off concepts indicate that investors' behavior changes according to their risk tolerances and risk perceptions. When investors perceive risk as low, they will engage in higher-risk investments. Similarly, when they perceive risk as high, they will engage in lower-risk investments.

Risk Parity

Risk parity is an investment portfolio allocation strategy using risk to determine how to optimally diversify a portfolio of stocks and bonds among specified assets. The goal is to earn the optimal level of return for the volatility and risk of the securities involved. The risk parity approach is heavily used by hedge fund managers who deploy very sophisticated models instead of traditional intuitive models.

Upside, Downside, and Hybrid Risks

There are upside risks (opportunities to benefit), downside risks (threats to success), and/or hybrid risks (contains both upside and downside risks) in any risk-related situations. **Risk techniques** are used in risk analysis and include upside risks, downside risks, and hybrid risks. Examples of **upside risks** include research and development efforts, business impact analysis, test marketing, sales prospecting, and market survey. Examples of **downside risks** include vulnerability analysis; threat analysis; fault tree analysis; and failure mode and effect analysis. Examples of **hybrid risks** include strengths, weaknesses, opportunities, threats (SWOT) analysis; business continuity planning methods; statistical analysis; event tree analysis; modeling and simulation techniques; decision making under conditions of risk and uncertainty; and business analysis focusing on economic, political, social, legal, technical, and environmental factors.

Key Risk Indicators

Key risk indicators (KRIs) are vital measurements of relationships between risk and volatility and show how those relationships affect the achievement of an organization's objectives and goals. KRIs are high-level, risk-related, and risk-managed essential elements that are needed for successful and effective risk management in a company. Examples of KRIs include risk coverage, risk discovery, risk mitigation, risk assurance, risk securitization, risk diversification, and risk competency. Note that KRIs are similar in concept to key performance indicators (KPIs).

Relative Risk

The principle of relative risk states that costs must be balanced against intended benefits. This means costs of doing anything should not exceed the benefits from doing anything.

Derisking

If "risking" means risk taking, then "de-risking" means risk-lessening, risk-downsizing, or risk modifying. It can also include reducing a current risk or a future risk with various methods of risk transferring (e.g., hold-harmless agreements, incorporation, business partnerships, insurance, reinsurance, hedging, new contracts, and re-contracting), risk sharing, risk diversifying, risk spreading with third-parties, risk-shifting (e.g., between stockholders and bondholders and vice versa), surety bonds, performance bonds, and blanket bonds. Examples of these methods include: self-insurance, reinsurance, coinsurance, captive insurance, financial engineering, joint ventures, risk securitization through using financial securities (e.g., financial bonds, financial options, and puts) as collateral for security, and incorporation methods (e.g., a public corporation is less risky than a private corporation; a regular corporation is less risky than a proprietorship or partnership; and a limited liability corporation is less risky than a regular corporation). Note that de-risking has an inverse (indirect and opposite) relationship with the residual risk in that while de-risking efforts reduce the overall risk, residual risk decisions result in adding risk to the overall risk.

Value at Risk

Value at risk (VaR) is the maximum amount of loss that can occur in a given time period (e.g., one year) and at a given confidence level (e.g., 95%). The VaR needs to be established for each risk type or risk category that is documented in risk descriptions and risk discussions. The amount of VaR is the amount of risk capital (i.e., capital at risk) needed to withstand a particular loss. Risk appetite is directly related to the VaR, meaning that the higher the risk appetite, the larger the amount of VaR, implying more value is at risk. The probability of ruin is directly related to the VaR in that as the probability of ruin increases, the VaR increases.

An example of VaR is that we are 95% confident that our organization will have to incur $500,000 loss in the next year due to cyberattacks, resulting from cyberrisks of data breaches. A **back-testing** of the VaR amount should be performed by comparing the actual VaR with the estimated VaR. The root causes for the major variances should be found.

Risk Management Methodologies, Tools, and Techniques

Here we present risk management tools and discuss how to manage corporate risks.

Risk Management Tools

Measuring risk can be difficult. A variety of approaches are used ranging from simply adjusting costs up or benefits down, adjusting risk levels, dollar amounts, and probabilities of events occurring, including quantitative methods and qualitative methods. Some of the more commonly used tools and techniques include business impact analysis, cost-benefit analysis, SWOT analysis (situation analysis), sensitivity analysis, fit-gap analysis, option analysis, outcomes analysis, economic analysis, root-cause analysis, expected value analysis, and subjective scoring methods. It is a good business practice to combine quantitative methods with the qualitative techniques to obtain broad perspectives and comprehensive picture of risks.

Business Impact Analysis

A business impact analysis (BIA) is a critical step to understanding the impact of various threats, exposures, and risks facing an organization. This analysis can be applied to any business function, operation, or mission. The results of the BIA are then integrated into business strategies, plans, policies, and procedures.

Cost-Benefit Analysis

In order to allocate resources and implement cost-effective security controls, organizations should conduct a cost-benefit analysis for each proposed control to determine which controls are required and appropriate for their circumstances. This analysis is done after identifying all possible controls and evaluating their feasibility and effectiveness.

The cost-benefit analysis can be qualitative and quantitative. Its purpose is to demonstrate that the costs of implementing the controls can be justified by the reduction in the level of risk. A cost-benefit analysis for proposed new controls or enhanced control encompasses:

- Determining the impact of implementing the new or enhanced controls.
- Determining the impact of *not* implementing the new or enhanced controls.
- Estimating the costs of the implementation. These may include hardware and software purchases; reduced operational effectiveness if system performance or functionality is reduced for increased security; cost of implementing additional policies and procedures; cost of hiring additional personnel to implement proposed policies, procedures, or services; and training and maintenance costs.
- Assessing the implementation costs and benefits against system and data criticality to determine the importance of implementing the new controls, given their costs and relative impact.

The organization will need to assess the benefits of the controls in terms of maintaining an acceptable mission posture for the organization. Just as there is a cost for implementing a needed control, there is a cost of *not* implementing it. By relating the result of not implementing the control to the mission, organizations can determine whether it is feasible to forgo its control implementation.

SWOT Analysis

The scope of situation analysis or SWOT analysis includes an assessment of an organization's key strengths (S), weaknesses (W), opportunities (O), and threats (T). It considers several factors, such as the firm itself, the organization's industry, its competitive position, functional areas of the firm, and firm management.

Sensitivity Analysis

Sensitivity analysis includes scenario (what-if) planning and simulation studies. It indicates how much change in outputs will occur in response to a given change in inputs. As applied to investments, sensitivity analysis indicates how much an investment's return (or net present value) will change in response to a given change in an independent input variable, with all other factors held constant. This technique can be used on one variable at a time or on a group of variables (sometime referred to as scenario analysis). Typically, investment returns are more sensitive to changes in some variables than to changes in others.

Fit-Gap Analysis

Fit-gap analysis determines the difference between the actual outcome and the expected outcome. It asks two basic questions: (1) How much fit is there? and (2) How much gap is there? The gap can be reduced, though not eliminated, through strategies, contingency plans, and specific action steps.

Option Analysis

Options analysis is more a framework for critical thinking than a model. It requires analysts to ask if all options for managing uncertainty have been considered. Options analysis may be subdivided into sequential decision analysis and irreversible investment theory.

Outcomes Analysis

Outcomes analysis is a comparison of a model's inputs to corresponding actual outputs. These comparisons can assess the accuracy of estimates or forecasts or provide evidence of poor performance. Statistical tests or expert judgment can be used in outcomes analysis. It is better to use a range of forecasts of tests instead of a single test, because a single test can have a built-in weakness. Back-testing is a form of outcomes analysis.

Economic Analysis

The scope of economic analysis includes breakeven analysis, capital budgeting analysis (e.g., payback period, net present value, internal rate of return (IRR), and profitability index), and financial ratio analysis such as return on investment, on value, on quality, on assets, on training, on equity, on data, and on sales). The analysis mainly deals with quantitative data in terms of dollars and ratios.

Root-Cause Analysis

Root causes are a fundamental deficiencies or problems that result in a nonconformance. These deficiencies or problems must be corrected to prevent their recurrence. Root causes link undesirable events to their sources. Measuring a problem's root causes involves determining the sources of identified risks (known risks) and understanding the positive and negative impacts of those known risks on other areas of an organization. Corrective controls must address and reduce the root causes of problems at their source, not just the symptoms. Root cause-analysis is a technique used to identify the conditions that initiate the occurrence of an undesirable activity, state, or an event. It is a part of risk management techniques.

Expected Value Analysis

Expected value analysis involves the assignment of probability estimates to alternative outcomes and summing the products of the various outcomes. For example, the price of crude oil per barrel today is $10.80 and there is a 25% probability of the price rising to $11.50 in the next year, a 25% chance it will fall to $10.50, and a 50% chance of a slight increase to $11.00. The expected value (EV) of the future price of one barrel of crude oil would be:

$$EV = 0.25 \times \$11.50 + 0.25 \times \$10.50 + 0.50 \times \$11.00 = \$11.00$$

Subjective Scoring Methods

Subjective scoring methods involve assigning weights to responses to questions addressing areas that may introduce elements of risk. The resulting "risk" score may be just one component of an overall subjective project or investment evaluation. Evaluation criteria are individually weighted to reflect the concept of inherent risk. Identified risk factors should be limited to a few points for manageability and understandability and for meaningful interpretation of the results.

Quantitative Methods

Quantitative methods include five specific approaches, which are described next.

Exposure Factor. This risk metric provides a percentage measure of potential loss—up to 100% of the value of the asset.

Single Loss Exposure Value. This value is computed by multiplying the asset value with the exposure factor. This risk metric presents the expected monetary cost of a threat event. For example, an earthquake may destroy critical information technology and communications resources, thereby preventing an organization from billing its clients for perhaps a week—until replacement resources can be established—even though the necessary information may remain intact.

Quantitative Methods (continued)

Financial losses from a single event could be devastating. Alternatively, the threat of operational errors costing individually from hundreds to a few thousands of dollars—none devastating or even individually significant—may occur many times a year with a significant total annual cost and loss of operational efficiency.

Annualized Rate of Occurrence. Threats may occur with great frequency, rarely, or anywhere in between. Seemingly minor operational threats may occur many times every year, adding up to substantial loss, while potentially devastating threats, such as a 100-year flood, fire, or hack that destroys critical files, may occur only rarely. Annualizing threat frequency allows the economic consequences of threat events to be addressed in a sound fiscal manner, much as actuarial data for insurance enables insurance companies to provide valuable services to their clients.

Probability of Loss. Probability of loss is the chance or likelihood of expected monetary loss attributable to a threat event. For example, loss due to operational error may extend from a 1/10 chance of losing $10 million annually to a 1/100 chance of losing $1 billion annually, provided the right combinations of conditions are met. Note that there is little utility in developing the probability of threat events for anything but relatively rare occurrences. The annualized probable monetary loss can be useful in budgeting.

Annualized Loss Expectancy. The simplest expression of annualized loss expectancy is derived by multiplying the annualized rate of occurrence (i.e., threat frequency) with the single loss exposure value. For example, given an annual rate of occurrence of 1/10 and a single loss exposure of $10 million, the expected loss annually is 1/10 × $10 million = $1 million. This value is central in the cost-benefit analysis of risk mitigation and in ensuring proportionality in resources allocated to protection of assets.

Qualitative Methods

Qualitative methods include judgment and intuitive (gut-feel) approach, checklists, self-assessments, focus groups, interviews, surveys, and the Delphi technique. In the Delphi technique, subject matter experts present their own views of risks independently and anonymously, and their views are centrally compiled. The process is repeated until consensus is obtained. The Delphi technique is a method used to avoid groupthink, as subject matter experts do not meet face-to-face to make decisions.

Managing Corporate Risks

Five **best practices** should be implemented to manage corporate risks on an ongoing basis.

1. **Manage existing safeguards and controls.** The day-to-day management of existing safeguards and controls ranges from the robust access control for information assets, to enforcement of systems development standards, to awareness and management of the physical environment and associated risks. Many other essential areas of safeguard and control must be administered and practiced daily. These include, but are not limited to, personnel procedures, change control, information valuation and classification, and contingency planning.

Managing Corporate Risks (continued)

2. **Periodically assess risks.** In order to determine whether all necessary and prudent safeguards and controls are in place and efficiently administered, associated risks must be assessed periodically, preferably with quantitative risk assessment. An insecure information technology environment may appear on the surface to be securely administered, but quantitative risk assessment can reveal safeguard or control inadequacies. Effective application of the results of that assessment, through risk mitigation and associated cost-benefit analysis, can lead to the assurance of efficient safeguards or controls of organization assets and improved bottom-line performance.

3. **Mitigate risks by implementing and efficiently administering safeguards and controls.** It is important to remedy situations where risk assessment shows that safeguards or controls are not in place or are not effectively administered.

4. **Risk assessment and strategic planning.** Quantitative risk assessment, applied in the consideration of alternative strategic plans, can reveal unacceptable risks in an otherwise sound business case. Failure to assess the risks associated with alternative strategic plans can result in the implementation of plans at significant monetary loss. That loss is a consequence of being unaware of, or inadequately considering, risks.

5. **Implement an enterprise risk management (ERM) program.**

GLOBALLY ACCEPTED RISK MANAGEMENT FRAMEWORKS

Several globally accepted risk management frameworks are available to provide a variety of perspectives with different and useful purposes in risk management. We define the enterprise risk management in general followed by eight specific risk management frameworks.

Enterprise Risk Management

In this section we define risk from two perspectives: pure risk and organization risk. From a pure risk viewpoint, risk is defined as the possibility of a loss (financial and/or nonfinancial). From an organization viewpoint, risk is defined as a risk of failure (upside risk) and a risk of success (downside risk).

Yesterday's Risk Management

Traditionally, an organization's risk management was focused on pure risks and handled on a piecemeal basis and in an ad hoc manner. Risk was recognized only when a disaster occurred and only when huge amounts of losses occurred (i.e., financial and/or nonfinancial losses). Some organizations have taken insurance coverage to protect against losses or some have operated with self-insurance. Each department, operation, function, or division handled risk in its own way, and senior management and the board do not know how much total risk the entire organization is facing at any point in time. Risk was not explicitly considered in the organization's governance processes and oversight mechanisms. There was no CRO position at the senior management level to handle the organization-wide risks.

Risks were not a part of business strategy and management performance, resulting in a mismatch between:

- Risk identification and risk containment.
- Risk-resource allocation and risk-resource usage.
- Risk planning and risk execution.
- Risk-based costs and risk-based benefits.
- Risk-based decisions and risk-based results.
- Responsibility for risks and accountability of risks.

Some organizations established a limited budget to cover financial losses; others did not. In summary, a silo approach was taken to handle risk management, and risk was not integrated within the entire organization.

Today's Risk Management

Today, many forward-looking organizations have established an enterprise risk management (ERM) business philosophy to manage risks in a comprehensive and integrated manner in one place. Senior management and the board knows how much total risk the entire organization is facing at any point in time due to ERM's holistic and big-picture views of all major risks. These organizations have established a chief risk officer position with budget and staff at the senior management level to handle the organization-wide risks. Risks are a part of business strategy and management performance. Some organizations establish a limited budget to cover financial losses; others do not. In summary, an integrated approach is taken to handle risk management.

The correct sequence of elements of a business strategy and management performance is shown next.

Mission/Vision/Core Values ⟶ Goals/Objectives ⟶ Strategies ⟶ Decisions ⟶ Results (Performance)

Strategies ⟶ Known and Unknown Risks (ERM) ⟶ Decisions ⟶ Results (Performance)

Risk Management before ERM and after ERM

A summary of an organization's risk management status from two timelines—before ERM and after ERM—is presented next.

Risk Management before ERM

- More emphasis was placed on pure risks dealing with insurance coverage and losses or self-insurance and little or no emphasis on organization risk.
- Risks had low visibility because they were discretely managed and monitored at lower levels of management.
- Risk was not an explicit part of an organization's s strategy and management's performance. Only the chief executive officer or president was responsible and accountable for risk management.
- The risk assessment process was considered as a scientific approach, left to mathematicians, technicians, and actuaries who develop risk models and come up with risk scenarios, which may not be useful to management due to misleading and confusing interpretations.
- Employees had little or no risk awareness due to lack of training and because risk awareness was not built into their job descriptions.
- Management considered only risk drivers arising inside of an organization (e.g., sales, revenue, costs, profits, technology, and employees). It ignored risk drivers coming from outside of the organization (e.g., competitive, supply-chain, production, reputation, social media, regulatory, and political risk; union strikes).
- More focus was placed on risk containment and less focus was placed on risk identification.

Risk Management before ERM (continued)

- More focus was placed on risk of failure and less focus was placed on risk of success.
- More focus was placed on known risks and less focus was placed on unknown risks (i.e., whitespace).
- More focus was placed on risk detection and correction and less focus was placed on risk anticipation and prevention.
- More focus was placed on reaction and less focus was placed on proactive responses.
- More focus was placed on a narrow view of risks and less focus was placed on a broad view of risks.
- The risk management process is less structured, organized, disciplined, managed, and integrated than what it should be.

Risk Management after ERM

- Equal emphasis is placed on both pure risks and organization risks.
- Risks take on high visibility because they are continuously managed and monitored at higher levels of management.
- Risk is explicitly part of an organization's strategy and management's performance. All senior management, board members, and all employees are responsible and accountable for risk management.
- The risk assessment process is considered as a combination of art (judgment and strategy) and science (risk models and model outcomes).
- Greater levels of risk awareness are found in employees due to constant and continuous training and because risk awareness is built into their job descriptions.
- Management considers risk drivers arising inside and outside of an organization.
- There is an equal focus on:
    - Risk containment and risk identification.
    - Risk of failure and risk of success.

Risk Management after ERM (continued)

- Known risks and unknown risks.
- Risk anticipation, prevention, detection, and correction.
- A broad view and a narrow view of risks.

- There is more focus on proactive responses and less focus on reaction.
- The risk management process is structured, organized, disciplined, managed, and integrated.

Risk Management Frameworks

Eight specific risk management frameworks are discussed here.

1. U.S. COSO's Framework for Enterprise Risk Management

The Framework highlights the importance of ERM in strategic planning and embedding it throughout an organization because risk influences and integrates strategy and performance across all departments and functions. The Framework is a set of 20 principles organized into five interrelated components:

Component 1: Governance and Culture. Governance sets the organization's tone, reinforcing the importance of and establishing oversight responsibilities for ERM. Culture pertains to ethical values, desired behaviors, and understanding of risk in the entity. This component is supported by the following principles of (1) exercises board risk oversight, (2) establishes operating structures, (3) defines desired culture, (4) demonstrates commitment to core values, and (5) attracts, develops, and retains capable individuals.

Component 2: Strategy and Objective-Setting. The ERM strategy and objective-setting work together in the strategic planning process. A risk appetite is established and aligned with strategy; business objectives put strategy into practice while serving as a basis for identifying, assessing, and responding to risk. This component is supported by the following principles of (1) analyzes business context, (2) defines risk appetite, (3) evaluates alternatives strategies, and (4) formulates business objectives.

Component 3: Performance. Risks that may impact the achievement of strategy and business objectives need to be identified and assessed. Risks are prioritized by severity in the context of risk appetite. The organization then selects risk responses and takes a portfolio view of the amount of risk it has assumed. The results of this process are reported to key risk stakeholders. This component is supported by the following principles of (1) identifies risk, (2) assesses severity of risk, (3) prioritizes risks, (4) implements risk responses, and (5) develops portfolio view.

Component 4: Review and Revision. By reviewing entity performance, an organization can consider how well the ERM components are functioning over time and in light of substantial changes, and what revisions are needed. This component is supported by the following principles of (1) assesses substantial change, (2) reviews risk and performance, and (3) pursues improvement in ERM.

Component 5: Information, Communication, and Reporting. ERM requires a continual process of obtaining and sharing necessary information, from both internal and external sources, which flows up, down, and

1. U.S. COSO's Framework for Enterprise Risk Management (continued)

across the organization. This component is supported by the following principles of (1) leverages information and technology, (2) communicates risk information, and (3) reports on risk, culture, and performance.

Examples of communicating methods include electronic messages; third-party materials; informal discussions and meetings; training and seminars; public events; internal documents; employee performance evaluations; annual management reviews; social media; newswires; whistleblower hotlines; and escalation protocols and procedures to report inappropriate behavior and exceptions in standards of conduct. High-quality information is accessible, accurate, appropriate, current, reliable, and above all has integrity.

COSO's Risk Responses

For all risks identified, management selects and deploys a **risk response strategy** from five categories: accept, avoid, pursue, reduce, and share.

1. **Accept.** No action is taken to affect the severity of the risk. This response is appropriate when the risk is already within risk appetite. A risk that is outside the entity's risk appetite and that management seeks to accept will generally require approval from the board or other oversight bodies.
2. **Avoid**. Action is taken to remove the risk, which may mean ceasing a product line, declining to expand to a new geographical market, or selling a division. Choosing avoidance suggests that the organization was not able to identify a response that would reduce the impact of the risk to an acceptable amount of severity. The decision to "avoid" is considered as a part of the alternative strategy-setting process that could introduce new risks to the organization.
3. **Pursue.** Action is taken that accepts increased risk to achieve increased performance. This may involve adopting more aggressive growth strategies, expanding operations, or developing new products and services. When choosing to exploit risk, management understands the nature and extent of any changes required to achieve desired performance while not exceeding the target residual risk.

COSO's Risk Responses (continued)

4. **Reduce.** Action is taken to reduce the severity of the risk. This involves any of myriad everyday business decisions that reduce residual risk to an amount of severity aligned with the target residual risk profile and risk appetite.

5. **Share.** Action is taken to reduce the severity of the risk by transferring or otherwise sharing a portion of the risk. Common techniques include outsourcing to specialist service providers, purchasing insurance products, and engaging in hedging transactions. As with the reduce responses, sharing risk lowers residual risk in alignment with risk appetite.

COSO's Lines of Accountability Model

The three lines of the accountability model are the core business function, support functions, and assurance functions.

COSO's Benefits of Enterprise Risk Management

With an ERM framework for optimizing strategy and performance, organizations that integrate ERM throughout the entity can realize many benefits. These benefits highlight the fact that risk should not be viewed solely as a potential constraint or challenge to setting and carrying out a strategy. Rather, the change that underlies risk and the organizational responses to risk give rise to strategic opportunities and key differentiating capabilities.

Risk is not a strategic constraint. Rather, risk is a strategic opportunity.

COSO's Guidance to Management and the Board

Organizations need to be more adaptive to change. They need to think strategically about how to manage the increasing volatility, complexity, and ambiguity of the world, particularly at the senior levels in the organization and in the boardroom where the stakes are highest.

COSO's ERM Misconceptions and Outlooks

The following is a list of misconceptions about COSO's ERM practices and a summary of future directions of ERM (outlooks). These outlooks consist of several emerging trends that will have either a positive or negative effect on the future ERM.

COSO's ERM Misconceptions

Misconception 1:	ERM is a separate function or department, similar to marketing and finance functions or departments.
Truth 1:	ERM is not a separate function or department as it is fully integrated into all functions or departments with the same strategy and objectives for all functions or departments.
Misconception 2:	ERM is simply a passive list of inventory of all risks.
Truth 2:	ERM has a broader view of risk-related active practices to manage all risks.
Misconception 3:	ERM is just an internal control mechanism found only in accounting, finance, and auditing functions.
Truth 3:	ERM focuses on many things such as internal control, governance, risk management, strategy, objectives, and performance. ERM's principles apply at all levels and across all functions of an organization.

COSO's ERM Misconceptions and Outlooks (continued)

Misconception 4:	ERM is just a checklist of yes or no.
Truth 4:	ERM is not a checklist as it is a set of principles, processes, and systems. It is a learning and monitoring mechanism with the goal of improving an organization's performance.
Misconception 5:	ERM is only good for large Fortune 500 for-profit companies.
Truth 5:	ERM can be useful to all sizes (i.e., small, medium, or large) and for all types of organizations (i.e., for-profit firms, not-for-profit organizations, social enterprises, governmental agencies, and government corporations).

ERM's Outlooks

Trend 1:	Use of big data, collected either from inside or outside of an organization, is rapidly growing to explore new business opportunities that can increase revenue and profits. New ways of analyzing the big data (data analytics) and new ways of presenting the big-data results (data visualization tools) can help the ERM strategies and practices to view them in a new light.
Trend 2:	New areas of technology are being researched and deployed. Examples include artificial intelligence software, robots, drones, proximity sensors, and other automation initiatives to make employees more productive and customers more satisfied than before.

COSO's ERM Misconceptions and Outlooks (continued)

Trend 3:	As value from risk management exceeds the cost of risk management, greater levels of implementation of ERM strategies and practices result.
Trend 4:	As an organization's resilience mechanisms get stronger and stronger, ERM's strategies and practices can handle new and high-impact risks.
Trend 5:	As an organization's risk appetite levels increase and its subsequent risk-taking practices increase, management will explore new business opportunities to improve an organization's overall performance. When these new opportunities are successful, they put more pressure on management to increase the risk appetite and risk-taking levels and vice versa. Note that an organization's risk culture can either help or hinder the risk-taking practices. A change in the risk culture is required to improve an organization's performance.

2. IIA's Enterprise Risk Management

Enterprise risk management (ERM) is prescribed as an organizational use of a risk framework. This section defines ERM, approaches to ERM, ERM tools, and implementation of ERM.

ERM Defined

ERM is defined as a rigorous and coordinated approach to assessing and responding to all risks that affect the achievement of an organization's strategic and financial objectives. This includes both upside and downside risks. ERM risks are classified as financial, hazard, strategic, and operational risks.

Financial risks—Risks arising from volatility in foreign currencies, interest rates, and commodities. They include credit risk, liquidity risk (bankruptcy risk), and market risk.

Hazard risks—Risks that are insurable, such as natural disasters, various insurable liabilities, impairment of physical assets, and terrorism.

Strategic risks—High-level and corporate-wide risk, which includes political risk, regulatory risk, reputation risk, leadership risk, and market brand risk. It is also related to failure of strategy and changing customer needs and business conditions.

Operational risks—Risks related to the organization's systems, processes, technology, and people.

Approaches to ERM

An ERM approach can be viewed in three dimensions. The first dimension represents the range of organization operations. This includes business units or locations, starting small as pilot projects and eventually rolling out to the entire enterprise (i.e., institutionalization). The second dimension represents the sources of risk (hazard, financial, operational, and strategic). This may include property catastrophe risk and currency risk. The third dimension represents the types of risk management activities or processes (risk identification, risk measurement, risk mitigation, and risk monitoring).

Within this ERM universe, two general models of ERM have emerged that are not mutually exclusive. These models are a measurement-driven approach and a process-control approach. A measurement-driven approach focuses on identifying the key risk factors facing an organization and understanding their materiality and probability of occurrence. Risk mitigation activities are focused on the most material risks with appropriate mitigation strategies. Specific steps in the measurement-driven model include assess risk (risk factors and profiles), shape risk (impacts, mitigate, and finance), exploit risk (plans and opportunities), and keep ahead (monitor change and loop). A process-control approach focuses on key business processes and accompanying uncertainties in the execution of the business plan. The emphasis is on linking the process steps, reporting relationships, methodologies, and data collection and reporting to ensure informed decision making. The goal is to manage risk events by achieving consistency of application across the business process spectrum, thereby limiting the possibility of surprise occurrence. The process-control model assumes that good processes can control risks.

Approaches to ERM (continued)

Some organizations are approaching ERM in two ways: the push approach and the pull approach. In the push approach, corporate or division management tries to implement the ERM throughout the organization. In the pull approach, individual business units will adopt the ERM at their own pace.

Scorecards, action plans, and monitoring are part of the ERM approach. Scorecards include metrics, a time frame for managing the risk, and a link to shareholder value. Action plans include identifying a risk champion and determining milestones. Monitoring includes progress reviews and review for validity of metrics.

Implementation of ERM

First, senior management support and commitment is needed to properly implement the ERM program in the organization. A dedicated group of cross-functional staff is needed to push it through the organization. Employees should see the ERM program as an enhancement to existing processes, rather than as a new, stand-alone process. The implementation should proceed incrementally and leverage early wins.

Most organizations are implementing the ERM program incrementally. Some begin by layering additional sources of risk, one at a time, into their existing processes for risk assessment and risk mitigation. Some embrace all sources of risk at the outset but tackle the processes one at a time, with most starting with risk assessment. Others take on all risk sources and all processes but on a small, manageable subset of their operations as a pilot project. Most all seek early wins that will help build momentum and confidence and promote further development toward their ideal ERM process.

3. U.S. OMB's Framework for ERM and Internal Control

This section presents two topics: the Framework for Enterprise Risk Management and the Framework for Internal Control. Although these two topics are discrete in nature, they must be connected for maximum benefit.

OMB's Framework for Enterprise Risk Management

A good risk management program should allow stakeholders to have increased confidence in an organization's governance process and the ability to fulfill or deliver its objectives.

OMB's Definition of Extended Enterprise

The OMB defines "extended enterprise" as consisting of interdependent relationships, parent – child relationships, and relationships external to an organization. This means that no organization is self-contained, and risk drivers can arise outside of organizations that extend beyond the internal enterprise.

Examples of outside risk drivers are listed next.

- A major disruption in a supply chain (i.e., supply-chain risk)
- A major fire in a supplier's manufacturing plant (i.e., production risk)
- A long employee-union strike in a supplier's manufacturing plant (i.e., production risk)
- Continued pressure from government regulators for compliance with laws and regulations (i.e., noncompliance risk when laws are not followed)

OMB's Definition of Extended Enterprise (continued)

- Customers' boycotting a company's products from purchase (i.e., reputation risk)
- Customers' backlash and negative comments posted on social media platforms (i.e., reputation risk)

These relationships give rise to a need for assurance that risk is being managed in that relationship both appropriately and timely. Although a normal enterprise cannot control the risks generated from the extended enterprise, it can constrain the risk-taking or risk-addressing plans undertaken by the internal enterprise. In other words, the internal enterprise needs to accommodate the risks from extended enterprise and must not ignore or disregard such risks.

Total risks = Risks from internal enterprise + Risks from extended enterprise

Relationships between Risk Management and Internal Controls

ERM seeks to encompass the range of major risks that threatens organizations' ability to implement their mission and strategy. Organizations should build their capabilities, first to conduct more effective risk management, then to implement ERM, rating those risks in terms of impact (high, medium, or low), and finally building internal controls to monitor and assess the risk development at various time-points. This relationship is shown next:

Conduct Risk Management (First) ⟶ Implement ERM (Next) ⟶ Build Internal Controls (Next) ⟶ Monitor and Assess Risks (Last)

OMB's Framework for Internal Control

Internal control is a process effected by an organization's oversight body (the board), management, and other personnel (employees) that provides reasonable assurance that the objectives of the organization are achieved. These objectives can be broadly classified into one or more of these categories:

- Operations—Effectiveness and efficiency of operations
- Reporting—Reliability of reporting for internal and external use
- Compliance—Compliance with applicable laws, rules, and regulations

OMB's Framework for Internal Control (continued)

Achieving the objectives of external reporting and compliance to it are largely based on laws, rules, regulations, and standards. These objectives in turn depend on how activities within the organization's internal controls are performed and reported. Generally, management and directors have greater discretion in setting internal reporting objectives that are not driven by external parties or bodies. However, organizations may choose to align internal reporting and external reporting objectives to all internal reporting to better support the external reporting.

Laws, Rules, Regulations, and Standards ⟶ External Reporting

Management and Directors ⟶ Internal Reporting

Total Reporting = External Reporting + Internal Reporting

Internal controls have built-in weaknesses. This means that no matter how well an internal control system is designed, implemented, or operated, it cannot provide absolute assurance that *all* of an organization's objectives are met. This is because factors outside the control or influence of management can affect an organization's ability to achieve its objectives. For example, natural disasters (e.g., fire, flood, tornados, or cyclones) or man-made disasters (e.g., violence, terrorism, strikes, and protests) can affect an organization's ability to achieve all of its objectives. Therefore, effective internal controls that are currently operating can provide reasonable assurance, not absolute assurance, that an organization achieves its objectives.

4. Switzerland ISO Risk Management—ISO Standard 31000

The International Organization for Standardization (ISO) in Geneva, Switzerland, develops and issues standards in several areas of business and industry. Two ISO standards related to risk management include Risk Management—Principles and Guidelines (ISO Standard 31000:2011) and Risk Management—Risk Assessment Techniques (ISO/IEC Standard 31010:2011).

ISO Standard 31000:2011 focuses on risk management. It sets out principles, a framework, and a process for the management of risk that is applicable to any type of organization in the public or private sector. It does not mandate a one-size-fits-all approach, but rather emphasizes the fact that the management of risk must be tailored to the specific needs and structure of the particular organization. Risks affecting organizations may have consequences in terms of societal, environmental, technological, safety, and security outcomes; commercial, financial, and economic disciplines; as well as social, cultural, and political reputation impacts. It also addresses crisis management, earthquakes, floods, storms, and hurricanes.

Using ISO 31000 can help organizations increase the likelihood of achieving objectives, improve the identification of opportunities and threats, and effectively allocate and use resources for risk treatment. The standard can be applied to any organization, regardless of size, activity, or sector. However, the Standard cannot be used for certification purposes although it does provide guidance for internal or external audit programs. Organizations using it can compare their risk management practices with an internationally recognized benchmark, providing sound principles for effective management and corporate governance.

4. Switzerland ISO Risk Management—ISO Standard 31000 (continued)

Major highlights of the ISO 31000 Standard are listed next.

- It was written from a technical point of view for risk management analysts and managers and for subject matter experts, not for business managers and analysts.
- It defines risk as "effect of uncertainty on objectives."
- It is globally applicable to all types of industries due to its flexibility, adaptability, and simplicity. It is most helpful to rapidly changing organizations.
- It moves the risk management from a reactive posture to a proactive posture in creating, capturing, and sustaining value, all in alignment with the organization's objectives.
- It contains three major components: core principles, framework, and processes in managing risks.
- It provides a solid foundation and practical and specific recommendations on how to implement the core principles of effective risk management.

5. *Switzerland ISO/IEC Risk Assessment—ISO Standard 31010*

The ISO/IEC Standard 31010:2011 focuses on risk assessment, which helps decision makers understand the risks that could affect the achievement of objectives as well as the adequacy of the controls already in place. The Standard focuses on risk assessment concepts, processes, and the selection of risk assessment techniques. The Standard can be applied to any type of risk, whatever its nature, whether having positive or negative consequences, and is not intended for the purpose of certification.

6. *RIMS ERM Risk Maturity Model*

The risk maturity model (RMM) of the Risk and Insurance Management Society (RIMS) is divided into seven attributes, 25 competency drivers, and 68 key readiness indicators. Organizations can benchmark their own ERM programs against the RMM methodology to assess their own strengths and weaknesses in risk management.

The risk maturity model consists of five stages from 1 to 5 where "1" is Ad hoc (the lowest, immature level), "2" is Initial, "3" is Repeatable, "4" is Managed, and "5" is Leadership (the highest, mature level). The goal of many organizations is to reach stage 3 in the short term and to reach stage 5 in the long term. For example, the repeatable stage (3) gives consistent and predictable results.

Two important questions that any organization should ask itself are (1) whether its risk management processes are formal/mature or informal/immature and (2) whether its risk framework is fully adopted or partially

6. RIMS ERM Risk Maturity Model (continued)

adopted. Several benefits and value can accrue to organizations when their risk management framework and processes are formal, mature, and fully adopted.

The seven attributes cover the planning and governance of an ERM program, execution of assessments, and aggregation of risk information. These seven attributes represent the best practices of an ERM program and are listed next.

1. **Adoption of ERM-based processes**—This attribute measures an organization's risk culture and considers the degree of management support for the ERM program.
2. **ERM process management**—This attribute measures the extent to which an organization has adopted an ERM methodology throughout its culture and decision making. It indicates how well the ERM program follows the best practices from identification to monitoring of risks.
3. **Risk appetite management**—This attribute evaluates the level of awareness around risk-reward trade-offs, accountability for risks, defining risk tolerances, and whether the organization is effective in closing the gap between the potential risks and actual risks.
4. **Root-cause discipline**—This attribute assesses the extent to which an organization identifies risk by source or root cause and distinguishes between real risks and symptoms of risks. Identification of root causes can strengthen management responses and risk mitigation efforts.

6. RIMS ERM Risk Maturity Model (continued)

5. **Uncovering risks**—This attribute measures the quality of and coverage of risk assessment efforts. It examines the methods of collecting risk information and risk assessment process; identifies trends and correlations that can be uncovered from risk information; and focuses on risk areas that may be uncovered in the "whitespace" that do not have a readily identifiable owner or associated control function. Risk coverage rates solely rest on risk discovery rates.

6. **Performance management**—This attribute determines the degree to which an organization executes its mission, vision, and strategy. It evaluates the strength of planning, communicating, and measuring the core enterprise goals and analyzes how actual progress deviates from expectations.

7. **Business resiliency and sustainability**—This attribute evaluates the extent to which business continuity planning and operational planning activities are carried out to ensure a long-term sustainability. It requires that the business continuity plans are agile and resilient.

Benefits of the RIMS-RMM framework for risk-mature organizations include (1) a positive correlation between the high risk scores and high credit ratings that can help in raising new capital in the capital markets and (2) an increase in the market value (capitalization value) through increased stock prices. These benefits accrue to organizations because their risks are properly controlled and well managed.

RIMS-IIA Collaboration

RIMS and the IIA define the ERM in different ways.

> RIMS—"ERM is a strategic business discipline that supports the achievement of an organization's objectives by addressing the full spectrum of its risks and managing the combined impact of those risks as an interrelated risk portfolio."

> IIA—"ERM is a structured, consistent, and continuous process across the whole organization for identifying, assessing, deciding on response to and reporting on opportunities and threats that affect the achievement of its objectives."

The RMM's definition of ERM focuses on best practices and disciplined approaches. The IIA's definition of ERM focuses on processes.

Both risk practitioners and internal auditors have a common focus on the same standards.

Note that both risk practitioners and internal auditors use the same specific risk management standards in their work, such as the ISO 31000, the IIA's International Professional Practices Framework, and COSO's ERM framework. They both face the same challenges regarding blending siloed risk strategies, handling of interrelated and interconnected risks, and uncovering unknown risks in the whitespace.

7. U.K.'s Federation of European Risk Management Association

Risk management is a process that increases the chance (probability) of success and reduces the chance (probability) of failure toward achieving an organization's objectives. It consists of four components: risk assessment, risk reporting, risk treatment, and risk monitoring.

Risk management = Risk assessment + Risk reporting + Risk treatment + Risk monitoring

Risk assessment is an overall process of risk analysis and risk evaluation. **Risk analysis** is further divided into risk identification, risk description, risk estimation, risk techniques, and risk profiles.

Risk identification reveals how much an activity is exposed to uncertainty and volatility. Tools and techniques to identify risks include brainstorming, questionnaires, business process studies, industry benchmarking, scenario analysis, risk assessment training and workshops, audits and inspections, and risk discovery with intense analysis.

Risk description presents or displays the identified risks in a structured format, such as a table, spreadsheet, matrix, graph, or a simple narrative.

Risk estimation quantifies the possible amounts of consequence (impact) and the probability of occurrence (likelihood) that are useful in calculating the amount of risk (i.e., Risk = Impact × Likelihood). Consequences are divided into three parts: upside risk (opportunities), downside risk (threats), and hybrid risk (contains both upside risk and downside risk).

7. U.K.'s Federation of European Risk Management Association (continued)

Risk techniques are used in risk analysis and include upside risks, downside risks, and hybrid risks. Examples of **upside risks** include research and development efforts, business impact analysis, test marketing, sales prospecting, and market survey. Examples of **downside risks** include vulnerability analysis; threat analysis; fault tree analysis; and failure mode and effect analysis. Examples of **hybrid risks** include SWOT analysis; business continuity planning methods; statistical analysis; event tree analysis; modeling and simulation techniques; decision-making under conditions of risk and uncertainty; and business analysis focusing on economic, political, social, legal, technical, and environmental factors.

Risk profiles are the output of risk analysis and indicate the significant rating given to each risk and provide a tool for prioritizing risk treatment efforts.

Risk assessment = Risk analysis + Risk evaluation

Risk analysis = Risk identification + Risk description + Risk estimation + Risk profiles

Risk evaluation is composed of two parts: risk criteria and risk treatment. In **risk criteria**, estimated risks are compared against the established risk criteria (risk standards). In **risk treatment**, risks are modified or mitigated to an acceptable level of risk in several ways such as accept, avoid, or transfer.

Risk evaluation = Risk criteria + Risk treatment

7. U.K.'s Federation of European Risk Management Association (continued)

Risk reporting includes both internal reporting (e.g., board, business units, and individuals) and external reporting (e.g., stakeholders wanting both financial and nonfinancial performance information).

Risk monitoring is a continuous process to identify, assess, and control all risks to management's satisfaction. This monitoring can be achieved through regular audits and compliance reviews.

Risk monitoring = Regular audits + Compliance reviews

8. U.K. BS 31100 Standard: Code of Practice for Risk Management

The British Standards Institution (BSI) issued a Standard BS ISO 31100:2011: "Code of Practice for Risk Management." For all practical purposes, the BS 31100 Standard is similar to the ISO 31000 Standard. What is different is that the BS 31100 Standard uses a risk maturity model to improve an organization's risk management capability.

EFFECTIVENESS OF RISK MANAGEMENT

The effectiveness of risk management is determined in part by how much an organization is using a risk management framework, its sources for discovery of risks, maturity level of the framework, and its outcomes. Topics such as risk maturity, risk discovery, risk sources, and risk outcomes are presented in this section, as is an approach to knowing how to use a risk management framework.

Risk Maturity

Use of an enterprise risk management is suggested as an organizational use of a risk framework. Organizations use this framework in different ways depending on whether they are risk mature or risk immature. Risk maturity deals with whether an organization is using a proper risk management framework to manage all of its risks. It asks two basic questions: (1) Has an organization established and does it use a proper risk management framework to assess all of its risks? and (2) Is that risk framework sufficient, current, and complete? Two possible outcomes (i.e., mature or immature) are shown next.

- **Mature** and sophisticated organizations use a formal risk management framework. A suggestion is to continue to improve.
- **Immature** and unsophisticated organizations use an informal risk management framework. A suggestion is to make more improvements.

Risk Discovery

Risk discovery means determining how much of the risk universe is identified, unearthed, or uncovered during a risk assessment exercise. Risk discovery or discovery rate depends on the risk coverage rate or risk penetration rate (i.e., digging deeper and deeper into the risk universe to find out major and unknown risks). The higher the coverage rate, the greater the discovery rate and vice versa. Note that there is an inverse relationship between residual risks and discovered risks, meaning that the lower the residual risks, the higher the discovered risks and vice versa. Risk discovery also depends on whether the risk assessment exercises are based on surface analysis or intense analysis. Surface analysis reveals superficial, insignificant, and minor risks (i.e., it is like picking low-hanging fruit); intense analysis reveals significant and major risks. Significant risks are big in scope (nature and extent), size (magnitude), and strength (impact). Auditors need to identify the significant risks only.

Risk Sources

Risk sources are the places where the potential risks can originate. These places consist of people, systems, facilities, equipment, machines and devices, processes, operations, functions, tasks and activities, policies, procedures, and practices. Each business initiative or project is a candidate for introducing or creating risks. Examples of these sources are when new products are developed and when new markets are entered with current and new products.

Before proceeding with managing risks, the auditor or manager needs to understand how risks arise in an organization in the first place, including their sources. An organization's management takes on new initiatives or projects from their strategic plans or business plans in order to: reduce costs; increase revenues, profits, and market share; improve employee morale, performance, and productivity; and for other purposes. *These new initiatives become new sources for new risks.*

Risk Outcomes

Risk outcomes are an integral part of business outcomes because they go hand in hand. The implementation or execution of business plans and policies can result in positive outcomes (positive effects lead to successes), negative outcomes (negative effects lead to failures), and hybrid outcomes (a mix of positive and negative effects). A source of these negative outcomes can be due to inherent risks and uncertainties built into those plans and policies. Note that these three outcomes are possible with any business activity, project, or process. Positive outcomes can be thought of as opportunities that should be seized or pursued; negative outcomes, as threats that should be reduced or avoided. The goal of risk managers is to turn negative outcomes into positive outcomes through risk mitigation efforts and control mechanisms. These outcomes are expressed in equation form below.

Positive outcomes = Opportunities

Negative outcomes = Threats or vulnerabilities

Negative outcomes → Positive outcomes

Vulnerabilities → Threats → Risks → Controls

Using a Risk Management Framework

A five-step suggested approach to using a risk management framework in an organization follows.

1. Identify the risk universe in full containing current risks, future risks, known risks, and unknown risks.
2. Select a specific risk area from the risk universe and identify all the vulnerabilities associated with this risk area. A meaningful question is "What are we vulnerable for today and tomorrow and how?"
3. Identify all the threat types, threat events, and threat sources associated with these vulnerabilities. A relevant question is "What threats are we facing now and in the future?"
4. Derive risks from the identified vulnerabilities and threats. Ask "What can go wrong?"
5. Inventory all the controls that are in place today and identify what controls are needed in the future to reduce or eliminate risks. Match the risks to controls with a risk and control matrix and risk maps. Make sure that each vulnerability, threat, and risk has a corresponding and effective control in place or planned to be in place. A particular question is "What controls do we need now and in the future?"

INTERNAL AUDIT'S ROLE IN THE RISK MANAGEMENT PROCESSES

Risk management is a systematic and disciplined process in managing and controlling organization-wide risks, which is often referred to as enterprise risk management. The scope and nature of this process is to identify, assess, manage, and control potential undesirable events or situations to provide reasonable assurance regarding the achievement of the organization's objectives because risks can impede the achievement of those objectives. Risks can be current risks and future risks as well as known risks and unknown risks.

Evolution of Risk Management

It is interesting to note how the risk management field has evolved over the past several years from a defensive strategy to an offensive strategy. The evolution was labeled as three stages, including the traditional stage, integrated stage, and contemporary stage with details as follows:

Traditional (basic) risk management used a defensive approach. It is cost-benefit driven with focus on risk transfer mechanisms such as insurance policies and hedging operations. It treated risks as an expense item in the budget through buying an insurance policy or participating in hedging operations. It primarily focused on handling insurable, contractual, hazard-based, and transactional risks. Moreover, it treated risks as siloed, treating each risk separately and discretely.

Evolution of Risk Management (continued)

Integrated (advanced) risk management is an improvement over traditional risk management but is not as comprehensive as it can be. It combined individual risk functions, such as premiums and claims, to minimize insurable losses through prevention methods and severity reductions. It identified, analyzed, and coordinated risks from other risk activities and functions within an organization. For example, its goal was to prevent automobile accidents, worker injuries, property damages, and human life losses.

Contemporary (modern) risk management is a comprehensive risk management effort due to its focus on the entire organization's risk management issues, ERM. ERM handles uncertainty and threats facing an organization and encourages a framework for board oversight of risk management. It is driven by risk – reward trade-off and takes an offensive role to assess interconnected or interrelated portfolios of risks that were ignored before. Here, the goal is to add value to organizations.

In summary, the three stages of evolution of risk management are shown next.

Traditional	→ Integrated	→ Contemporary
(Defensive strategy)		(Offensive strategy)

Role of Internal Audit in ERM

The role of internal audit in ERM is divided into three discrete sections: assurance activities, consulting services, and forbidden services. Five core assurance activities should be undertaken, seven risk-based consulting services can be performed with appropriate safeguards and proper disclosures and disclaimers, and six forbidden activities should *not* be undertaken except in emergency situations or in a very small business environment. The activities are forbidden because they may lead internal auditors to take on management roles and responsibilities in risk management that could impair their independence and objectivity standards.

- Specific activities in the ERM program are shown next.

Assurance activities:	Reviewing the management of key risks
	Evaluating the reporting of key risks
	Evaluating risk management processes
	Giving assurance that risks are correctly evaluated
	Giving assurance on the risk management processes

Role of Internal Audit in ERM (continued)

Consulting services:	Developing ERM strategy for board approval
	Championing the establishment of ERM
	Maintaining and developing the ERM framework
	Consolidated reporting on risks
	Coordinating ERM activities
	Coaching management in responding to risks
	Facilitating identification and evaluation of risks
Forbidden activities:	Setting the risk appetite
	Imposing risk management processes
	Management assurance on risks
	Taking decisions on risks responses
	Implementing risk responses on management's behalf
	Accountability for risk management program

If an organization has established a formal risk management function staffed with risk managers and risk specialists, internal auditors should focus more on providing assurance services and less on providing consulting services to provide more value to the organization with assurance services.

Collaboration between Risk Professionals and Internal Auditors

A joint report between the IIA and RIMS states that risk management and internal audit functions will be more effective when they work together than separately, especially when there is a common understanding of each other's roles. The next four collaborative practices can result in recognizable value.

1. Link the audit plan and the enterprise risk assessment and share other work products. Doing so provides assurance that significant risks are being identified effectively.
2. Share available resources wherever and whenever possible. Doing so allows for efficient use of scarce resources (e.g., financial, staff, and time).
3. Cross-leverage each function's respective competencies, roles, and responsibilities. Doing so provides communication depth and consistency, especially at the board and senior management levels.
4. Assess and monitor strategic risks. Doing so allows for deeper understanding and focused action on the most significant risks.

Audit Roles

The chief audit executive (CAE) is an ERM champion and should use risk-based audit plans that are consistent with the organization's goals. Internal auditing is the implementation arm of an ERM program. Internal auditors act as facilitators in cross-functional risk assessment workshops conducted in the business units. **Best practices** in running workshops include length of the workshop, preparation for the workshop, risk agreement, capturing the discussion, software selection, anonymous voting, instantaneous reporting and feedback, and selection and training of the facilitator.

Internal auditors must be process owners and subject matter experts. Both internal auditors and other employees of the organization should view ERM as a value-added activity since it is both inward looking and forward thinking.

Internal auditors should think like managers and focus on business objectives rather than an audit universe. Doing this requires new skill levels for internal auditors, including facilitation skills, skills in risk scorecards, and developing risk frameworks and metrics.

Audit Tools

Traditional audit tools, such as checklist approaches and internal control questionnaires, may not work in implementing an ERM program. Internal auditors should move away from the perception of being policemen. ERM can improve the efficiency of internal auditing function since they accomplish more with less.

Some organizations have set up ERM committees consisting of representatives from strategic planning, human resource, internal auditing, risk management, and loss prevention.

When companies fail to manage risk, opportunities are missed and shareholder value can be lost. Consequently, both internal pressures and external pressures develop to improve corporate governance. With respect to corporate governance, internal auditors can play an important role in ensuring that senior management, the audit committee, and the board of directors are fully informed of the organization's risk profiles and exposures.

INTERNAL CONTROL CONCEPTS AND TYPES OF CONTROLS

Three types of controls are discussed: business control systems, management control systems, and corporate control systems.

Business Control Systems

Control Characteristics

Control is any positive and negative action taken by management that would result in accomplishment of the organization's goals, objectives, and mission. Controls should not lead to compulsion or become a constraint on employees. Controls should be natural and should be embedded in the organizational functions and operations. Moreover, controls should be accepted by the employees using or affected by them. Use and implementation of controls should be inviting, not inhibiting. Controls should be seen as beneficial from the employee's personal and professional viewpoints. Ideally, controls should facilitate the achievement of employee's and organizational goals and objectives. In other words, any control that does not help or promote in achieving the goals and objectives should not be implemented. Controls should be effective and efficient. Controls should not cost more than the benefits derived.

Control Requirements

The auditor needs to understand the control requirements of an application system or a business operation before assessing control strengths and weaknesses. In other words, there should be a basis or baseline in place (i.e., standards, guidelines, and benchmarks) prior to control measurement and assessment. In the absence of a baseline of standards, auditor's findings, conclusions, and recommendations will be questioned and will not be accepted by the auditee.

Combination Controls

Rarely would a single control suffice to meet control objectives. Rather, a combination of controls or complementary controls is needed to make up a whole and to provide a synergistic effect. An example of a combination of controls is a situation where fire-resistant materials are used in the computer center (a preventive control) to prevent a fire while smoke and fire detectors are used to detect smoke and fire (a detective control) and fire extinguishers are used to put out the fire (a corrective control). Here a single preventive control would not be sufficient. All three controls are needed to be effective.

Complementary Controls

Complementary controls (hand-in-hand controls) have an important place in both the manual and the automated control environment. Complementary controls are different from compensating controls in that, in the latter, category weak controls in one area or function are balanced by strong controls in other areas or functions, and vice versa. A function or an area need not be weak to use complementary controls. Complementary controls can enhance the effectiveness of two or more controls when applied to a function, program, or operation. These individual, complementary controls are effective as standalones and are maximized when combined or integrated with each other. In other words, complementary controls have a synergistic effect.

The following areas can complement each other: administrative controls, physical security controls, personnel security controls, technical security controls, emanations security controls, operations controls, applications controls, procedural controls, environmental controls (heat, humidity, air-conditioning), and telecommunications security controls.

Compensating Controls

Normally the auditor will find more control-related problems if it is a first-time audit of an area. Generally, the more frequently an area is audited, the less the probability of many control weaknesses. Therefore, determining the nature of efficient and effective operations needs both audit instinct and business judgment. During the control evaluation process, the auditor should consider the possibility of availability of compensating controls as a way to mitigate or minimize the impact of inadequate or incomplete controls. In essence, the concept of compensating controls deals with balancing weak internal controls in one area with strong internal controls in other areas of the organization. Here the word "area" can include a section within an end user department or IT department.

An example of a weak control is a situation where data control employees in the IS department are not reconciling data-input control totals to data-output control totals in an application system. This control weakness in the IS department can be compensated for by strong controls in the user department where end users reconcile their own control totals with those produced by the application system. Sometimes automated compensating controls and procedures are needed to shorten the lengthy manual controls and procedures (e.g., replacing a manual report balancing system with an automated report balancing system).

Contradictory Controls

Two or more controls are in conflict with each other. Installation of one control does not fit well with the other controls due to incompatibility. This means implementation of one control can affect other, related control(s) negatively. Some examples follow:

- Installation of a new software patch can undo or break another related, existing software patch either in the same system or other related systems. This incompatibility can be due to errors in the current patch(s) or previous patch(s) or that the new patches and the previous patches were not fully tested either by the software vendor or by the user organization.
- Telecommuting work and organization's software piracy policies could be in conflict with each other if a noncompliant telecommuter implements such policies improperly and in an unauthorized manner when he purchases and loads unauthorized software on the home/work personal computer.

Control Assessment

During an assessment of control strengths and weaknesses, the auditor might run into situations where a business function, system, or manual/automated procedure is overcontrolled or undercontrolled. This means that there may be too many controls in one area and not enough controls in other areas. Also, there may be duplication or overlapping of controls between two or more areas. Under these conditions, the auditor should recommend the elimination of some user controls, some IT controls, some manual controls, some automated controls, or a combination of them. The same may be true of situations where a system or operation is over-secured or undersecured, and where an application system is overdesigned or underdesigned. This assessment requires differentiating between relevant and irrelevant information; considering compensating controls; considering interrelationships of controls; and judging materiality and significance of audit findings taken separately and as a whole.

Cost-Benefit Analysis

A cost-benefit analysis is advised during the process of designing each type of control into an application system during its development and maintenance as well as during its operation. Ideally, costs should never exceed the benefits to be derived from installing controls. However, costs should not always be the sole determining factor because it may be difficult or impractical to quantify benefits such as timeliness, improved quality and relevance of data and information, and improved customer service and system response time. When controls are properly planned, designed, developed, tested, implemented, and followed, they should meet one or more of the following 12 attributes: (1) practical, (2) reliable, (3) simple, (4) complete, (5) operational, (6) usable, (7) appropriate, (8) cost-effective, (9) timely, (10) meaningful, (11) reasonable, and (12) consistent.

Costs versus Controls versus Convenience

Costs of controls vary with their implementation time and the complexity of the system or operation. Control implementation time is important to realize benefits from installing appropriate controls. For example, it costs significantly more to correct a design problem in the implementation phase of an application system under development than it does to address in the early planning and design phases.

There are **trade-offs** among costs, controls, and convenience factors. The same is true between system usability, maintainability, auditability, controllability, and securability attributes of systems.

Controls by Dimension

Control can be viewed through three different dimensions of timing: pre-control (proactive control), concurrent control (ongoing control), and post-control (reactive control).

Pre-control (e.g., policy) anticipates problems and is proactive in nature. Concurrent control is exercised through supervision and monitoring. Post-control identifies deviations from standards or budgets and calls for corrective action, and is similar to feedback control. Pre-control and feedforward control are interrelated since they deal with future-directed actions. Forecasting, budgeting, and real-time computer systems are examples of feedforward controls. Pre-control is the most preferred action; the least preferred action is post-control. The difference is when a corrective action is taken—the sooner the better.

A feedback control is used to evaluate past activity in order to improve future performance. It measures actual performance against a standard to ensure that a desired result is achieved. Feedback control has been criticized because corrective action takes place after the fact (reactive).

Feedback control can allow costs to build up due to their back-end position. An example is human resource managers holding exit interviews with employees who have resigned to go to work for competitors. Management tabulates the interviewee's responses and uses the information to identify problems with training, compensation, working conditions, or other factors that have caused increased turnover. Other examples include customer surveys, increased finished goods inspections, increased work-in-process (WIP) inspections, variance analysis, postaction controls, monitoring product returns, and evaluating customer complaints.

Controls by Dimension (continued)

A feedforward control attempts to anticipate problems and effect timely solutions (proactive), and hence is important to management. An example is when a key auditee employee will not be available for a few weeks for audit work due to illness, and the audit supervisor reschedules the audit work to be done in this auditable area. Other examples include: defect prevention by quality control inspection of raw materials and WIP, quality control training programs, budgeting, forecasting inventory needs, and advance notice of a purchase.

Controls by Function

Controls prevent adverse effects of risks. Controls can be classified according to the function they are intended to perform. Among the different types of control functions are directive controls, preventive controls, detective controls, corrective controls, manual controls, and computer controls.

Directive controls ensure the occurrence of a desirable event. Specific examples of directive controls include: requiring all members of the internal auditing department to be Certified Internal Auditors and providing management with assurance of the realization of specified minimum gross margins on sales. Other examples include policies, directives, guidance, and circulars.

Preventive controls are needed to avoid the occurrence of an unwanted event. Examples include segregation of duties, use of checklists, use of systems development methodology, competent staff, use of passwords, authorization procedures, and documentation. Segregation of duties means duties are divided among different people to reduce the risk of error or inappropriate actions. For example, it includes dividing the responsibilities for authorizing transactions, recording them, and handling the related asset. A manager authorizing credit sales would not be responsible for maintaining accounts receivable records or handling cash receipts. Similarly, salespersons would not have the ability to modify product price files or commission rates. It calls for a separation of the functional responsibilities of custodianship, record keeping, operations, and authorization. Other examples include (1) separating threats from assets to minimize risks and (2) separating resource allocation from resource use to prevent resource misuse.

Controls by Function (continued)

Detective controls are needed to discover the occurrence of an unwanted event. The installation of detective controls is necessary to provide feedback on the effectiveness of the preventive controls. Examples include reviews and comparisons, bank reconciliations, account reconciliations, and physical counts.

Corrective controls are needed to correct after an unwanted event has occurred. They fix both detected and reported errors. Examples include correction procedures, documentation, and control and exception reports.

Manual controls include budgets, forecasts, policies and procedures; reporting; physical controls over equipment, inventories, securities, cash, and other assets, and periodically counted and compared with amounts shown on control records.

Computer controls include general controls and application controls. General controls include data center operations controls, system software controls, access security controls, and application system development and maintenance controls. Application controls are designed to control application processing, helping to ensure the completeness and accuracy of transaction processing, authorization, and validity. Many application controls depend on computerized edit checks. These edit checks consist of format, existence, reasonableness, and other checks on the data, which are built into each application during its development. When these checks are designed properly, they can help provide control over the data being entered into the computer system. Computer controls are performed to check accuracy, completeness, and authorization of transactions.

Controls by Objectives

Data objectives such as data completeness, data accuracy, data authorization, data consistency, and data timeliness are examples of controls by objectives.

Data completeness refers to the presence or absence of information. All required data elements must be present for a transaction or record to be complete. Examples include all numeric places should be filled and a check cannot be issued unless all fields have a valid value. Examples of data completeness controls include use of prenumbered forms, obtaining transaction authorization, and system logging of transactions.

Data accuracy asks whether data values have been entered into the system correctly and whether data values have been distorted during processing. The sources of the data in terms of where they came from and incorruptibility of data are also important here. This means that the received data are unchanged (no additions, changes, and deletions from the original order, without repetition and omission) with positive assurance and an acceptable degree of confidence. Examples include checking for numeric ranges, spelling errors, data duplication, and data omission. Examples of data accuracy controls include use of batch and hash totals, check digits, balance controls, and system-assigned numbers to documents.

Controls by Objectives (continued)

Data authorization looks at whether transactions are authorized by appropriate personnel for proper accountability. The person who is approving the transactions is also important here. Moreover, authorization function should be tailored or responsive to the requirements of the application system. Examples of data authorization controls include management approvals, two-person controls, and management overrides.

Data consistency asks whether policies, procedures, and standards have been uniformly applied. This refers to the relation between intra-data elements and intra- and inter-records and files. Examples include a Requestor's name cannot equal an Approver's name, and an Approver's name cannot equal a Signatory's name in a check-approval scenario. The causes of data inconsistencies can be due to invalid, untimely, incomplete, and inaccurate data.

Data timeliness means that data are not stale for intended use and that they are current. Management needs to understand the need for establishing controls to ensure data integrity. This understanding makes the system more effective and useful. Examples of data timeliness controls include use of electronic mail to send urgent messages instead of phone and use of facsimile to send urgent letters instead of regular mail.

Management Control Systems

Topics such as control systems, closed control systems, open control systems, and specific management controls are discussed in this section.

Control Systems Defined

All control systems contain two variables such as input variable (reference value) and output variable (controlled value). Control systems are of two types; closed control systems and open control systems. The main difference is that closed systems have a feedback mechanism while open systems do not have a feedback mechanism. Hence, closed systems are much stronger, more effective, and fully complete than open systems. In a feedback mechanism, actual output of a system is fed back to the input end (reference value) for comparison with the desired output (controlled value).

Most business control systems (e.g., paying bills to vendors by checks and when a check is cleared a bank is the feedback mechanism) and engineering control systems (e.g., a thermostat to control a room temperature where the thermostat is the feedback mechanism) are examples of closed control systems due to their feedback mechanisms. Here, closed control systems provide feedback to indicate (1) whether a control has worked or not worked operationally, (2) whether a control is effective or ineffective in achieving objectives, (3) whether an error or a deviation has occurred or not occurred, and (4) whether errors and deviations were corrected or not corrected. There is no improvement in management's plans and actions without timely feedback.

Closed Control Systems

Closed control systems contain six elements to operate, including a process element, measurement element, comparison element, error element, control element, and correction element. Note that the measurement element, comparison element, and error element are the basic functions of a feedback mechanism. Each element with its purpose is described below.

- **Process element** transforms inputs to outputs.
- **Measurement element** observes output and sends error signals to comparison element to decide if there are errors or deviations (feedback).
- **Comparison element** is a person or device comparing inputs to measured output and sends error signals.
- **Error element** sends error or deviation signals from input to the control element.
- **Control element** decides what actions to take when it receives error or deviation signals.
- **Correction element** makes changes in the process to remove errors and deviations.

Open Control Systems

Open control systems contain three elements to operate, including a process element, control element, and correction element. What is missing in an open control system is the measurement element, comparison element, and error element, which are the basic functions of a feedback mechanism. An example of an open control system is an electric fireplace to heat a room where the room temperature cannot be regulated due to lack of a thermostat, which acts as a feedback mechanism.

Management Controls

Management controls, in the broadest sense, include the plan of organization, methods, and procedures adopted by management to ensure that its goals and objectives are met. Management controls, also known as internal controls, include accounting and administrative controls.

Management control systems must be integrated with ongoing management practices and, where appropriate and effective, with other management initiatives, such as productivity improvement, quality improvement, business process improvement, reengineering, and performance measures and standards. Examples of management practices include periodic staff meetings, quarterly management reviews, budget planning and execution, and variance analysis.

Management control systems must be effective and efficient—balancing the costs of control mechanisms and processes with the benefits the systems are intended to provide or control. They should identify who is accountable and provide accountability for all activities.

Traditional Management Controls

Management controls include the process for planning, organizing, directing, and controlling the entity's operations. They include the management control systems for measuring, reporting, and monitoring operations. Specifically, they include automated and manual systems, policies and procedures, and other ongoing management activities that help ensure risks are managed and controlled. Internal auditing is an important part of management control.

Managerial control can be divided into feedforward and feedback controls. A feedforward control is a proactive control such as defect prevention, inspection, training, and budgeting. A feedback control is used to evaluate past activity to improve future performance. It measures actual performance against a standard to ensure that a defined result is achieved. Examples of feedback controls include surveys and variance analysis.

Contemporary Management Controls

Many new management controls have evolved over the years, including economic-value-added (EVA), market-value-added (MVA), activity-based costing (ABC), open-book management, and the balanced scorecard system.

EVA is a financial control technique that is defined as a company's net (after-tax) operating profit minus the cost of capital invested in the company's tangible assets. It captures all the things a company can do to add value

Contemporary Management Controls (continued)

from its activities, such as running the business more efficiently, satisfying customers, and rewarding shareholders. Each job, department, or process in the organization is measured by the value added.

MVA measures the stock market's estimate of the value of a company's past and projected capital investment projects. For example, when a company's market value (the value of all outstanding stock plus the company's debt) is greater than all the capital invested in it from shareholders, bondholders, and retained earnings, the company has a positive MVA, an indication that it has created wealth. A positive MVA usually goes hand-in-hand with a high EVA measurement.

ABC attempts to identify all the various activities needed to provide a product or service and allocate costs accordingly. Because ABC allocates costs across business processes, it provides a more accurate picture of the cost of various products and services. In addition, it enables managers to evaluate whether more costs go to activities that add value or to activities that do not add value. They can then focus on reducing costs associated with non-value-added activities.

Open-book management first allows employees to see for themselves—through charts, computer printouts, meetings, and reports—the financial condition of the company. Second, it shows individual employees how their job fits into the big picture and affects the financial future of the organization. Finally, it ties employee rewards to

Contemporary Management Controls (continued)

the company's overall success. The goal of open-book management is to get every employee thinking like a business owner rather than like a hired hand—what money is coming in and where it is going. Open-book management helps employees appreciate why efficiency is important to the organization's success. It turns the traditional control on its head.

The **balanced scorecard system** is a comprehensive management control system that balances traditional financial measures with measures of customer service, internal business processes, and the organization's capacity for learning and growth. The financial perspective reflects a concern that the organization's activities contribute to improving short- and long-term financial performance (e.g., net income and return on investment). Customer service indicators measure such things as how customers view the organization, as well as customer retention and satisfaction. Internal business process indicators focus on production and operating statistics, such as order fulfillment or cost per order. The learning and growth indicator focuses on how well resources and human capital are being managed for the company's future. Metrics may include employee retention and the introduction of new products.

Specific Management Controls

Management controls are a part of closed control systems because management always wants feedback on their plans and actions. Management controls can be divided in several ways, such as positive controls, negative controls, feedforward controls, concurrent controls, feedback controls, proactive controls, ongoing controls, reactive controls, pre-controls, current controls, and post-controls.

Positive controls will increase the motivation levels of employees in making them sincere, honest, efficient (productive), and effective (achieving goals) in their work (e.g., bonuses, promotions, and wage increases).

Negative controls will decrease the motivation levels of employees in making them sincere, honest, efficient (productive), and effective (achieving goals) in their work (e.g., punishments, demotions, and wage decreases).

Feedforward and feedback controls are based on actions. A feedforward control is a proactive control, such as error prevention, inspection of incoming materials and products, employee training and development, and operating and capital budgeting. A feedback control is a reactive control used to detect errors and to evaluate past activity to improve future performance. It measures actual performance against a standard to ensure

Specific Management Controls (continued)

that a defined result is achieved. Examples of feedback controls include surveys from customers, employees, and suppliers and variance analysis from budgets.

Management controls can also be viewed through three different dimensions of timing: pre-control (proactive control), concurrent control (ongoing control), and post-control (reactive control).

Feedforward Controls ⟶ Proactive Controls ⟶ Pre-Controls

Concurrent Controls ⟶ Ongoing Controls ⟶ Current Controls

Feedback Controls ⟶ Reactive Controls ⟶ Post-Controls

Corporate Control Systems

Definition of Controls

Control strategies should be linked to business strategies in that controls and the control environment in an organization should facilitate the achievement of business goals and objectives. Control is any positive and negative action taken by management that would result in accomplishment of the organization's goals, objectives, and mission. Controls should not lead to compulsion or become a constraint on employees. Controls should be natural and should be embedded in the organizational functions and operations. More so, controls should be accepted by the employees using or affected by them. Use and implementation of controls should be inviting, not inhibiting.

Controls should be seen as beneficial from the employee's personal and professional viewpoints. Ideally, controls should facilitate the achievement of employee's and organizational goals and objectives. In other words, any control that does not help or promote in achieving the goals and objectives should not be implemented.

Controls should be effective and efficient. Controls should not cost more than the benefits derived. Controls reduce risks, but they cannot completely eliminate all risks due to their high-cost nature. Note that current controls address current risks only; as new risks always emerge, new controls are needed in a timely manner to address new risks; otherwise, new control-related problems can occur.

Classification of Controls

Controls can be classified into five major categories: management controls, accounting controls, administrative controls, operational controls, and internal controls. The reason for classifying controls into different ways is that different controls work best in different departments or functions.

Management controls, in the broadest sense, include the plan of organization, methods, and procedures adopted by management to ensure that its goals and objectives are met (i.e., these goals ensure goal congruence principle). Management control systems must be effective and efficient—balancing the costs of control mechanisms and processes with the benefits the systems are intended to provide or control. They should identify who is accountable and provide accountability for all activities.

Management control systems must be integrated with ongoing management practices and, where appropriate and effective, with other management initiatives, such as productivity, quality, and business process improvement; reengineering; and performance measures and standards.

Accounting controls are defined in professional standards published by accounting authorities. They help ensure there is full accountability for physical assets and that all financial transactions are recorded and reported in a timely and accurate fashion.

Administrative controls help ensure resources are safeguarded against waste, loss, fraud, abuse, and misappropriation and support the accomplishment of organization's goals and objectives.

Classification of Controls (continued)

Operational controls are the day-to-day procedures and mechanisms used to control operational activities. The goal is to ensure that they are carried out effectively and efficiently. They also address computer security methods focusing on mechanisms primarily implemented and executed by people and computer systems. These controls are put in place to improve the security of a particular computer system or group of systems. They often require technical or specialized expertise and often rely on management controls and technical controls.

Internal control is a process within an organization designed to provide reasonable assurance regarding the achievement of five primary objectives:

1. The reliability and integrity of information
2. Compliance with policies, plans, procedures, laws, regulations, and contracts
3. The safeguarding of assets
4. The economical and efficient use of resources
5. The accomplishment of established objectives and goals for operations and programs

GLOBALLY ACCEPTED INTERNAL CONTROL FRAMEWORKS

Seven globally accepted internal control frameworks or models are discussed in this section.

1. COSO's Integrated Framework for Internal Control in the United States

COSO's Definition of Internal Control

Internal control is not a static, serial, and independent process but a dynamic and integrated process. The Framework applies to all types of entities: large-size, mid-size, small; for-profit and not-for-profit entities; and government bodies. Note that a smaller entity's system of internal control may be less formal and less structured than that of a larger entity, yet it still may have effective internal control.

Internal control is defined as follows: "Internal control is a process, affected by an entity's board of directors, management, and other personnel, designed to provide reasonable assurance regarding the achievement of objectives relating to operations, reporting, and compliance.

COSO's Objectives of Internal Control

The COSO Framework provides for three categories of objectives, which allow organizations to focus on differing aspects of internal control.

1. **Operations objectives**—Pertain to effectiveness and efficiency of the entity's operations, including operational and financial performance goals and safeguarding of assets against loss.
2. **Reporting objectives**—Pertain to internal and external financial and nonfinancial reporting and may encompass reliability, timeliness, transparency, or other terms as set forth by regulations, recognized standard setters, or the entity's policies.
3. **Compliance objectives**—Pertain to adherence to laws and regulations to which the entity is subject.

COSO's Components of Internal Control

Internal control consists of five interrelated and integrated components: control environment, risk assessment, control activities, information and communication, and monitoring activities. These components are derived from the way management runs a business and are integrated with the management processes.

Control Environment

The control environment is the set of standards, processes, and structures that provide the basis for carrying out internal control across the organization. The board of directors and senior management establish the tone at the top regarding the importance of internal control, including expected standards of conduct. Management reinforces expectations at various levels of the organization. The control environment comprises:

- The integrity and ethical values of the organization.
- The parameters enabling the board of directors to carry out the governance oversight responsibilities.
- The organizational structure and assignment of authority and responsibility.
- The process for attracting, developing, and retaining competent individuals.
- The rigor around performance measures, incentives, and rewards to drive accountability for performance. The resulting control environment has a pervasive impact on the overall system of internal control.

Risk Assessment

Every entity faces a variety of risks from external and internal sources. Risk is defined as the possibility that an event will occur and adversely affect the achievement of objectives. Risk assessment involves a dynamic and iterative process for identifying and assessing risks to the achievement of objectives. Risks to the achievement of these objectives from across the entity are considered relative to established risk tolerances. Thus, risk assessment forms the basis for determining how risks will be managed.

A precondition to risk assessment is the establishment of objectives, linked at different levels of the entity. Management specifies objectives within categories relating to operations, reporting, and compliance with sufficient clarity to be able to identify and analyze risks to those objectives. Management also considers the suitability of the objectives for the entity. Risk assessment also requires management to consider the impact of possible changes in the external environment and within its own business model that may render internal control ineffective.

Precondition (Actions & changes) → Condition (Objectives) → Postcondition (Risks)

Control Activities

Control activities are the actions established through policies and procedures that help ensure that management's directives to mitigate risks to the achievement of objectives are carried out. Control activities are performed at all levels of the entity, at various stages within business processes, and over the technology environment. They may be preventive or detective in nature and may encompass a range of manual and automated activities, such as authorizations and approvals, verifications, reconciliations, and business performance reviews. Segregation of duties is typically built into the election and development of control activities. Where segregation of duties is not practical, management selects and develops alternative control activities.

Information and Communication

Information is necessary for the entity to carry out internal control responsibilities to support the achievement of its objectives. Management obtains or generates and uses relevant and quality information from both internal and external sources to support the functioning of other components of internal control. Communication is the continual, iterative process of providing, sharing, and obtaining necessary information.

Internal communication is the means by which information is disseminated throughout the organization, flowing up, down, and across the entity. It enables personnel to receive a clear message from senior management

Information and Communication (continued)

that control responsibilities must be taken seriously. The full scope of internal communication can be upward, downward, horizontal, and diagonal communication.

External communication is twofold: It enables inbound communication of relevant external information, and it provides information to external parties in response to requirements and expectations. Examples of external parties are regulators, external auditors, business partners, and government authorities.

Monitoring Activities

Ongoing evaluations, separate evaluations, or some combination of the two are used to ascertain whether each of the five components of internal control, including controls to effect the principles within each component, is present and functioning. Ongoing evaluations built into business processes at different levels of the entity provide timely information. Separate evaluations, conducted periodically, will vary in scope and frequency depending on assessment of risks, effectiveness of ongoing evaluations, and other management considerations. Findings are evaluated against criteria established by regulators, recognized standard-setting bodies, management, and the board of directors. Industry criteria and best practices should also be considered during the evaluation of findings. Deficiencies are communicated to management and the board of directors as appropriate.

COSO's Limitations of Internal Controls

Internal controls have limitations because they cannot prevent bad judgment, cannot prevent bad decisions, and cannot prevent external adverse events or incidents (e.g., customers boycotting buying a company's products due to that company's management's negative views on some social issues; increase in inflation and interest rates) that can cause an organization to fail to achieve its operational goals. In other words, even an effective system of internal control can experience a failure. Management needs to understand the next limitations when selecting, designing, developing, and implementing internal control systems:

COSO's Limitations of Internal Controls (continued)

- Suitability of objectives established as a precondition to internal control
- Reality that human judgment in decision making can be faulty and subject to bias
- Breakdowns that can occur because of human failures, such as simple errors
- Ability of management to override internal control
- Ability of management, other personnel, and/or third parties (e.g., vendors and suppliers) to circumvent controls through collusion
- External adverse events beyond the organization's control (e.g., a foreign country's government seizing a domestic U.S. company's assets for political reasons)

These limitations preclude the board and senior management from having absolute assurance of the achievement of the entity's objectives; in other words, internal control provides reasonable assurance but not absolute assurance.

Reasonable Assurance ⟶ Yes

Absolute Assurance ⟶ No

Factors to Be Considered When Understanding Limitations of Internal Controls

The six factors listed next need to be considered when understanding limitations of internal controls.

1. **Reasonable assurance.** Reasonable assurance certainly does not imply that an internal control system will frequently fail. Many factors, individually and collectively, serve to provide strength to the concept of reasonable assurance. The cumulative effect of controls that satisfy multiple objectives and the multipurpose nature of controls reduce the risk that an entity may not achieve its objectives. However, because of the inherent limitations discussed earlier, there is no guarantee that, for example, an uncontrollable event, a mistake, or an improper reporting incident could never occur. In other words, even an effective internal control system can experience a failure. *Reasonable assurance is not absolute assurance.*

2. **Judgment.** The effectiveness of controls will be limited by the realities of human frailty in the making of business decisions. Such decisions must be made with human judgment in the time available, based on information at hand, and under the pressures of the conduct of business. Some decisions based on human judgment may later, with the clairvoyance of hindsight, be found to produce less than desirable results, and may need to be changed.

Factors to Be Considered When Understanding Limitations of Internal Controls (continued)

The fact that decisions related to internal control must be made based on human judgment is described further in the discussion of breakdowns, management override, and costs versus benefits.

3. **Control breakdowns.** Even if internal controls are well designed, they can break down. Personnel may misunderstand instructions. They may make judgment mistakes. Or they may commit errors due to carelessness, distraction, or fatigue. Temporary personnel executing control duties for vacationing or sick employees might not perform correctly. System changes may be implemented before personnel have been trained to react appropriately to signs of incorrect functioning.

4. **Management override.** An internal control system can only be as effective as the people who are responsible for its functioning. Even in effectively controlled entities—those with generally high levels of integrity and control consciousness—a manager might be able to override internal control.

   The term "management override" is used here to mean overruling prescribed policies or procedures for illegitimate purposes with the intent of personal gain or an enhanced presentation of an entity's financial condition or compliance status. Override practices include deliberate misrepresentations to bankers, lawyers, accountants, and vendors, and intentionally issuing false documents. such as purchase orders and sales invoices.

Management override should not be confused with management intervention, which represents management's action to depart from prescribed policies or procedures for legitimate purposes. Management intervention is necessary to deal with nonrecurring and nonstandard transactions or events that otherwise might be handled inappropriately by the control system.

5. **Collusion.** The collusive activities of two or more individuals can result in control failures. Individuals acting collectively to perpetrate and conceal an action from detection often can alter financial data or other management information in a manner that cannot be identified by the control system. For example, there may be collusion between an employee performing an important control function and a customer, supplier, or another employee. On a different level, several layers of sales or divisional management might collude in circumventing controls so that reported results meet budgets or incentive targets.

6. **Costs versus benefits.** Resources always have constraints, and entities must consider the relative costs and benefits of establishing controls. In determining whether a particular control should be established, the risk of failure and the potential effect on the entity are considered along with the related costs of establishing a new control.

   Costs and benefit measurements for implementing controls are done with different levels of precision. Generally, it is easier to deal with the cost side of the equation, which, in many cases, can be quantified in a fairly precise manner. The benefit side often requires an even more subjective valuation. Nevertheless,

Factors to Be Considered When Understanding Limitations of Internal Controls (continued)

certain factors can be considered in assessing potential benefits: the likelihood of the undesired condition occurring, the nature of the activities, and the potential financial or operating effect the event might have on the entity.

The complexity of cost-benefit determination is compounded by the interrelationship of controls with business operations. Where controls are integrated with, or "built in" to, management and business processes, it is difficult to isolate either their costs or benefits.

Similarly, many times a variety of controls may serve, individually or together, to mitigate a particular risk. Cost-benefit determinations also vary considerably depending on the nature of the business. High-risk activities definitely require cost-benefit analysis while low-risk activities might not.

The challenge is to find the right balance. Excessive control is costly and counterproductive. For example, customers making telephone orders will not tolerate order acceptance procedures that are too cumbersome or time-consuming. Too little control, however, presents undue risk of bad debts. An appropriate balance is needed in a highly competitive environment. And, despite the difficulties, cost-benefit decisions will continue to be made.

COSO's Three-Lines-of-Defense Model

The benefits of clearly defining responsibilities related to governance, risks, and control are that gaps in controls and duplication of duties related to risk and control are minimized. Succinctly, the Three-Lines-of-Defense (LOD) model advocates for clearly defined responsibilities for three aspects of risk: risk ownership, risk monitoring, and risk assurance.

Risk ownership is the first LOD and deals with functions that own and manage risks. These owners create and manage risks and take the right risks. This LOD focuses on management controls and internal control measures and involves front-line managers, mid-level managers, process owners, and business owners.

Risk monitoring is the second LOD and deals with various risk control and compliance functions that monitor risks. It provides management and/or oversight functions and involves support functions, such as financial control; physical and information security; risk management; quality; health and safety; inspection; compliance; legal; environmental; and supply chain.

Risk assurance is the third LOD and deals with internal audit, which provides independent assurance on the effectiveness of control and compliance functions. It provides assurance to senior management and the board over the first and second LOD efforts and involves internal auditors who do not perform management functions to protect their objectivity and independence. Internal auditors have a functional reporting line to the audit committee of the board and administrative reporting line to the CEO and/or president. Regulatory auditors, external auditors, quality auditors, tax auditors, environmental auditors, and other outside auditors or entities are not involved in providing assurance services.

2. CoCo Model in Canada

The Canadian Institute of Chartered Accountants (CICA) has issued 20 "criteria of control" (CoCo) as a framework for making judgments about control. The term "control" has a broader meaning than internal control over financial reporting. CoCo defines control as "those elements of an organization (including its resources, systems, processes, culture, structure, and tasks) that, taken together, support people in the achievement of the organization's objectives." It defines three categories of objectives.

1. Effectiveness and efficiency of operations
2. Reliability of internal external reporting
3. Compliance with applicable laws, regulations, and internal policies

CoCo is the basis for understanding control in an organization and for making judgments about the effectiveness of control. The criteria are formulated to be broadly applicable. The effectiveness of control in any organization, regardless of the objective it serves, can be assessed using these criteria. The criteria are phrased as goals to be worked toward over time; they are not minimum requirements to be passed or failed.

2. CoCo Model in Canada (continued)

CoCo defines four types of criteria: purpose, commitment, capability, and monitoring and learning. The **purpose** type groups criteria that provide a sense of the organization's direction and addresses objectives (including mission, vision, and strategy); risks (and opportunities); policies; planning; and performance targets and indicators. The **commitment** type groups criteria that provide a sense of the organization's identity and values and addresses ethical values, including integrity, human resource policies, authority, responsibility, accountability, and mutual trust. The **capability** type groups criteria that provide a sense of the organization's competence and addresses knowledge, skills, and tools; communication processes; information; coordination; and control activities. The **monitoring and learning** type groups criteria that provide a sense of the organization's evolution and addresses monitoring the internal and external environment, monitoring performance, challenging assumptions, reassessing information needs and information systems, follow-up procedures, and assessing the effectiveness of control.

3. Control Self-Assessment Model in the United States

Control self-assessment (CSA) deals with evaluating the system of internal control in any organization. CSA is a shared responsibility among all employees in the organization, not just internal auditing or senior management. The examination of the internal control environment is conducted within a structured, documented, and repetitive process. The formal assessment approach takes place in workshop sessions with business users as participants (process owners) and internal auditors as facilitators (subject matter experts) and as nonfacilitators (note takers). The purpose of the sessions is conversation, mutual discovery, and information sharing.

Audit-Facilitated Approach to CSA

Two types of people conduct internal audit engagements: internal auditors and non-internal auditors. Auditors conduct audit engagements based on an audit plan; these types of audits include assurance audits, consulting audits, and compliance audits.

Nonauditors performing audit-related work conduct self-assessments of risks and controls, which are proactive in nature, meaning nonauditors are reviewing, assessing, and evaluating their own work. These self-assessments, although not traditional audits, are conducted by audit clients (a business unit's functional employees and managers), consultants, and process owners where the latter is a part of audit clients.

Audit-Facilitated Approach to CSA (continued)

Self-assessments mean self-reviews, self-examinations, self-tests, self-evaluations, self-rating, self-ranking, self-grading, self-certifications, and self-reporting of a business function, department, operation, process, or system, which are conducted by nonauditors after they are trained and are facilitated by internal auditors, using questionnaires, templates, and checklists. Note that internal auditors do not prepare or develop the questionnaires; do not conduct the self-assessments; and do not write the self-assessment reports. Instead, nonauditors perform these tasks. Here, internal auditors act as facilitators of self-assessments; they do not act as regular auditors.

There are obvious **benefits** to audit clients and internal auditors from these self-assessments. Benefits to audit clients include (1) identifying strengths and weaknesses in their business functions, (2) establishing controls to minimize significant risks, and (3) promoting self-assessments as an exercise of risk awareness and control consciousness. Benefits to internal auditors are that the self-assessments can reduce the overall scope of audit to some extent and can increase audit efficiency to some extent due to time and effort saved from prior work done by the audit clients during the self-assessments.

Four **participants** in the self-assessments exercise have specific roles:

1. Audit client employees, supervisors, and consultants conduct self-assessments.

2. Process owners perform self-evaluations.

Audit-Facilitated Approach to CSA (continued)

3. Audit client managers issue self-certifications, similar to the CEO and CFO, certifying their company's financial statements.

4. Internal auditors act as trainers, facilitators, and subject matter experts on risk and control matters, including as note takers (nonfacilitators) during training classes and workshops given to audit clients. Note that the original audit clients who were trained by internal auditors can later train other employees (i.e., train the trainer) either in the same department or in other departments.

Auditors should use professional skepticism and professional judgment when reviewing, understanding, and using the results of self-assessments prepared by the audit client due to audit clients' built-in bias of reviewing and evaluating their own work (i.e., a strong motive to look good). When audit clients conduct risk and control self-assessments, two outcomes are possible because they have little or no experience in conducting such assessments: false positive results and false negative results. A **false positive result** can occur when a business activity or control is rated as effective when it is ineffective. A **false negative result** can occur when a business activity or control is rated as ineffective when it is effective. Internal auditors need to understand the reasons for these ratings of effective or ineffective and proceed further with caution.

4. Cadbury Report in the United Kingdom

The Cadbury Report of the Committee on the Financial Aspects of Corporate Governance issued in December 1992 consists of internal controls, fraud, audit (internal and external), financial reporting practices, audit committees, shareholders, corporate governance, the board of directors, and the code of best practice.

Regarding internal controls, the report says that directors maintain a system of internal control over the financial management of the company, including procedures designed to minimize the risk of fraud. The directors should make a statement in the report and accounts on the effectiveness of their system of internal control and the auditors should report thereon.

Regarding fraud, the report says that prime responsibility for the prevention and detection of fraud and other illegal acts is that of the board, as part of its fiduciary responsibility for protecting the assets of the company. The auditor's responsibility is to properly plan, perform, and evaluate his or her audit work so as to have a reasonable expectation of detecting material misstatements in the financial statements.

Regarding the internal audit, the report states that the function of the internal auditors is complementary to, but different from, that of the external (outside) auditors. The committee regards the internal audit as good practice for companies to establish internal audit function to undertake regular monitoring of key controls and procedures. Such regular monitoring is an integral part of a company's system of internal control and helps to ensure its

4. Cadbury Report in the United Kingdom (continued)

effectiveness. An internal audit function is well placed to undertake investigations on behalf of the audit committee and to follow up any suspicion of fraud. It is essential that heads of internal audit should have unrestricted access to the chairman of the audit committee in order to ensure the independence of their position.

Regarding the external audit, the report says that an essential first step is to be clear about the respective responsibilities of directors and external auditors for preparing and reporting on the financial statements of companies, in order to begin to narrow the "expectation gap." This gap is due to lack of understanding of the nature and extent of the external auditors' role. The gap is the difference between what audits do achieve and what it is thought they achieve or should achieve. The expectations gap is damaging not only because it reflects unrealistic expectations of audits but also because it has led to disenchantment with the value of audits to the various interested parties.

The external auditors' role is to report whether the financial statements give a true and fair view, and the audit is designed to provide a reasonable assurance that the financial statements are free of material misstatements. The auditors' role is not (to cite a few of the misunderstandings) to prepare the financial statements, or to provide absolute assurance that the figures in the financial statements are correct, or to provide a guarantee that the company will continue to exist.

5. Turnbull Model in the United Kingdom

In 1998, the London Stock Exchange developed a Combined Code for corporate governance. The code requires that company directors should, at least annually, conduct a review of the effectiveness of the system of internal control and should report to shareholders that they have reviewed the effectiveness of all three types of controls, including financial, operational, and compliance control.

6. King Model in South Africa

The Institute of Directors in South Africa has established the King Committee on Corporate Governance that produced the King Report in 1994. The committee has developed a Code of Corporate Practices and Conduct, and compliance with the code is a requirement to be listed in the Johannesburg Stock Exchange (JSE) Securities Exchange in South Africa.

7. KonTraG Model in Germany

In 1998, the German government proposed changes for the reform of corporate governance. The model affects control and transparency in business. Specifically, it impacts the board of directors, supervisory board, corporate capitalization principles, authorization of no-par-value shares, small non-listed stock corporations, banks investing in industrial companies, and the acceptance of internationally recognized accounting standards.

EFFECTIVENESS AND EFFICIENCY OF INTERNAL CONTROLS

Control Defined

Control is any action, either positive or negative, taken by management, the board, and other parties to manage risks and to increase the likelihood that established objectives and goals will be achieved. Management plans, organizes, and directs the performance of sufficient actions to provide reasonable assurance that objectives and goals will be achieved. Thus, control is the result of proper planning, organizing, and directing by management. The control environment includes six elements:

1. Integrity and ethics values
2. Management's philosophy and operating style
3. Organizational structure
4. Assignment of authority and responsibility
5. Human resource policies and practices
6. Competence of personnel

Internal Control Defined

Internal control (IC) is defined as a process used by an organization's management to help achieve its business objectives, such as (1) run its operations effectively and efficiently (i.e., operations); (2) report reliable information about its operations for internal and external use (i.e., reporting); and (3) comply with all applicable laws, rules, and regulations (i.e., compliance). Organizations design, implement, and operate ICs to achieve their objectives related to operations, reporting, and compliance, as shown:

Objectives Identified ⟶ Controls Designed ⟶ Controls Established ⟶ Objectives Achieved

Internal controls represent management's specific plans, programs, projects, and activities, which are then embedded and built into an organization's policies, operating procedures, business practices, manual systems, and automated systems operating in core business functions, such as operations, marketing, and finance. Internal controls are also built into activities of business partners, outsourced partners, and third-party entities through written contracts. Internal controls safeguard assets (physical and nonphysical), protect people (employees and nonemployees), and secure vital data and information. In simple terms, internal controls can come across as a list of do's and don'ts, as well as very complicated language in contracts.

Internal Control System

An **internal control system** is a continuous built-in component of operations, effected by people, that provides reasonable, but not absolute, assurance that an organization's objectives will be achieved. Here, "people" means:

1. Board of directors with their oversight responsibilities regarding overseeing management's design, implementation, and operation of an internal control system.
2. Management with its strategic, tactical, and operational responsibilities, specifically in the design, implementation, and operating effectiveness of an internal control system.
3. Employees with their day-to-day work activities and job responsibilities, specifically helping management in the design, implementation, and operation of an internal control system and in reporting issues related to internal controls.

Internal Control System (continued)

4. Auditors and compliance officers with their responsibilities in reviewing and evaluating the effectiveness and efficiency of internal controls.

The systems of control exist to ensure the achievement of intended results, to promote operating efficiency, and to encourage compliance with policies and other established constraints. Although internal auditors have a definite interest in verifying the results of business activity, their primary concern must be the continuing effectiveness of the systems of control that influence business results.

The important qualities that must be evaluated are adequacy, effectiveness, and efficiency. It is not intended that the auditor should evaluate adequacy or effectiveness in absolute terms, nor is it intended that the auditor judge efficiency in absolute terms.

Adequate Internal Controls

In evaluating adequacy, the auditor analyzes systems to determine that they include design features proper to the circumstances and reasonably sufficient to effect control. The evaluation of adequacy begins with the comparison of "what should be" to "what is." Initial audits and audits of proposed procedures or organization structures focus primarily on the adequacy of control.

The systems of control must detect and correct errors and irregularities when preventive controls fail. Sound systems of control contain safeguards that will counteract failures in other controls.

The features of the control system that encourage compliance with these requirements include the separation of duties, the employment of persons likely to comply, the establishment of authority limits, and the communication of expected conduct.

Effective Internal Controls

In general, **effectiveness** is the degree to which an organization achieves a stated goal or objective. Effective control is present when management directs systems and people in such a manner as to provide a reasonable assurance that the organization's objectives and goals are achieved.

In evaluating effectiveness, the auditor measures the degree of compliance with control features and the extent to which compliance serves the intended purposes. The question that must be answered is: "Do the controls work?"

Efficient Internal Controls

In general, **efficiency** is the use of minimal resources, such as raw materials, machinery, energy, money, and people, to provide a desired volume of output or outcome. Efficiency is related to performance and productivity in that efficient performance accomplishes objectives and goals in an accurate and timely fashion with minimal use of resources. In contrast, economical performance accomplishes objectives and goals at a cost commensurate with the risk.

The systems of control should promote operational efficiency. The features of control systems that promote operational efficiency include the processes used to select and train personnel, establish procedures, set performance requirements, measure results, and provide incentives. Managerial policies, laws, regulations, and sound fiduciary principles establish bounds within which the organization can conduct its business.

In evaluating efficiency, the auditor judges the practicality of controls in terms of their cost relative to their intended benefit. An internal auditor's evaluation of efficiency is restricted to the controls themselves; it does not extend to the measures of operating performance associated with the functioning of such controls. In judging efficiency, the internal auditor must conclude whether the benefits provided by the controls exceed their cost.

Issues in Internal Controls

Three major issues in internal controls are presented next.

1. People are the major limiting factor or roadblock in ensuring the adequacy, effectiveness, and efficiency of internal controls because:
   a. The behavior of people is unexpected or unpredictable.
   b. People design and develop products and services.
   c. People establish processes, policies, and procedures.
   d. People evaluate the adequacy, effectiveness, and efficiency of internal controls.
   e. People have built-in strengths and weaknesses.
2. Internal controls could be overridden or manipulated, thus hurting an organization financially, operationally, and strategically.
3. Retrofitting a weak internal control system costs excessive amounts of money due to replanning, redesigning, redeveloping, retesting, and reimplementing the retrofitted controls.

COMPLIANCE MANAGEMENT

Roles of Regulators and Compliance Managers

The roles of government regulators and the compliance managers at the affected organizations are different and opposite; regulators issue laws, rules, and regulations (LRRs) while compliance managers implement those LRRs. Various governmental authorities (regulators) at local, state, and federal levels pass LRRs to control the conduct of business organizations for the good of the society and to collect tax revenues for proper functioning of government. The government needs these tax revenues to provide services to citizens and businesses. Corporate management can get a reasonable assurance about compliance with LRRs through compliance audits. The government has the constitutional power and the legal right to fine and punish business organizations for failing to comply with the required LRRs.

To fulfill their roles, government regulators can perform retrospective analysis and flexibility analysis while compliance managers can conduct barrier analysis and cost-benefit analysis.

Regulatory analysis = Retrospective analysis + Flexibility analysis + Barrier analysis
+ Cost-benefit Analysis

Regulators = Retrospective analysis + Flexibility analysis

Compliance managers = Barrier analysis + Cost-benefit analysis

Compliance Costs and Benefits

Corporate management says it costs a significant amount of resources to comply with the often confusing and duplicating laws, rules, and regulations in terms of record-keeping and monitoring activities. Management does not readily see a direct and positive benefit from compliance. Yet regulators say these LRRs are developed with a purpose for the benefit of the entire society and that the cost of compliance should be treated as a cost of doing business. This is a never-ending debate, but in the end, the government wins due to its constitutional power. A trade-off analysis should be performed between the cost of compliance and the cost of noncompliance.

Total Cost of Compliance

The **total cost of compliance** is both compliance costs and noncompliance costs.

Compliance costs are a combination of these costs:

- Planning costs
- New equipment, installation, software, and hardware costs
- Hiring costs
- Training costs
- Subject matter expert consulting costs
- Collecting and compiling compliance data

Total Cost of Compliance (continued)

- Implementation costs
- Reporting costs
- Continuous monitoring costs
- Overall administrative and management costs for supervision and follow-up efforts

Noncompliance costs are a combination of these costs:

- Government fines and penalties
- Legal fees
- Court costs
- Case preparation costs
- Legal expert consulting fees
- Nonquantified loss of image and reputation costs resulting from negative publicity in news media and public's rejection of purchase and use of the affected company's products and services

In a way, noncompliance costs are data evidence costs, meaning data was shown to regulatory authorities as a proof-of-evidence when regulators allege organizations for noncompliance with laws and regulations.

Domain 6: Fraud Risks (10%)

This domain discusses several topics related to fraud risks, including interpretation of fraud risks; types of fraud; indicators of fraud; awareness of fraud; controls to prevent or detect fraud risks; audit tests to detect fraud, including discovery sampling; integrating analytical relationships to detect fraud; interrogation or investigative techniques; forensic auditing and computer forensics; use of computers in analyzing data for fraud and crime; Government Accountability Office's (GAO's) framework for managing fraud risks; Committee of Sponsoring Organizations of the Treadway Commission's (COSO's) framework for fraud risk management; fraud analytics; and fraud and the internal auditor.

INTERPRETATION OF FRAUD RISKS

Fraud Defined

Fraud is a generic term and embraces all the multifarious means that human ingenuity can devise, which are resorted to by one individual, to get an advantage over another by false representations. It includes all surprise, trick, cunning, and unfair ways by which another is cheated. *Fraud* is a term of law, applied to certain facts as a conclusion from them, but is not in itself a fact. It has been defined as any cunning deception or artifice used to cheat or deceive another.

Cheat and defraud means every kind of trick and deception, from false representation and intimidation to suppression and concealment of any fact and information by which a party is induced to part with property for less than its value or to give more than it is worth for the property of another. The terms *fraud* and *bad faith* are synonymous when applied to the conduct of public offenders.

Characteristics of Fraud

An organization's management should consider the potential for fraud when identifying, analyzing, and responding to risks. Three risk factors contribute to the design, implementation, and operating effectiveness of assessing fraud risks: the types of fraud, fraud risk factors, and response to fraud risks. The three risk factors include incentive/pressure, opportunity, and attitude/rationalization. Note that these three fraud risk factors do not necessarily indicate that fraud exists but are often present when fraud occurs.

Characteristics of Fraud (continued)

1. **Incentive/pressure**—Management, other employees, or external parties (e.g., for some improper payments) have an incentive or are under pressure, which provides a motive to commit fraud.
2. **Opportunity**—Circumstances exist, such as the absence of controls, ineffective controls, or the ability of management to override controls, that provide an opportunity to commit fraud.
3. **Attitude/rationalization**—Individuals involved are able to rationalize committing fraud. Some individuals possess an attitude, character, or ethical values that allow them to knowingly and intentionally commit a dishonest act. Generally, the greater the incentive or pressure, the more likely an individual will be able to rationalize the acceptability of committing fraud.

Management uses the fraud risk factors to identify fraud risks. While fraud risk may be greatest when all three risk factors are present, one or more of these factors may indicate a fraud risk. Other information provided by internal and external parties can also be used to identify fraud risks. This information may include allegations of fraud or suspected fraud reported by the office of the inspector general or internal auditors, personnel, or external parties who interact with the entity.

Management can perpetrate fraud by directly or indirectly manipulating accounting records; overriding controls, sometimes in unpredictable ways; or committing other fraudulent or improper acts.

Response to Fraud Risks

Management analyzes and responds to identified fraud risks so that they are effectively mitigated. Fraud risks are analyzed through the same risk analysis process performed for all identified risks. Management analyzes the identified fraud risks by estimating their significance, both individually and in the aggregate, to assess their effect on achieving the defined objectives. As part of analyzing fraud risk, management also assesses the risk of management override of controls. The oversight body oversees management's assessments of fraud risk and the risk of management override of controls so that they are appropriate.

Management responds to fraud risks through the same risk response process performed for all analyzed risks. Management designs an overall risk response and specific actions for responding to fraud risks. It may be possible to reduce or eliminate certain fraud risks by making changes to the entity's activities and processes. These changes may include stopping or reorganizing certain operations and reallocating roles among personnel to enhance segregation of duties. In addition to responding to fraud risks, management may need to develop further responses to address the risk of management override of controls. Further, when fraud has been detected, the risk assessment process may need to be revised.

Fraud Risks from Misstatements

Fraud risk is a part of audit risk, making up a portion of inherent and control risk. Fraud risk consists of the risk of fraudulent financial reporting and the risk of misappropriation of assets that cause a material misstatement of the financial statements. The auditor should specifically assess and document the risks of material misstatements

Fraud Risks from Misstatements (continued)

of the financial statements due to fraud and should consider fraud risk in designing audit procedures. The auditor may determine the risks of material fraud concurrently with the consideration of inherent and control risk but should form a separate conclusion on fraud risk. The auditor should evaluate the risk of fraud throughout the audit.

The auditor must plan and perform the audit to obtain reasonable assurance about whether the financial statements are free of material misstatement, whether caused by error or fraud. Accordingly, the auditor should evaluate the **risks of material misstatement due to fraud (fraud risk)**. The primary factor that distinguishes fraud from error is that the action causing the misstatement in fraud is *intentional*.

Two types of misstatements are relevant to the auditor's consideration of fraud in an audit of financial statements—misstatements arising from fraudulent financial reporting and misstatements arising from misappropriation of assets:

1. **Misstatements arising from fraudulent financial reporting**—Intentional misstatements or omissions of amounts or disclosures in financial statements to deceive financial statement users. They could involve intentional alteration of accounting records, misrepresentation of transactions, intentional misapplication of accounting principles, or other means.
2. **Misstatements arising from misappropriation of assets**—Involve thefts of an entity's assets that result in misstatements in the financial statements. They could involve theft of property, embezzlement of receipts, fraudulent payments, or other means. Safeguarding controls relate to protecting assets against loss from unauthorized acquisition, use, or disposition.

Other Types of Misstatements

Because fraud risk takes on many forms, it is difficult to list or interpret the fraud risks correctly due to problems in identifying and detecting various fraudulent activities. However, fraud risks can be broadly interpreted as falling into these major categories:

- Over- or underreporting of:
    - Production unit count in a manufacturing factory or plant
- Unit count of sales or dollar count of sales
- On-hand inventory count in a factory, plant, warehouse, and retail store
- Product and service invoices and shipping dates
- Customer merchandise returns to a retailer or manufacturer
    - Operating, marketing, and administrative expenses
    - Gross income and net income
- Credit or debit card chargeback fraud
- Payroll fraud with ghost employees
- Advertising fraud due to intentional false billing errors
- Investment fraud (bitcoin fraud, affinity fraud, and microcap fraud)

ACTS, TRAITS, AND PROFILES OF FRAUD PERPETRATORS

A list of fraudulent behavior acts about which an internal auditor must be concerned is presented next.

- Significant changes in the behavior of the defrauder (e.g., easygoing attitude, irregular work habits, and expensive social life)
- Knowledge that the defrauder is undergoing an emotional trauma at home or in the workplace
- Knowledge that the defrauder is betting heavily
- Knowledge that the defrauder is drinking heavily
- Knowledge that the defrauder is heavily in debt
- Audit findings of errors or irregularities that are considered immaterial when discovered
- The defrauder works quietly, works hard, works long hours, often works alone.
- The defrauder appears to be living beyond his/her means.
- The defrauder has an expensive car or clothes.

Traits of Managers

Traits of managers associated with frauds include wheeler-dealers and management that is feared, impulsive, too numbers-oriented, and insensitive to people (especially to employees).

Traits of Employees

The next traits of employees are suggested as indicating fraudulent behavior.

- Managers and executives seem to be the major sources of ethical attitudes within organization. That is, there is pressure from superiors to commit unethical behavior. Superiors pressure subordinates to support incorrect viewpoints, sign false documents, overlook superiors' wrongdoing, and do business with superiors' friends. The chief executive officer sets the ethical tone of the organization.
- Be wary of employees who never take vacations, live beyond their means, or suffer from mood swings.
- About two males are arrested for embezzlement to every one female.
- About one-third of male and female embezzlers are 22 to 29 years of age; they constitute the largest groupings of all.

White-Collar Crime

White-collar crime is a breach of trust, confidence, or fiduciary duty. White-collar crime is classified as that directed against consumers and that directed against employers. It is caused by greed and by weak internal control mechanisms.

The common characteristics of each of the so-called white-collar crimes are intentional deception (fraud theft, embezzlement, and corruption), destruction of property (industrial sabotage), gross negligence (product liability), and failure to comply with government regulations on environmental pollution, unfair pricing practices, untrue advertising, unsafe and unhealthy products, stock fraud, tax fraud, and so on. *High-level employee crimes are perceived to be based on economic greed while low-level employee crimes are perceived as based on economic need.*

Profile of Corporate Fraudsters

Corporate fraudsters tend to:

- Make extravagant purchases or live a lavish lifestyle.
- Have unexplained mood swings or compulsive behavior (e.g., workaholics, alcohol, or drug abusers, over-eaters, and gamblers).

Profile of Corporate Fraudsters (continued)

- Be unable to deal with pressure.
- Be able to rationalize theft.
- Be able to exploit internal control weaknesses to cover up fraud.
- Be reluctant to take vacations or to stay away from the office.

Profiles of Organizational Crime

Researchers have found that organizations committing crimes tended to have these profiles:

- The oil, pharmaceutical, and motor vehicle industries and their management were the most likely to violate the law.
- Firms that were relatively more prosperous tended to pollute illegally more often.
- Larger corporations in general commit no more violations per unit size than do smaller corporations. In some cases, larger corporations had more infractions generally, but smaller corporations had more violations per unit size.
- More diversified firms will violate more often. (This is because they are exposed to a greater number of regulations. More diversified firms seem more likely to violate labor and manufacturing laws than those less diversified.)
- Firms with more market power had slightly fewer violations per unit size than less dominant firms, which suggests that market power may diminish pressures to violate the law.
- Firms and industries with greater labor concentration tend to have more official censures for labor violations.

TYPES OF FRAUD

Three elements of fraud include (1) an intent to defraud, (2) commission of a fraudulent act, and (3) accomplishment of the fraud. Several types of fraud exist, depending on the purpose, place, and people who are perpetrating the fraudulent activities. Because fraud has so many dimensions, it can be classified in eight ways:

1. Management fraud
2. Employee fraud
3. Identity fraud
4. Investment fraud
5. Internet fraud
6. Stock promotion fraud
7. Chargeback fraud
8. Miscellaneous fraud

Management Fraud

Management considers the types of fraud that can occur within the entity to provide a basis for identifying fraud risks. Fraud involves obtaining something of value through willful misrepresentation. The court system (judicial or adjudicative) will determine whether an act qualifies as fraud.

The three types of management fraud are listed next.

1. **Fraudulent financial reporting**—Intentional misstatements or omissions of amounts or disclosures in financial statements to deceive financial statement users. This could include intentional alteration of accounting records, misrepresentation of transactions, or intentional misapplication of accounting principles.
2. **Misappropriation of assets**—Theft of an entity's assets. This could include theft of property, embezzlement of receipts, or fraudulent payments.
3. **Corruption**—Bribery and other illegal acts.

Some accounting-related transaction-based red flags include:

- Cash flow is diminishing.
- Sales and income are diminishing.
- Payables and receivables are increasing.

Management Fraud (continued)

- Unusual or second endorsements on checks.
- Inventory and cost of sales are increasing.
- Income and expense items are continually reclassified.
- Suspense items are not reconciled at all or reconciled in an untimely manner.
- Suspense items are written off without explanation.
- Accounts receivable writeoffs are increasing.
- Journal entries are adjusted heavily at year-end.
- Old outstanding checks.
- Heavy customer complaints.

Accounting Fraud by High-Level Managers

- Early booking of sales
- Expense deferrals
- Inventory overstatement
- Expense account padding

Employee Fraud

Embezzlement and corruption are two major types of employee fraud. The crime of embezzlement consists of the fraudulent misappropriation of the property of an employer by an employee to whom the possession of that property has been entrusted. Here is the difference between embezzlement and larceny: Embezzlement occurs when the embezzler gains initial possession of property lawfully but subsequently misappropriates it. Larceny is committed when property is taken without the owner's consent.

Common embezzlement techniques include these schemes:

- **Cash disbursement embezzlement** involves the creation of fake documents or false expense entries using phony invoices, time cards, and receipts.
- **Cash receipts fraud** involves the lapping of cash or accounts receivable. Here the embezzler "borrows" from today's receipts and replaces them with tomorrow's receipts. Other examples are skimming, where the proceeds of cash sales are intercepted before any entry is made of their receipts, and granting fake credits for discounts, refunds, rebates, returns, and allowances, possibly through collusion with a customer.
- **Theft of property** involves assets such as tools, supplies, equipment, finished goods, raw materials, and intellectual property, such as software, data, and proprietary information.

Accounting Fraud by Lower-Level Employees

- Check kiting
- Lapping of receivables
- Phony vendor invoices
- Phony benefit payment claims
- Expense account padding

Corruption is another common type of employee fraud. Vendors, suppliers, service providers, and contractors often corrupt the employees of an organization on both a small-scale level (e.g., gifts and free tickets of nominal value) and a large-scale level (e.g., commissions, payoffs, free trips, free airline tickets and hotel accommodations).

Identity Fraud

Identity theft means a fraud committed or attempted by one person using the identifying information of another person without the explicit authority of the second person. **Identifying information** means any name or number that may be used, alone or in conjunction with any other information, to identify a specific person, including any:

- Name, Social Security number, date of birth, official state or government issued driver's license or identification number, alien registration number, government passport number, employer or taxpayer identification number.
- Unique biometric data, such as fingerprint, voice print, retina or iris image, or other unique physical representation.
- Unique electronic identification number, address or routing code (e.g., a bank's routing number and account number), and credit/debit card number with personal identification number (PIN).
- Telecommunication identifying information or access device, such as cell/mobile phone number and a personal device's serial number.

Investment Fraud

Three types of investment fraud include affinity fraud, bitcoin Ponzi schemes, and microcap fraud.

Affinity fraud involves either a fake investment or a normal investment where the fraudster lies about important details, such as the risk of loss, the track record of the investment, or the background of the promoter of the investment scheme. It is called affinity fraud because the fraud victims are members of identifiable groups of people, such as friends, family, relatives, and colleagues; religious groups; ethnic communities; or elderly persons.

Bitcoin Ponzi schemes involve using virtual currency or digital currency where fraudsters can lure investors into Ponzi and other schemes and use these currencies to facilitate fraudulent, or simply fabricated, investments or transactions. The fraud may also involve an unregistered offering or trading platform. These schemes often promise high returns for getting in on the ground floor of a growing Internet phenomenon. A major attraction to using virtual currencies in transactions is their greater privacy benefits and less regulatory oversight than transactions in conventional (flat) currencies, such as the U.S. dollar. Virtual currencies are traded on online exchanges for conventional currencies or used to purchase goods or services online, such as clothes and shoes.

Common red flags of fraud for Ponzi schemes are listed next.

- High investment returns with little or no risk
- Overly consistent returns
- Unregistered investments

Investment Fraud (continued)

- Unlicensed sellers
- No minimum investor qualifications required
- Investments not in writing
- Difficulty in receiving payments
- Investments enlisted by national, ethnic, or religious affiliation groups or sponsored by respected leaders, prominent members, or celebrities

Microcap fraud is involved in the over-the-counter (OTC) market for securities where the market is designed for and comprised of companies with small amounts of assets and low stock prices. Microcap stocks are low-priced stocks issued by the smallest of companies, including penny stocks, which are the very lowest-priced stocks. As such, they are more susceptible to stock manipulation. Publicly available information about microcap companies often is scarce, making it easier for fraudsters to spread false information. In addition, it is often easier for fraudsters to manipulate the price of microcap stocks because microcap stocks historically have been less liquid than the stock of larger companies. Liquid investments are those stocks that can be sold easily.

Investment Fraud (continued)

Some Red Flags to Watch for when Investing in a Microcap Stock

- Little or no assets, false press releases, and minimal revenues.
- Insiders own large amounts of stock.
- Unusual external auditing issues.
- Odd items appear in the footnotes of financial statements.
- Stock trading was suspended due to spam and for other reasons.
- Frequent changes in company name or type of business.
- Company issues a lot of shares without a corresponding increase in the company's assets.
- Increase in stock price or trading volume linked to promotional activities.

Internet Fraud

Internet-based frauds are occurring at an alarming rate because the Internet is where most people (mass audience) are going to search, learn, study, research, share, listen, entertain, and do other things. In addition, the Internet is a useful way to reach a mass audience without spending a lot of time or money. A website, online messages, or spam emails can reach large numbers of people with minimum effort. It is easy for fraudsters to make their messages look real and credible, and sometimes hard for investors to tell the difference between fact and fiction.

Four ways how fraudsters can trick investors using online channels include online investment newsletters, online bulletin boards, pump-and-dump schemes, and spam emails.

Stock Promotion Fraud

Fraudsters who conduct stock promotions are often paid promoters or company insiders who stand to gain by selling their shares after creating a buying frenzy and pumping up the stock price. The promoters or insiders make profits for themselves by creating losses for unsuspecting investors.

Fraudsters may promote a stock in seemingly independent and unbiased sources, including social media, investment newsletters, online advertisements, emails, Internet chat rooms, and direct mail. The red flags of investment fraud include (1) aggressive stock promotion, (2) guaranteed high investment returns, (3) pressure to buy immediately, and (4) unsolicited stock recommendations.

Chargeback Fraud

A **chargeback** occurs when a customer who purchased merchandise from a retailer or a product from a company (e.g., a manufacturer, reseller, distributor, and wholesaler) was not happy either with the product or with non-product-related matters and files a claim with a bank to get his or her money back. The customer paid the retailer or other seller with a charge card (debit or credit card). When the customer files a chargeback claim, the bank contacts the seller and gives a temporary credit to the customer and charges the seller for the amount of the purchase until after final investigation among the customer, bank, and the seller is completed. Most chargeback claims by customers are genuine, but some are fraudulent claims. In summary, a chargeback claim, which is a financial claim, involves a customer (buyer), an intermediary (customer's bank that issued the charge card and paid the seller), and a retailer (seller). In a way, a chargeback fraud is a financial fraud.

Miscellaneous Fraud

Miscellaneous fraud addresses topics such as theft of assets, fraud by frequency, fraud involving conspiracy, and varieties of fraud. There are many varieties of frauds, limited only by the ingenuity of the perpetrators. From a discovery point of view, fraud can be classified in a number of ways. The reason for this classification is that different approaches and procedures are required to discover each type of fraud and to control each type's occurrence.

Miscellaneous Fraud (continued)

Four **types of fraud** include: (1) theft of assets (e.g., fraud open on the books, fraud hidden on the books, and fraud off the books), (2) fraud by frequency (i.e., repeating or nonrepeating), (3) fraud by conspiracy (i.e., collusion), and (4) varieties of fraud (e.g., specialized fraud and garden varieties of fraud).

Examples of specialized fraud include embezzlement of assets entrusted by depositors to financial institutions (e.g., banks, savings and loans, credit unions, pension funds) (called custodial fraud) and false insurance claims for life, health, auto, and property coverage.

Eight types of **garden-variety frauds** are common today:

1. Kickbacks
2. Defective pricing
3. Unbalanced contracts or purchase orders
4. Reopening completed contracts
5. Duplicate payments
6. Double payments
7. Shell payments
8. Defective delivery

INDICATORS OF FRAUD

Risk Factors in Fraud

Internal auditors should be aware of risk factors related to general fraud as well as computer fraud. The degree of fraud can be linked to an organization's environment.

- **High-fraud environment**—Low management integrity, poor control environment, loose accountability, and high pressure for results
- **Low-fraud environment**—A culture of honesty, management openness, employee assistance programs, and total quality management

  Specifically, risk factors or red flags related to corporate fraud are listed next.

- Infighting among top management
- Low morale and motivation among employees
- Understaffed accounting departments
- High level of complaints against the organization from customers, suppliers, or regulatory authorities

Risk Factors in Fraud (continued)

- Inconsistent and surprising cash flow deficiencies
- Decreasing sales or income while accounts payable and receivable are rising
- Company's line of credit is used to its limit for long periods of time
- Significant excess inventory
- Increasing number of year-end adjusting journal entries

Red Flags for Computer Fraud

Red flags do not signal that a fraud has occurred but rather that the opportunity for a fraud exists. Examples of red flags include concealed assets, missing or destroyed records and documents, split purchases, excessive voids or refunds, and rapid turnover of financial managers and executives.
The eight factors that contribute to computer fraud are listed next.

1. Inadequate design of the information system
2. Aggregation of the information system's transaction processing steps so that a review of what is taking place becomes impossible

Red Flags for Computer Fraud (continued)

3. Insufficient discrimination as to the legitimacy of the transactions processed by the information system
4. Error toleration by the information system, either in data content or in processing results
5. Detachment of the information system's ongoing operation from the physical or functional reality that it is supposed to reflect
6. Unrestrained, unmediated remote access to an information system that is subject to possible compromise or manipulation
7. Restricted ability to collect sufficient knowledge about the fraud itself, especially its scope and the extent of the loss that has occurred
8. Limits in the investigative tools for analyzing the knowledge that auditors may gain about the fraud

Professional Skepticism in Fraud

The planning and performance of an audit are to be carried out by an auditor with an attitude of professional skepticism. This means that the auditor neither assumes that management is dishonest nor assumes unquestioned honesty. An objective evaluation of the situation and management integrity are important considerations for the auditor. *The auditor needs to balance between excessive audit costs due to suspicion and time constraints.*

The sequence of audit activities related to professional skepticism include:

1. Reviewing internal control structure
2. Performing audit planning work
3. Determining the audit scope
4. Collecting audit evidence
5. Reviewing accounting estimates
6. Issuing an audit opinion

Management Representations versus Risk to Consider in Audit

The auditor needs to assess the risk of management misrepresentations and to consider the effects of such risks in establishing an overall audit strategy and the scope of the audit.

Review of Accounting Estimates for Misstatements and Bias

Many assumptions go into accounting estimates. The internal auditor should understand these assumptions and should evaluate to determine whether the assumptions are subjective and are susceptible to misstatements and bias.

Examples of Accounting Estimates

- Uncollectible receivables
- Allowance for loan losses
- Revenues to be earned on contracts
- Subscription income
- Losses on sales contracts
- Professional membership or union dues income
- Valuation of financial securities

Review of Accounting Estimates for Misstatements and Bias (continued)

- Trading versus investment security classifications
- Compensation in stock option plans and deferred plans
- Probability of loss
- Obsolete inventory
- Net realizable value of inventories
- Losses in purchase commitments
- Property and casualty insurance accruals
- Loss reserves
- Warranty claims
- Taxes on real estate and personal property

In addition to review, the auditor should test management's process of developing accounting estimates or develop an independent estimation. The auditor can compare prior estimates with subsequent results to assess the reliability of the process used to develop estimates. The auditor should also review whether the accounting estimates are consistent with the entity's operational plans and programs.

AWARENESS OF FRAUD

Fraud-awareness initiatives include fraud training and education for managers, supervisors, employees, and stakeholders (e.g., customers and suppliers) with responsibility for implementing antifraud programs and efforts. Benefits of these initiatives are to (1) prevent potential fraud, (2) create a culture of integrity and compliance within an organization, and (3) better detect potential fraud.

Examples of Leading Practices in Antifraud Efforts

- Provide training and educational programs when employees are hired and retrain periodically. Maintain records of training to show compliance with requirements.
- Provide more frequent and more targeted training to employees working in high-risk positions or functional areas. Maintain records of training to show compliance with requirements.
- Blend antifraud training programs with existing ethics training, code of conduct training, and compliance training programs.
- Provide information on how and where to report fraud incidents, including information on reporting mechanisms and what to report.

AWARENESS OF FRAUD (CONTINUED)

- Send a positive message with benefits of fraud risk management programs (e.g., increased revenues and profits and good morale), the cost of fraud, and consequences of engaging in fraud, such as sanctions, disciplinary actions, and other punishments.

Examples of educational activities related to fraud control include newsletters highlighting the results of cases or information on fraud schemes; fraud risk indicators that communicate red flags to employees; and computer-based trainings that are available on-demand, such as audios or videos about fraud issues.

CONTROLS TO PREVENT OR DETECT FRAUD RISKS

Fraud prevention results in big savings because when fraud is prevented, there are no detection or investigation costs. This means a dollar spent in preventing fraud saves many more dollars later on. Therefore, greater attention should be paid to preventive controls rather than detective controls and recovery controls.

Preventive Controls in General

Some examples of preventive controls are listed next.

- Sharing the company vision with all employees
- Distributing fraud policies and programs
- Conducting proactive audits using discovery sampling techniques
- Database query facilities and data mining tools
- Providing a hotline for fraud reporting by employees and others
- Monitoring employee performance
- Enforcing employee vacation privileges
- Discouraging collusion between employees, customers, or vendors with policies clearly explained to them

Preventive Controls in General (continued)

- Establishing a sound system of internal controls (both formal and informal)
- Providing fraud awareness training programs
- Providing employee assistance programs to deal with personal and work-related pressures
- Establishing physical security and information systems security controls
- Enforcing existing internal controls and fraud policies with the understanding that dishonesty will be punished
- Establishing separation of duties, dual custody, and dual controls
- Establishing total quality management programs
- Creating a positive work environment with open-door policy to facilitate open communications
- Creating teamwork with self-directed teams or quality circles
- Assigning responsibility for fraud prevention programs
- Hiring honest employees
- Publishing a code of ethics
- Establishing a system of authorizations and independent checks and balances
- Encouraging employee empowerment

Detective Controls in General

Some examples of detective controls are listed next.

- Building audit trails in business transactions (whether automated or not)
- Testing controls
- Conducting regular internal audits
- Conducting surprise internal audits
- Conducting employee performance evaluations
- Watching employee lifestyle changes
- Observing employee behavior toward work, the organization, and other employees
- Periodically taking physical inventory of assets, financial securities, and other valuable items

Computer Fraud–Related Controls

Good business practices **include management (directive) controls**, such as performing preemployment screening procedures, requiring employees to sign a code of conduct, and conducting periodic training programs in computer security and privacy policies and procedures. System-based preventive, detective, corrective, and recovery controls are also needed to efficiently combat computer crime and fraud.

Preventive controls can help in restricting the access of potential perpetrators to the computer facility, computer terminals, data files, programs, and system libraries. Separation of duties, rotation of duties, backup personnel, and a good system of internal controls are some examples of preventive controls.

Detective controls can help in discovering fraud in the event perpetrator slips past established prevention mechanisms. Some tips and procedures for fraud detection are listed next.

- Auditors should take a fresh approach to looking at the data (middle-of-the-month review instead of month-end).
- They should break the normal pattern of reporting (obtain early or late reports, ad hoc reports instead of scheduled), change review timing to throw things off their track (random times, not month-end, quarter-end, or year-end), and run normal reports at unusual times.

Computer Fraud–Related Controls (continued)

Audit hooks can help in monitoring the computer fraud. Audit hooks are embedded in application programs and are flagged when incoming and processed transactions meet prescribed criteria. If auditors requested and designed the audit hooks, they should provide the test data and assist in testing the computer system.

Corrective and recovery controls can help to limit losses (financial or other) resulting from a well-planned and well-executed computer fraud and crime.

Prior to auditing for fraud, the organization must answer these questions:

- What does it have that someone would want to steal?
- How would someone go about stealing from it?
- How vulnerable is it?
- How can it detect fraud and crime?

AUDIT TESTS TO DETECT FRAUD, INCLUDING DISCOVERY SAMPLING

Audit Steps to Detect Fraud

It has been said that most frauds are detected by accident, not by planned effort. This should not stop auditors from planning to detect fraud. Some known approaches to detect fraud include testing, statistical sampling, computer-assisted audit techniques, data query, and data mining tools. Some examples of audit tests include analytical techniques, charting techniques, recalculations, confirmations, observations, physical examinations, inquiries, and document reviews.

Steps to Take when Fraud Is Suspected

1. Document examination.
2. Examining accounting records.
3. Documenting fraud. Documenting fraud is a continuous effort from inception to completion of the fraud investigation.

Steps to Take when Fraud Is Suspected (continued)

4. Obtaining documentary evidence. Three principal methods exist for obtaining documentary evidence: subpoenas, search warrants, and voluntary consent.

5. Types of evidence. Evidence falls into one of two categories, either direct or circumstantial.

6. Organization of evidence.

7. Charting techniques. Three types of charting techniques for documenting fraud are link network diagrams, time flow diagrams, and matrices.

8. Business and individual records. Original documents are preferred and should be obtained wherever possible. If necessary, the examiner should furnish the record custodian a receipt for the property. If the originals cannot be obtained, the examiner can settle for copies.

9. Memorandum of interview. It is a good practice to write a memorandum addressed to the case file any time evidence comes into or leaves the hands of the fraud examiner or auditor. Whether it is included in the final report or workpapers or not, each official contact during the course of a fraud examination should be recorded on a "memorandum of interview" on a timely basis.

Steps to Take when Fraud Is Suspected (continued)

10. Writing fraud reports. Some reasons why a written report is so important are listed next.

    - The report is an evidence of the work performed.
    - The report conveys to the litigator all the evidence needed to evaluate the legal status of the case.
    - The written report adds credibility to the examination and to the examiner.
    - The report forces the fraud examiner to consider his or her actions before and during the interview, so that the objectives of the investigation can be best accomplished.
    - The report omits immaterial information so that the facts of the case can be clearly and completely understood.

11. Characteristics of fraud reports. Important characteristics of good report writing include accuracy, clarity, impartiality, relevance, and timeliness.

12. Written reports. There should be five major sections: cover page, witness statements, cover letter, workpapers, and index.

Steps to Take when Fraud Is Suspected (continued)

13. Privileged reports. There is no privilege for investigative reports and notes, or for any fraud examination, forensic audit, or similar services. However, there are two exceptions.

    a. If the examiner is conducting an investigation at the request of an attorney in anticipation of litigation, the report is considered in most courts as an attorney/client work product (i.e., privileged).

    b. If a public authority, such as the police, federal agents, the courts or grand jury, or the like, is conducting the investigation, the report can be considered privileged.

14. Mistakes to avoid in writing fraud reports:

    - Conclusions. Under no circumstances should conclusions be made, as they may come back to haunt the examiner in litigation.
    - Opinions. Under no circumstances should an opinion be written concerning the guilt or innocence of any person or party.
    - Informant and source information. Under no circumstances should the name of a confidential source or informant be disclosed in the report or anywhere else in writing.

Legal Rules of Evidence

There are strict legal rules regarding the handling of evidence and the chain of custody thereof. If the examiner is operating under a lawful order of the courts that compels a custodian of records to furnish original documents, the documents should be copied, preferably in the presence of the custodian, before being removed from the premises. The custodian keeps the copies. If not operating under a court directive and the records are being provided voluntarily by the custodian, the examiner may retain copies instead of originals.

Discovery Sampling

Discovery sampling is a type of sampling procedure that has a specified probability of including at least one item that occurs very rarely in the population. It is used when there is a possibility of finding such things as fraud and avoidance of internal controls. In discovery sampling, the auditors can specify the probability of including in the sample at least one item with a particular characteristic, if the characteristic occurs at a specified rate in the population. If the sample does not turn up an item with this characteristic, the auditors can make a probability statement that the characteristic's rate of occurrence is less than that specified.

Discovery sampling can be regarded as a special case of attribute sampling. However, in its usual applications, it does not yield an estimated rate of occurrence, and usually it is used only if the particular characteristic's rate of occurrence is thought to be very small—that is, close to zero. For example, discovery sampling is usually used in financial audits to guard against an intolerable rate of fraud.

INTEGRATING ANALYTICAL RELATIONSHIPS TO DETECT FRAUD

Major Impetus

The major impetus for the need to integrate analytical relationships in detecting fraud was the recommendation of the Treadway Commission that analytical procedures should be used more extensively to identify areas with a high risk of fraudulent financial reporting.

The Treadway Commission defined fraudulent financial reporting as intentional or reckless conduct, whether by act or omission, that results in materially misleading financial statements. Fraudulent financial reporting can involve many factors and take many forms. It may entail gross and deliberate distortion of corporate records, such as inventory count tags, or falsified transactions, such as fictitious sales or orders. It may entail the misapplication of accounting principles. Company employees at any level may be involved, from top to middle management to lower-level personnel. If the conduct is intentional, or so reckless that it is the legal equivalent of intentional conduct, and results in fraudulent financial statements, it comes within the Commission's operating definition of the term "fraudulent financial reporting."

Fraudulent financial reporting differs from other causes of materially misleading financial statements such as unintentional errors. The Commission also distinguished fraudulent financial reporting from other corporate improprieties, such as employee embezzlements, violation of environmental or product safety regulations, and tax fraud, which do not necessarily cause the financial statements to be materially inaccurate.

Types of Analytical Procedures

- Trend analysis (i.e., identifying patterns and deviations)
- Ratio analysis (e.g., comparative ratios and single ratios)
- Modeling techniques (i.e., using simulation methods and sensitivity analysis)

INTERROGATION OR INVESTIGATIVE TECHNIQUES

Fraud Investigation

The objectives of fraud investigation are to determine whom, why, and how. Possible approaches include:

- Testimonial evidence, documentary evidence, physical evidence (forensic analysis), and personal observation
- Theft act investigative methods, such as surveillance and covert operations, invigilation (close supervision of suspects)
- Concealment investigative methods, such as document examination, audits, computer searches, and physical asset counts
- Conversion investigative methods, such as public record searches and net-worth analysis
- Inquiry investigative methods, such as interviewing and interrogation

Investigative Process

The investigative process for a fraud incident can be divided into three phases.

1. **Initiating the investigation**—Securing the crime scene, collecting evidence, developing an incident hypothesis, and investigating alternative explanations.
2. **Analyzing the incident**—Analysis of the evidence collected in the first phase along with alternative explanations to determine whether a crime has occurred.
3. **Analyzing the evidence**—Preparing to present the incident with findings and recommendations to management or law enforcement authorities.

Team Composition

Investigating a fraud or computer-related crime requires a team approach with many participants. Each participant has a specific task to complete, consistent with his or her skills and experience. These participants (specialists) can include representatives from corporate investigations, law enforcement officials, system auditors, corporate counsel, consultants, information technology security management, and functional user management.

Target

A victim organization should practice a delay technique when its computer system is attacked. If a system perpetrator can be delayed longer while attacking, investigative authorities can trace the perpetrator's origins and location.

Objects/Subjects

An investigation revolves around two things: objects (e.g., computers, networks, switches, processes, data, and programs) and subjects (e.g., former and current employees and outsiders [e.g., hackers, crackers, virus writers, cloners, and phrackers]).

Search and Seizure

Ownership, occupancy, and possession are three influencing factors in a crime warrant search. A search warrant or court order is necessary to use the "trap and trace" technique, which involves the telephone company and Internet Service Provider finding the intruder. Traps can be placed on in-circuit emulators, network protocol analyzers, and hardware analyzers.

Search and Seizure (continued)

If computer equipment involved in a computer crime is not covered by a search warrant, the investigator should leave it alone until a warrant can be obtained. A court order is also required to access the evidence and to conduct surveillance techniques. To get a court-ordered search, one has to show that there is probable cause to believe that the suspect is committing an offense and that normal procedures have failed or are unlikely to work or are dangerous to health and life. An independent judge must issue the court order, not a police officer, security investigator, law enforcement agent, or prosecutor.

Interrogation

During evidence collection activities, the investigative team interviews and interrogates many individuals. The interviewing and interrogation processes are quite different in terms of objectives, techniques, and timing. The goal of the interview is obtaining information about the incident. Here, the intent is finding the answers to the five Ws: *who, what, when, where, and why.* This requires talking to as many witnesses as possible. The goal of interrogation, however, is to establish enough evidence to consider the subject a suspect.

FORENSIC AUDITING AND COMPUTER FORENSICS

Forensic Auditing

Auditing for fraud is called forensic auditing. The purpose of forensic auditing or examination is to establish whether a fraud has occurred. One of the major purposes of financial auditing is to attest the financial statements of an organization. Unlike financial auditing, forensic auditing has no generally accepted auditing standards. In fact, most self-proclaimed forensic auditors are certified public accountants or internal auditors specializing in fraud detection. Basically, forensic auditors or investigators conduct interviews, make onsite and offsite inspections, and perform document analysis during their work. The scope of forensic auditing work can be divided into four phases: (1) problem recognition and planning, (2) evidence collection, (3) evidence evaluation, and (4) communication of results.

Computer Forensics

Forensics is the process of using scientific knowledge for collecting, analyzing, and presenting evidence to the courts. Forensics deals primarily with the recovery and analysis of latent (hidden) evidence. Computer forensics is defined as the discipline that combines elements of law and computer science to collect and analyze data from computer systems, wired networks, wireless communications, mobile devices, and storage devices in a way that is admissible as evidence in a court of law.

Computer Forensics (continued)

An organization is said to possess a solid computer forensic capability when it develops a robust cyber-incident response plan; uses security monitoring tools; conducts vulnerability assessment exercises periodically; deploys intrusion prevention software (IPS); deploys intrusion detection software (IDS); uses web application proxies; places firewalls at multiple levels for a stronger protection; uses web content filtering software to block unwanted website traffic; rotates regular data backup files between onsite and offsite, and hires competent staff. All these combined capabilities are aimed at reporting on the security status of an organization's computer systems and networks with a defense-in-depth protection strategy.

An organization having a computer forensics capability can accrue several benefits, such as (1) it provides a defense-in-depth approach to network and computer security in that it provides multiple layers of different types of protection from different computer vendors, thus giving a substantially better protection, (2) should a computer intrusion or security incident lead to a court case, the organization with computer forensics capability will be at a distinct advantage because it followed the "due care" legal principle and safeguarded the security and privacy of company's data, (3) it is a proof of complying with computer security best practices and sound security policies, (4) it can potentially avoid lawsuits by customers and employees or regulatory audits by government agencies, resulting from negligence; and (5) it is complying with laws that hold businesses liable for breaches in the security or integrity of computer systems and networks, resulting in data theft, data loss, and data destruction. Examples of these federal laws include SOX, HIPAA, GLB, and Privacy Act. Simply stated,

Computer Forensics (continued)

the court system prefers to see that organizations take a proactive role in establishing and monitoring strong security control mechanisms to handle computer incidents.

Two basic types of data are collected in computer forensics, persistent data and volatile data. *Persistent data* is the data that is stored on a local hard drive or cloud storage and is preserved when the computer is tuned off. *Volatile data* is any data that is stored in computer memory, or exists in transit, that will be lost when the computer loses power or is turned off. Volatile data resides in computer registers, cache, and random-access-memory (RAM). Since volatile data is temporary, it is essential that an investigator knows reliable ways to capture it for evidence before it disappears. In addition, it is important that system administrators, security analysts, and network administrators must understand the computer forensic process and methods to recover data from backup files, computer hard drives, and mobile devices so it can help identify and analyze a security incident.

Digital Forensics Analysis Methodology

Forensically needed data whether it is residing on computers (e.g., files on a hard drive of desktop, laptop, or notebook computers) or on mobile devices (e.g., smartphones, digital tablets, and flash drives) requires a systematic and structured methodology to collect, extract, and analyze such data so that a forensic report can be issued to the interested parties showing the legal evidence. This methodology can take five specific steps in the following order:

Step 1: Collect imaging forensic data.

Step 2: Extract the required data.

Step 3: Identify relevant data.

Step 4: Analyze the relevant data.

Step 5: Issue a forensic report.

Each step is explained next.

Collect imaging forensic data means receiving an exact, sector-by-sector copy of a hard disk. Software capable of creating such copies of hard drives preserves deleted files, slack space, system files, and executable files (program files), which can be critical for later analysis of a security incident.

Digital Forensics Analysis Methodology (continued)

Extract the required data means the verification of the integrity of forensic data, selecting forensic tools, and extracting the requested data. Examples of forensic tools include virus and spyware detection software, login scripts, sinkhole routers, IPS and IDS software, packet sniffers, host and file scans, file sharing tools, antivirus and antispyware software, network device logs, protocol analyzers, audit software, password cracking programs, disk imaging software, auditing tools, operating system file utility programs, file zip and unzip utility programs, cable testers, and network line monitors. These and other tools can help investigators identify deleted files, infected files, damaged files, or encrypted files where the latter can represent ransomware attacks.

Identify relevant data requires deciding whether the data is relevant to the forensic request and making a relevant data list with all the associated metadata elements with their attributes.

Analyze the relevant data asks a basic question whether the collected and current data is enough to proceed further or whether more data is needed. If more data is needed, relevant questions include "what," "where," "when," "who," and "how" to get more data. At this time, the data is analyzed and findings are documented.

Issue a forensic report to all the interested parties based on the findings noted.

Relatively speaking, extracting data from computers could be easier than extracting data from mobile devices due to (1) difficulty in knowing what data to collect with so many smaller and novelty devices on the market, (2) difficulty in knowing where the data is located (i.e., local on the device or remote in the cloud), and (3) difficulty in differentiating between employee-owned mobile devices (BYOD) and company-owned mobile devices.

Digital Forensics Analysis Methodology (continued)

Investigators need to find out the number of web-based email accounts, text messages, social media accounts, apps, and file storage locations to allow them to take an inventory of all the data needed in order to preserve and perform data extraction and recovery efforts.

Investigators can collect the following data from mobile devices, including (1) stand-alone data files such as audio, graphic, and video files, (2) phone call logs showing incoming, outgoing, and missed calls, (3) text messages such as short message service (SMS) and enhanced message service (EMS) messages, (4) multimedia message service (MMS) messages showing audio, graphic, and video files without a text message, (5) browser and email data, (6) social media data containing user profiles with or without pictures, video, or audio files, (7) data on subscriber identity module (SIM) card on a smartphone, and (8) other data of interest, including equipment and subscriber data; digital wallet data; and data in personal notes and calendars.

USE OF COMPUTERS IN ANALYZING DATA FOR FRAUD AND CRIME

Collection and Preservation of Computer Evidence

Investigation of computer-related crimes more often than not involves highly technical matters, making it imperative during a search that appropriate steps are taken to ensure both the proper handling and preservation of evidence. There are seven recognized considerations involved in the care and handling of evidence.

1. Discovery and recognition
2. Protection
3. Recording
4. Collection
5. Identification
6. Preservation
7. Transportation

Chain of Computer Evidence

This section addresses various aspects of properly maintaining computer-related evidence. These procedures are important in avoiding problems of proof caused by improper care and handling of such evidence.

- Maintaining evidence in the form of computer storage media presents problems that differ from handling other types of evidence. Because they are subject to erasure and easily damaged, magnetic or electronic storage devices must be carefully guarded and kept under controlled temperature and humidity to avoid deterioration.
- In investigating and prosecuting a case involving such evidence, one of the early steps a prosecutor should take is to retain an appropriate computer expert or technical assistance. This can be critical in avoiding problems resulting from inept maintenance procedures or inadvertent loss of key information.
- Sometimes the contents of dozens or even hundreds of computer disks must be copied to allow the business to continue operating while the case is being prosecuted. This must be done under the close supervision of an expert who can ensure that the copying is done right and also can determine the least costly procedure.
- Initials of the seizing agent and the date should be scratched on each storage media container, and a **chain of custody** sheet or log should be made for every container. The log should show, at a minimum, the date, place, and specific location of the seizure and the name of the agent making the seizure.

The agents investigating the case are likely to have considerable expertise in maintaining computer evidence, gained from training and experience. Their advice and assistance can be invaluable to the prosecutor in minimizing problems of proof inherent in computer-related crimes.

Computer Fraud and Crime Examples

- Military and intelligence attacks include espionage in the form of industrial espionage, economic espionage, and foreign government espionage.
- Technical attacks include wiretapping (electronic eavesdropping) and data leakage.
- Business attacks include employee sabotage, data diddling, superzapping of computer files, and spreading a computer virus.
- Financial attacks include the salami technique, wire transfer fraud, and toll fraud through telephone cloning.
- Hacker attacks include holding data as hostage and demanding ransom money for stolen data and programs as in ransomware attacks.
- Grudge attacks include actions taken by disgruntled employees and the general public.
- “Fun” attacks include actions taken by people for challenge and publicity; money is not the goal.

GAO'S FRAMEWORK FOR MANAGING FRAUD RISKS

The U.S. Government Accountability Office (GAO) has issued *A Framework for Managing Fraud Risks in Federal Programs* as guidance to prevent, detect, and respond to fraud situations.

Fraud Defined

Fraud is defined as obtaining something of value through a willful misrepresentation. Fraud can take place in several ways, such as improper payments, illegal activities, and collusion. An improper payment is defined as any payment that should not have been made or that was made in an incorrect amount, including overpayments and underpayments.[1]

A pay-and-chase model refers to the practice of detecting fraudulent transactions and attempting to recover funds after payments have been made. This is an example of a reactive practice. Organizations should change the reactive practice of pay-and-chase model to a proactive practice of match-and-pay model, where fraud is identified before payments are made. This model improvement is made possible with data-mapping, data-matching, and data-mining techniques.

Before: Reactive practice = Pay-and-chase model = Detective control

After: Proactive practice = Match-and-pay model = Preventive control

[1]*A Framework for Managing Fraud Risks in Federal Programs* (July 2015), GAO-15-593SP, www.gao.gov.

Fraud Defined (continued)

One of the major goals of this framework is to reduce false positives during fraud audit and investigations. A high proportion of false positives can be reduced with this framework because a false positive shows an improper identification of suspect individuals who were not engaged in fraud. Use of multiple analytical tools and techniques (e.g., text mining, web scraping, data mapping, data matching, data mining, data visualization, data dashboards, fraud-data analytics, and statistical analyses) can reduce the occurrence of false positives, which in turn can increase the fraud detection rates.

Control Activities and Components

The GAO's Framework presents three control activities and five components for effectively managing fraud-related risks. The three control activities are prevention, detection, and response controls, which can recover fraudulent payments and delinquent debts. The five components are commit, assess, design and implement, evaluate and adapt, and monitoring and feedback.

Control activities for managing fraud risks include the policies, procedures, techniques, and mechanisms related to three categories of control activities that are interdependent and mutually reinforcing—prevention, detection, and response.

Fraud risks = Prevention controls + Detection controls + Response controls

Prevention controls mitigate the risk of fraud occurring and include antifraud strategy, employee background checks, fraud-awareness trainings, system-based edit checks, data matching to verify eligibility prior to payment, predictive analytics, segregation of duties, standards of conduct, and transaction limits.

Detection controls discover potential fraud that has already occurred and include internal and external assurance audits to detect fraud, data matching after payments have been made, data-mining applications, document reviews, hotlines and whistleblower reporting mechanisms, and surprise physical site visits and inspections.

Response controls investigate potential fraud, take corrective actions, and remedy the harm caused by fraud. They include investigations, prosecutions, disciplinary actions, suspensions, debarments, and payment recoveries.

Control Activities and Components (continued)

The **five components** for effectively managing fraud-related risks are described next. **Commit** requires a commitment to combating fraud by creating an organizational culture and structure conducive to fraud risk management. Assess requires a plan to assess risks in a regular fraud situation and to determine a fraud risk profile. **Design and implement** requires a strategy with specific control activities to mitigate assessed fraud risks and collaborate to help ensure effective implementation. **Evaluate and adapt** requires evaluating outcomes using a risk-based approach and adapting activities to improve fraud risk management. **Monitoring and feedback** mechanisms include ongoing practices that apply to the other four components. These mechanisms allow managers to continually incorporate new information, such as changing risks or the effects of actions taken to mitigate risks. Incorporating feedback to continually adapt fraud risk management activities requires constant data collecting, analyzing, and adapting processes.

Data Analytics for Fraud

A risk-based approach to data analytics for fraud is recommended that considers both costs and benefits. Here, costs include the cost of investing in specific data-analytics technologies (e.g., software, hardware, and staff costs) and benefits include reduced improper payments and fraud.

The most commonly used data-analytics tools and techniques in fraud prevention and detection are listed next.

- **Data mapping**—Requires linking or tracing audit tests to the corresponding data elements in order to evaluate the test results and to determine whether the test results achieve the defined objectives.
- **Data matching**—A computer matching process in which information from one source is compared with information from another source to identify any inconsistencies in data. These sources can be either a single file or multiple files and can be of any computer data file or database, either internal to a company or external to a company.
- **Data mining**—Analyzes data for relationships that have not been discovered previously. It identifies suspicious activity or transactions, including anomalies, outliers, and other red flags in the data. To this end, it applies data filters, log filters, fraud filters, and data rules that can help identify transactions that exhibit signs of fraud.
- **System-based edit-checks**—Help ensure that data meets requirements before it is accepted into computer systems and before payments are made. These edit checks are instructions programmed into a computer system to help ensure data quality (i.e., data are complete, accurate, valid, and recorded in the proper format). These checks identify missing, incorrect, or miscoded data.

Data Analytics for Fraud (continued)

- **Predictive analytics**—Includes a variety of automated systems and tools that can be used to identify particular types of human behavior, including fraud, before transactions are completed. Three models exist: rules-based models, anomaly-detection models, and predictive models.
- **Rules-based models**—Filter claims and behaviors that an individual submitted for an unreasonable number of services. These are the simplest types of models since the analysis conducted using them only involves counting or identifying types of claims and comparing the results to established threshold of rules.
- **Anomaly-detection models**—Identify abnormal patterns of an individual relative to the patterns of peers. These models generate analyses that are more complex because they require identification of patterns of behavior based on data collected over a period of time. Then actual patterns are compared to the established patterns that have been determined to be reasonable.
- **Predictive models**—Use historical data to identify patterns associated with fraud and then use these historical data to identify certain potentially fraudulent behaviors when applied to current claims data. Predictive models are the most complex type of model because they not only require analysis of large amounts of data but also may require detection of several patterns of behavior that individually may not be suspicious but, when conducted together, can indicate fraudulent activity. Link analysis is a part of predictive models because it discovers knowledge about an individual who is linked to known bad individuals through addresses or phone numbers.

Success of Data Analytics in Fraud

Measuring the success of data analytics programs to prevent fraud, waste, and abuse is not easy due to difficulties in estimating the savings associated with funds that were never stolen or wasted. However, data analytics can be used to analyze trends over time:

- How much fraud money was recovered?
- How many suspected individuals were arrested?
- How much reduction was noticed in fraudulent activities?

COSO'S FRAMEWORK FOR FRAUD RISK MANAGEMENT

The U.S. Committee of Sponsoring Organizations of the Treadway Commission (COSO) has issued a fraud risk management guide to prevent, detect, and respond to fraud situations.[2]

Fraud Defined

Fraud is defined as any intentional act or omission designed to deceive others, resulting in the victim suffering a loss and/or the perpetrator or fraudster achieving a gain.

Fraud → Victim → Loss

Fraud → Fraudster → Gain

A potential for fraud risk exists in all functions of a business, not just in accounting and finance. For example, the procurement function has a great potential for heavy fraud risk because it handles huge amounts of money. Simply stated, fraud can exist wherever and whenever money changes hands.

[2]COSO, *Fraud Risk Management Guide,* Executive Summary (September 2016), *www.coso.org.*

Fraud Risk Management Program

COSO's Framework for fraud risk management provides guidance on:

- Establishing fraud risk governance policies where they are a part of the corporate governance and internal control environment. Here, corporate governance addresses fiduciary responsibilities of the board of directors and the internal control environment creates the discipline supporting the assessment of risks.
- Performing a fraud risk assessment where its scope includes fraudulent financial reporting, fraudulent nonfinancial reporting, asset misappropriation, and illegal acts (including corruption).
- Designing and deploying fraud preventive and detective control activities. Here, preventive controls are designed to avoid a fraudulent event or transaction at the time of initial occurrence. Detective controls are designed to discover a fraudulent event or transaction after the initial processing has occurred.
- Conducting fraud investigations where the Framework develops and implements a system for prompt, competent, and confidential review, investigation, and resolution of instances of noncompliance and allegations involving fraud and misconduct.
- Monitoring and evaluating the total fraud risk management program where it requires ongoing evaluations are built into an organization's business processes at varying levels to provide timely information. A not-so-good alternative to ongoing evaluations is periodically conducting separate evaluations with varying degrees of scope and time of work.

Fraud Risk Management Process

An ongoing and comprehensive fraud risk management process consists of the five steps discussed next.

Step 1: Policy—Establish a fraud risk management policy as part of organizational governance.

Step 2: Risk assessment—Perform a comprehensive fraud risk assessment.

Step 3: Fraud-related controls—Select, develop, and deploy preventive and detective fraud control activities.

Step 4: Report and correct—Establish a fraud reporting process and coordinated approach to investigation and corrective action.

Step 5: Monitor and improve—Monitor the fraud risk management process, report results, and improve the process.

This comprehensive approach recognizes and emphasizes the fundamental difference between internal control weaknesses resulting in **errors** (i.e., errors could be due to unintentional human mistakes and/or poorly designed system-related problems) and internal control weaknesses resulting in **fraud**. This fundamental difference is **intent**.

Errors have *no* intent.

Fraud has intent.

Fraud Risk Management Process (continued)

An organization that simply adds the fraud risk assessment to the existing internal control assessment may not thoroughly examine and identify possibilities for intentional acts designed to misstate financial or nonfinancial information, misappropriate assets, or perpetrate illegal acts or corruption.

Implementing a specific and more focused fraud risk assessment as a separate or stand-alone fraud risk management process provides greater assurance that the assessment's focus remains on intentional acts.

Total risk assessment =	Fraud risk assessment +	Internal control assessment
(Two exercises)	(Separate exercise)	(Separate exercise)

COSO's Framework recommends ways in which governing boards, senior management, staff at all levels, and internal auditors together can deter fraud in their organization. Fraud deterrence is a process of eliminating factors that may cause fraud to occur. Applying fraud data analytics can play an important role in fraud deterrence. Deterrence is achieved when an organization implements a fraud risk management process that

- Establishes a visible and rigorous fraud risk governance process where it is a part of corporate governance and the internal control environment. Here, the internal control environment creates the discipline supporting the assessment of risks.
- Creates a transparent and sound antifraud culture.

Fraud Risk Management Process (continued)

- Periodically performs a thorough fraud risk assessment.
- Designs, implements, and maintains preventive and detective fraud-related control processes and procedures.
- Takes swift action in response to allegations of fraud, including, where appropriate, actions against those involved in wrongdoing.

The focus of fraud data analytics is on fraud prevention, detection, and response (correction). It uses tools such as data mapping, data matching, data mining, data visualization, text mining, web scraping, data dashboards, statistical analyses (e.g., discovery sampling), link analysis, and social media platforms. These tools are in addition to the traditional tools of inspecting, tracing, observing, counting, reconciling, comparing, and contrasting.

FRAUD ANALYTICS

Data analytics is applying quantitative and qualitative tools and techniques to big data in order to gain new insights and new opportunities. Analytics help either individually or collectively in detecting and preventing fraudulent activities. Various types of data analytics are discussed next.

Predictive Analytics

Predictive analytics is the process of estimating future outcomes based on the analysis of past data and/or current data. It describes what could happen. For example, the U.S. Department of Health and Human Services has applied the following analytic techniques to identify improper payments and fraudulent activities perpetrated by healthcare providers (bad actors) in its Centers for Medicare and Medicaid Services.

- A rules-based technique filters fraudulent claims and associated behaviors with predefined rules. It identified providers that bill using a Medicare identification number that was previously stolen and used improperly.
- An anomaly-based technique detects individual and aggregated abnormal patients versus a peer group. It identified providers that bill for more services in a single day than the number of services that 99% of similar providers bill in a single day.

Predictive Analytics (continued)

- A predictive-based technique assesses against known fraud cases. It identified providers that have characteristics similar to those of known bad actors.
- A network-based technique discovers knowledge with associative link analysis. It identified providers that are linked to known bad actors through addresses or phone numbers.

  For example, these predictive analytics can be applied to any industry:

  - Identifying new revenue opportunities by products or by markets
  - Forecasting workforce requirements by type and skill
  - Identifying the factors leading to employee satisfaction and productivity
  - Identifying factors for customers' filing a fraudulent claim
  - Discovering the underlying reasons for employees' attrition rates
  - Predicting what type of customers will default on a loan payment or credit card payment
  - Predicting employee turnover rates
  - Predicting equipment breakdowns before they disrupt operations

Embedded Data Analytics

Many organizations are using embedded data analytics, such as data visualization tools, reporting routines and methods, and data dashboards, in their business-oriented application systems, providing a real value to end users of such systems. Embedded analytics is a part of predictive analytics and predicts future events and outcomes. Compare the embedded data analytics to the traditional data analytics where the latter presents past events and outcomes.

Forensic Data Analytics

The focus of fraud-related forensic data analytics is on fraud prevention, detection, and response (correction). It uses tools such as data visualization, text mining, web-scraping tools, data dashboards, statistical analysis (e.g., discovery sampling), link analysis, and social media. These tools are in addition to the traditional tools of inspecting, tracing, observing, counting, reconciling, comparing, and contrasting. Usually business rules, such as a dollar amount of claims or the frequency of claims, are used to detect fraud.

Streaming Data Analytics

Streaming data analytics is performed in real time and in memory where it collects data from electronic sensors to produce time-series data. The use of streaming analytics increases as machine-generated data sources increase. Temporal analysis, which is based on the concept of time and which is a part of streaming data analytics, helps to understand the different scenarios that are based on changing times. For example, a retail store selling, activating, or redeeming thousands of gift cards within a short period of time (e.g., three to four hours), which can be an indication of fraud, or a sudden surge of activity, is an application of streaming data analytics. Here, the gift card activity is unusual and abnormal thus indicating fraud.

Data stream processing presents current events as they are occurring. Compare the streaming data analytics to the traditional data analytics and embedded data analytics where the traditional data analytics present past events and where the embedded data analytics predict future events.

Traditional Data Analytics ⟶ Shows Past Events

Streaming Data Analytics ⟶ Shows Current Events

Embedded Data Analytics ⟶ Shows Future Events

Social Media Data Analytics

Social media analytics takes thousands and thousands of data items from online posts, followers, fans, page views, reviews, comments, pins, and mentions in various social media websites to evaluate marketing campaigns, advertisements, and promotions and to conclude what marketing efforts worked and what did not work.

Web-Based Data Analytics

Web scraping is a web-based data extraction and data mining approach. For example, it can search Twitter, a social media network, for keywords relating to fraud.

Text-Based Data Analytics

Text analytics focuses on prescriptive analytics and descriptive analytics, where they focus much on written materials and mobile text messages using short message service (SMS) and multimedia message service (MMS). Text analytics also includes information from web call-center notes, comment fields posted on social media platforms, traditional reports, customer inquiries, web chats, and print books. Text-based data are unstructured data and are useful as a text-mining tool to detect fraud-related words on various data sources.

Open-Source Data Analytics

Open-source analytical tools and techniques are available, including open-source software, interoperable systems, and data-sharing facilities, at low cost or no cost. The open-source algorithms can be consolidated in a central location to allow for ease of access across several organizations to identify fraud, waste, and abuse. Moreover, the use of open-source tools could lessen the challenge of developing licensing agreements for proprietary software tools. Open-source data libraries could help in audits, inspections, and investigations.

Data Modeling Analytics

Data modeling analytics means building data models, using simulation models, and testing them with what-if questions to see their answers in the form of changing outputs (outcomes) when inputs to the model change.

Visual Analytics

Visual analytics uses data visualization tools, such as line, bar, scatter, bubble, and pie charts, to present relationships among big data in an easy-to-understand format. Senior managers prefer visual analytics, similar to data dashboards.

Descriptive Analytics

Descriptive analytics describes what already happened and includes content analysis and context analysis.

Content analysis is a set of procedures for transforming unstructured written material into a format for analysis. It is a methodology for structuring and analyzing unstructured written material in documents and reports. For example, two or more documents can be analyzed to discover a fraud-related content using specific words, symbols, names, events, outcomes, and addresses.

For example, using text-data analytics, governmental agencies are looking at social media platforms for specific words posted or commented to identify terrorist activities; to discover fraudulent activities in the food stamp program; and to pinpoint fraud, waste, and abuse in healthcare payments.

Context analysis is possible because data can be contextual, meaning some data is related to a specific context (in context). Hence, to analyze data trends and patterns, a pool of data must be separated into in-context data and out-of-context data.

Examples of in-context data include insurance companies analyzing claims data during natural disasters, and retail companies analyzing sales data during holiday shopping seasons, such as Thanksgiving, Christmas, and New Year's Eve; analyzing sales data during special promotions lasting one week (e.g., blast sales, flash sales, or tent sales); and analyzing sales data during a season (in context) and nonseason (out of context) if the focus is on seasonal sales.

Prescriptive Analytics

Prescriptive analytics helps decide what should happen and thrives on big data. When faced with a number of potential decisions, it analyzes for the best possible outcome.

Two examples include optimal allocation of a company's stock market portfolio after considering expected returns and dividends and airline companies determining ticket prices after considering travel variables such as customer demand, travel timings, travel locations, and holidays (e.g., ticket prices are higher during holidays).

First-Digit Tests

As part of fraud investigations, internal auditors can apply **Benford's law** or the first-digit test to detect unusual data patterns arising from human errors, data manipulations, or fraudulent transactions. If the first digit is 1 in a financial account number or business transaction number, chances are good that it is a naturally occurring number (i.e., fraud-free). If the first digit is 9, chances are good that it might be a purposefully assigned number (i.e., fraudulent) to perpetrate fraud. The test looks into the first digit of account numbers to see if it is 1 or 9 because the digit 1 occurs in that location 30% of the time while the digit 9 occurs in that location only 5% of the time. In general, lower numbers (1–5) are known to be fraud-free more often than the higher numbers (6–9), which are known to be fraudulent on the scale of 1 to 9.

FRAUD AND THE INTERNAL AUDITOR

The roles and responsibilities of internal auditors in fraud prevention and detection are often filled with confusion and controversy due to misconceptions and incorrect expectations about the complex roles and responsibilities of auditors. The roles and responsibilities of an organization's internal auditors and management are listed next.

- Auditors need to be familiar with how fraud is initiated and committed in their organizations.
- An organization's internal control system provides the primary assurance with respect to fraud prevention and detection, not the internal audit function, not an individual auditor, and not a group of auditors.
- An organization's management is fully responsible for fraud prevention and detection because management planned, designed, developed, tested, and implemented the entire internal control system, whether it is a manual system or an automated system.
- Auditors have the professional responsibility to evaluate fraud exposures and to evaluate the capability of the internal control system to prevent and detect fraud.
- Auditors must accept responsibility for those irregularities resulting from their failure to report known weaknesses in the system of internal control.

FRAUD AND THE INTERNAL AUDITOR (CONTINUED)

- Auditors cannot detect fraud when (1) irregular transactions were not recorded and no evidence of traceability and accountability exists; (2) isolated transactions occurred with infrequent frequency; and (3) irregular transactions were concealed by collusion.
- Auditors have the professional responsibility to report to the company's audit management, senior management, board of directors, and the audit committee when a fraud is suspected during the course of their routine and regular audit work.
- Auditors have the professional responsibility to exercise due professional care by considering the probability of significant errors, irregularities, fraud, or noncompliance issues.
- When in doubt, auditors have the responsibility to apply additional audit tests and reviews to determine if fraud has actually occurred.
- Auditors have the responsibility to remember the principle of relative risk, meaning that costs to detect fraud should not exceed the benefits from detecting fraud.
- In summary, internal auditors cannot guarantee the prevention and detection of fraud, just as the board of directors cannot guarantee the effective and efficient functioning of corporate governance processes and mechanisms.

RISKS TO INTERNAL AUDIT ACTIVITY

Like other functions, the internal audit function is a risk-prone activity, as there is no function in an organization that is risk-resistant. Risks to internal audit activities fall into three broad categories: audit failure risks, false assurance risks, and reputation risks.

Audit Failure Risks

In addition to control breakdowns and fraud occurrences, the internal audit activity itself could be a contributing factor to audit failures due to its own doing. Problems could involve auditors:

- Showing negligence in performing their professional work.
- Not following professional standards.
- Not identifying high-risk auditable areas during the planning of individual audits.

Audit Failure Risks (continued)

- Not paying attention to fraud alerts and red flags.
- Not doing the right audits at the right time.
- Wasting resources on doing the wrong audits at the wrong time.
- Not delivering a quality audit product.

Specific causes leading to audit failure risks include these failures:

- Failure to design effective internal audit procedures to test the "real" risks and the right controls.
- Failure to evaluate both the design adequacy and the control effectiveness as part of internal audit procedures.
- Failure of adequate internal audit supervision.
- Failure to exercise professional skepticism and judgment.
- Failure to undertake extended internal audit procedures related to negative findings or control deficiencies.
- Failure to communicate fraud suspicions to the right people at the right time.
- Failure to assign competent auditors to perform complex audit engagements.

Audit Failure Risks (continued)

Remedies to address the audit failure risks include:

- Periodic reviews of the audit universe and audit plan.
- An effective audit planning process and audit design of the system of internal controls.
- Escalation procedures within the internal audit activity indicating when and what types of issues to escalate to which level of audit management's hierarchy.
- Ensuring that high-risk audit engagements are staffed with auditors possessing a combination of right experience, knowledge, skills, competencies, or talents (i.e., right mix of audit resources with a blend of hard skills and soft skills).
- Ensuring that lead auditors have strong project management skills to complete an audit engagement on time and within the budget.
- Implementing an effective QAIP conducting internal assessments and external assessments.

False Assurance Risks

False assurance is a level of confidence or assurance based on perceptions or assumptions, not on facts. False assurance risk results when auditors are unknowingly overselling themselves or underperforming and making empty promises to audit clients who take those promises very seriously and who hold auditors accountable for what they promised. Simply put, false assurances result from what was said, when it was said, and how it was said. Examples of empty promises or false assurances that could raise **expectation gaps** include phrases like "We will take care of it," "We will help you, don't worry about," or "I will talk to my audit management and let me see what I can do for you."

Specific causes leading to false assurance risks include:

- Not keeping the proper mental distance between auditors and audit clients.
- Not monitoring an auditor's independence and objectivity issues.
- Not clearly defining and documenting the auditor's roles and responsibilities (role gap) when business units request the audit staff's help in implementing a new computer system project in accounting department or analyzing customer service department's problems with product warranty and guarantee claims (loaned audit resources).

False Assurance Risks (continued)

- Not communicating scope inclusions (what is covered, in scope) and scope exclusions (what is not covered, out of scope) in the audit's work when conducting risk assessments, developing internal audit plans, and performing internal audit engagements (expectation gap). Auditors need to realize that they may have a role gap and expectation gap in the minds of audit clients.

  Auditors' role gap = Audit clients' perceived role of auditors – Auditors' actual role

  Auditors' expectation gap = Audit clients' expected deliverables – Auditors' actual deliverables

  Loaned audit resources can create false assurance risks, in part due to expectation gaps.

  Remedies to address the false assurance risks include:

- Communicating frequently and clearly to all the affected parties about the auditors' role, their professional mission and mandate, and adherence to the professional *Standards*.
- Communicating scope inclusions and exclusions in every audit engagement project.
- Documenting "project risk" information at the beginning of a project describing the types and sources of risks a project is facing, including its risk immunity levels (risk resistant or risk prone) and risk sensitivity levels (sensitive or insensitive).
- Installing a "project acceptance" process at the beginning of a project where auditors document their specific roles and project outcomes and deliverables, the type of project risks being handled, the type of audit talent and competencies required or available, and the independence of auditors.

Reputation Risks

Reputation risks primarily deal with positive or negative impressions or images of auditors in the eyes of audit clients. Positive image can take many years to earn, whereas it takes very little time to earn a negative image; it can be gained through one high-profile and high-impact adverse event. Both audit failure risks and false assurance risks in combination can result in reputation risks, as they are interconnected.

Reputation risks = Audit failure risks + False assurance risks

For example, when auditors are assigned to a business function to assist its day-to-day work due to that function's staff shortages or to participate in a special project of considerable duration (say three to six months), these auditor-loaned resources can create false assurance situations and reputation risks. This is because nonauditors think that auditors are highly experienced and highly knowledgeable people carrying a strong "brand" name for perfection and excellence and that they never make mistakes. When something goes wrong in an auditor-assisted work, auditors are the first ones to be blamed for problems because auditors are outsiders and because it is assumed they do perfect work and that they know, or should know, everything. Examples of loaned audit resources can be found in the accounting, finance, treasury, corporate tax, insurance, and loss prevention departments.

Reputation Risks (continued)

Specific causes leading to reputation risks include:

- Using auditors as loaned resources to other business functions, whether short term or long term.
- Auditors' behavior and performance as loaned resources in other business functions and the associated impressions and images left on the minds of employees and managers of that business function.
- The auditors' inability to understand, protect, and maintain their own strong audit "brand" name (goodwill), leading to credibility issues (**credibility gaps**). There is a clear connection between the reputation gap, role gap, expectation gap, and credibility gap, as shown:

  Reputation gap = Role gap + Expectation gap + Credibility gap

Remedies to address the reputation risks are listed next.

- Training all internal auditors about the scope and nature of false assurances, reputation risks, and brand name protections.
- Educating auditors in that each auditor is a source for creating or de-source for eliminating audit failures, false assurances, and reputation risks.

Reputation Risks (continued)

- Conducting a self-audit of the internal audit department by outsiders, similar to what internal auditors do at an internal audit-client location.
- Maintaining an audit incident log describing all the audit failures, false assurances, and reputation issues and not revealing the auditors' names and locations.
- Posting, publicizing, and notifying every internal auditor about the lessons learned from recent observations and experiences regarding audit failures, false assurances, and reputation risks.
- Installing a suggestion box system within the internal audit department for improving or removing audit failures, false assurances, and reputation risks.
- Selecting internal auditors for job rotational assignments in nonaudit functions (job rotations) based on a careful blend of hard skills and soft skills they possess and those that can protect internal audit's brand reputation. Note that it requires the CAE to be open-minded (transparent), forward-thinking, and proactive in nature for maintaining an audit incident log, similar to a security incident log maintained in the IT function. The security incident log documents all the data security breaches and cyberattacks that occurred on data files and websites respectively.

THE IIA'S THREE-LINES-OF-DEFENSE MODEL

Similar to information systems security requiring multiple layers of defense (i.e., security controls using defense-in-depth and defense-in-breadth concepts) to protect technology assets (e.g., computers, networks, and mobile devices), organizations need three lines of defense (three layers of defense) to protect and preserve human assets (e.g., employees, customers, suppliers, vendors, visitors, and contractors), tangible assets (e.g., buildings, inventory, plant, and equipment), intangible assets (e.g., copyrights, trademarks, service marks, and patents), financial assets (e.g., cash, stocks, and bonds), and information assets (e.g., data, plans, policies, procedures, and practices). The scope of the three-lines-of-defense model applies to risk management and control activities and processes. The nature of this model includes vigilant employees observing people and things for unusual and strange behavior, manual control procedures, automated control procedures, and daily work rules and practices.

The idea behind the three-lines-of-defense model is that:

- If the first line of defense does not work for some reason, then the second line of defense comes into play to protect and preserve the assets.
- If the first line and second line of defense do not work for some reason, the third line of defense (last line of defense) should work in protecting and preserving the assets.

The concept behind the three-lines-of-defense model is that two hands are stronger than one hand and that multiple lines of defense provide a much stronger support and protection than a single line of defense. This model can be installed at two levels: organization-level and internal audit-level.

Organization-Level: Three Lines of Defense

Examples of organization-level three lines of defense follow:

First line of defense:	Operational and functional management working in manufacturing, marketing, merchandising, procurement, information technology, human resources, accounting, loss prevention, finance, and operations departments. This first defense is a form of initial exercise of controls through management controls and internal control measures. This defense is provided by risk owners and managers who own, manage, and oversee risks. These risk owners implement corrective actions to address process weaknesses and control deficiencies.
Second line of defense:	Employees working in compliance function, health and safety department, customer service department, technical support group, environmental management, IT security analysts, physical security guards, legal staff, risk analysts, financial control analysts, product quality inspectors, internal quality assurance providers, and external quality assurance providers. This second defense is a form of intermediary exercise of controls and provides risk control and compliance.

Organization-Level: Three Lines of Defense (continued)

Third line of defense:	Internal auditors, physical security guards, fraud specialists, public relations officers, insurance claims adjusters, and corporate gatekeepers (e.g., accountants, auditors, and attorneys). This third defense is a form of final exercise of controls and provides risk assurance.
Fourth line of defense:	Although not officially and explicitly defined, external auditors and regulatory auditors can be treated and recognized as providing fourth-line-of-defense services. These outside auditors can be asked to provide a separate and comprehensive review of an organization's risk management framework and practices (e.g., ERM), to assess the adequacy of the three lines of defense, and to report their review results to senior management, the board, and shareholders.

Both the second line and third line of defense provide oversight and/or assurance services over risk management. The key difference between the second and third lines is the concepts of independence and objectivity of internal auditors. (Source: Internal Audit and the Second Line of Defense, IPPF's Supplemental Guidance, Practice Guide, IIA, January 2016, www.theiia.org).

Responsibilities may become blurred across internal audit function and second-line-of-defense functions when internal auditors were asked to assume second-line-of-defense activities due to their special skills and talents. Examples of these assumed activities include new regulatory requirements (e.g., assistance in training and

Organization-Level: Three Lines of Defense (continued)

implementation of Sarbanes-Oxley Act of 2002 (SOX 2002), change in business (e.g., entry into new markets, new products, and new line of business), resource constraints (internal auditors are requested to fill the staffing and management gap), and efficiency in performing compliance and risk management functions better than the others.

Where safeguards to maintain internal audit's independence and objectivity are not possible, the responsibility for performing the second-line-of-defense activities should be reassigned to an internal non-audit function or outsourced externally to a third-party provider. Moreover, the second-line-of-defense activities performed by internal audit should be referenced in the audit's charter document and/or included in the board update report issued at least annually by the internal audit department.

Internal auditors should avoid activities that compromise their independence and objectivity, including:

- Setting the risk-appetite levels
- Owning, managing, and overseeing risks
- Assuming responsibilities for accounting, business development, and other first-line-of-defense functions
- Making risk-response decisions on the organization's management behalf
- Implementing or assuming accountability for risk management or governance processes
- Providing assurance on second-line-of-defense activities performed by internal auditors

Audit-Level: Three Lines of Defense

Similar to the three lines of defense found at the organization level, internal audit activity has three lines of defense or three layers of defense within its own department or function, as follows:

First line of defense	Staff auditor who is assigned to an audit engagement (engagement auditor), who developed the audit program, who prepared audit workpapers, and who drafted the initial audit reports can act as the first line of defense. Signoff letters received from the engagement auditor after completing the audit work support and strengthen the audit work.
Second line of defense	In-charge auditor or lead auditor who reviewed the audit program, workpapers, and audit reports to confirm adherence to the audit plan, objectives, and scope can act as the second line of defense. Signoffs received from the in-charge auditor or lead auditor support and strengthen the audit work completed.
Third line of defense	Audit supervisor or manager who reviewed the audit plan, audit program, workpapers, and audit reports to confirm adherence to the IIA's *Standards*, including the audit quality assurance standards, can act as the third line of defense. Signoffs received from the audit supervisor or manager support and strengthen the audit work completed. Note that the audit supervisors and managers should act as the last line of defense (last resort) because there is no one after them to protect and defend the audit work.

AUDIT METRICS AND KEY PERFORMANCE INDICATORS

Internal audit activity is a function requiring a measurement of its performance similar to other functions in an organization. Audit metrics and KPIs are self-checks for internal auditors to measure and manage progress of their own performance levels. Audit metrics and KPIs can be organized, structured, and monitored in terms of management KPIs, operational KPIs, strategic KPIs, professional KPIs, financial KPIs, and board-level KPIs.

Management KPIs

- Time to complete an audit engagement in hours or days (time to audit in hours or days).
- Average time to complete an audit engagement in hours or days (average time to audit in hours or days).
- Elapsed time between the audit fieldwork completion and audit report issuance. Longer time periods require improvements.
- Average time to issue audit reports in days or weeks. This measures how much time was taken to issue an audit report after an audit engagement was completed.
- Time since the last audit (in years). This actual time should be compared with the planned audit cycle time, and proper actions should be taken.

Management KPIs (continued)

- Elapsed time between the audits (in years). This actual time should be compared with the planned audit cycle time, and proper actions should be taken.
- Time to take corrective actions by audit client management regarding audit recommendations. Longer time periods require audit monitoring and follow-up.
- The longest time an auditor's job is open for months, quarters, and years.
- The shortest time an auditor's job is open for months, quarters, and years

Operational KPIs

- Percentage of the annual audit plan completed. Higher percentages indicate successful audits while lower percentages indicate unsuccessful audits, where the latter results in residual risks.
- Percentage of actual risks addressed, assured, or covered to the total number of risks discovered or uncovered. The difference results in an assurance gap.
- Percentage of audit reports issued as scheduled or planned. This shows that the audit activity can deliver its reports on time and that it is disciplined in doing so.
- Percentage of follow-up audits conducted as scheduled or planned. This indicates auditors' lack of seriousness and shows that auditors are there just to make recommendations and that they are not serious about whether they help the organization that they work for. It is a sign of disservice to the organization.
- Percentage of recommendations implemented resulting from internal assessments and external assessments regarding the internal audit activity's QAIP program.

Strategic KPIs

- Percentage of audit recommendations accepted by audit clients at a point in time. This indicates the usefulness (benefit) of audit recommendations to audit clients.
- Percentage of audit recommendations rejected by audit clients at a point in time. This indicates the nonuse of (no benefit) of audit recommendations to audit clients.
- Percentage of audit recommendations implemented after they are accepted by audit clients at a point in time. This indicates that audit recommendations are practical and useful.
- Percentage of unimplementable audit recommendations after they were accepted by audit clients at a point in time. This indicates that audit recommendations are theoretical in nature with no practical benefits.
- Percentage of significant audit recommendations (vital few of 20/80 rule) to the total number of audit recommendations made in a year. This indicates that internal auditors are clearly adding and enhancing value to their organization.
- Percentage of insignificant audit recommendations (trivial many of 20/80 rule) to the total number of audit recommendations made in a year. This indicates that internal auditors are not at all adding value to their organization.

Professional KPIs

- Percentage of auditors certified in internal auditing with the CIA designation.
- Percentage of auditors with audit-related multiple certifications.
- Average number of professional certifications held by auditors.
- Average number of continuing professional development hours earned in a year by auditors.
- Average number of auditors' work experience in years in internal auditing.
- Percentage of technology auditors to nontechnology auditors.
- Average turnover of audit staff in a year.

Financial KPIs

- Percentage of audits completed over the budget.
- Percentage of audits completed under the budget.
- Variance analysis between budgeted hours and actual hours.

Board KPIs

- Percentage of independent directors to total board members. The goal should be a higher percentage in the industry.
- Percentage of a company's executives on the board to total board members. The goal should be a smaller percentage in the industry.
- Percentage of shadow directors to total board members. The goal should be a zero percentage because shadow directors (e.g., outsiders such as lobbyists, activists, friends, family members, consultants, and majority shareholders) can exercise greater pressure on and influence over the board.
- Percentage of nonexecutive directors to risk management committee members. The goal should be a higher percentage because executive directors, such as chief executive, chief financial, and chief risk officers, can exercise greater influence on the risk committee, which is not good for the company.
- Percentage of independent directors to audit committee members. The goal should be a higher percentage because the audit committee oversees the entire financial reporting process and coordinates between internal auditors and external auditors, which is a major responsibility. The audit committee should not oversee the risk management and regulatory compliance functions as they are the responsibilities of senior management (executives).

Board KPIs (continued)

- Percentage of female directors to total board members. The goal should be a comparable percentage in the industry and nation's data.
- Percentage of directors with little or no compensation or remuneration paid. The goal should be a zero percentage because it follows the simple principle of no money, no work. Two outcomes are possible here: say on pay and no pay, no say. Without a comparable compensation and remuneration, directors are hired just for their names only to act as a rubber stamp for the CEO; they simply become routine box-checkers in their work, and they have no strong voice (or no teeth) in the board's matters and decisions.
- Percentage of board-level qualitative metrics to the total number of board-level metrics. Total metrics include both qualitative and quantitative metrics, which should be given equal importance. Examples of quantitative metrics include: (1) sales, revenues, profits, market share, company stock prices year over year; and (2) earnings per share and returns on investment, assets, equity, and capital. Examples of qualitative metrics include: low employee morale; negative comments posted on social media by unhappy customers; and cyber-, supply chain, product recall, public relations, and customer dissatisfaction risks.

CHARACTERISTICS OF EFFECTIVE AUDITORS AND AUDIT FUNCTION

In general, effectiveness means achieving the stated mission, vision, goals, objectives, plans, programs, or activities in the most economical manner after considering their costs and benefits. In this section, we present characteristics that define internal auditors as effective and the internal audit function as effective; they are not the same.

Characteristics of Effective Auditors

A list of characteristics that can define internal auditors as effective is presented next. Note that the list is not all-inclusive. Effective auditors can make an audit function effective due to their professionalism and competency levels.

Effective auditors possess competencies and skills in these areas:

- Business acumen
- Critical thinking
- Communications
- Basic legal and ethical principles

Characteristics of Effective Auditors (continued)

- Audit and legal evidence
- Forensics and investigations
- Analytical and functional knowledge
- Assurance services and consulting services
- Risk management and insurance
- Sampling and statistics
- Information technology in systems development and systems security
- Big-data analytics and data mining
- Industry knowledge

  Effective auditors acquire the core knowledge of the business or industry they work in. This means possessing:

- Business acumen when working for business organizations.
- Core knowledge about how a government operates when working for governmental agencies.

Characteristics of Effective Auditors (continued)

- Core knowledge about academic world (e.g., schools, colleges, and universities) when working in educational institutions.
- Core knowledge about how hospitals and medical research institutions operate when working in healthcare industry.
- Core knowledge about how nongovernmental organizations (NGOs) operate when working for NGOs.

It is very difficult for auditors to understand, operate, and contribute when they do not have the required core knowledge of their work.

- Effective auditors adhere to professional standards and possess the required core business knowledge combined with the right mix of business skills (hard skills and soft skills) to implement such professional standards. Up-skilling auditors is the major focus here (i.e., unskilled auditors must be up-skilled, reskilled, and cross-skilled).
- Effective auditors play several roles, such as:
    - Trusted advisors
    - Control assessors

Characteristics of Effective Auditors (continued)

  - Control evaluators
  - Cyberadvisors
  - Internal business consultants/partners to the board of directors (board) and senior management (company executives and officers)
- During their work in providing assurance and consulting services, effective auditors can link:
  - Audit strategy to business strategy.
  - Audit objectives to business objectives.
  - Audit risks to business risks.
  - Audit value to business value.
- Effective internal auditors can work with external auditors in coordinating and communicating during standard assurance services (e.g., financial audit) and special services, such as during governance, risk, and control reviews.
- Effective auditors pay equal attention to financial reporting (revenues, costs, and profits) and nonfinancial reporting (e.g., operations, marketing, legal, ethical, and social improvements and issues).

Characteristics of Effective Auditors (continued)

- Effective auditors are independent in appearance and action and are objective in mind and in reporting their work results.
- Effective auditors can use data analytics techniques and data mining software tools to assess data integrity and security controls over databases, data warehouses, and data marts.
- Effective auditors can use statistical analyses, such as regression analysis, factor analysis, cluster analysis, link analysis, and correlation analysis, to detect fraudulent transactions.
- Effective auditors can use data analytics and data mining software tools to assess the overall control environment after identifying systemic breakdowns in controls.
- Effective auditors can use big-data analytics as a part of their analytical reviews conducted during audit planning and engagement work.
- Effective auditors apply critical thinking skills and possess judgment rules when collecting and analyzing audit evidence and when reaching audit conclusions and recommendations. They know the differences between:
    - Strong evidence and weak evidence.
    - False evidence and true evidence.

Characteristics of Effective Auditors (continued)

  - Good conclusions and bad conclusions.
  - Big recommendations (vital few) and small recommendations (trivial many).
  - Value-creating opportunities and value-destroying events.

  An auditor's recommendations must be big in scope, size, and significance.

- Effective auditors are good at identifying or differentiating between value-creating and value-destroying plans, programs, policies, procedures, and practices. This can save an organization from undertaking value-destroying plans. The same thing applies to value-adding tasks and activities and non-value-adding tasks and activities.
- The chief audit executive (CAE) wears several hats, such as supervisor, manager, leader, change agent, coach, mentor, delegator, motivator, inspirer, agile performer, and above all futurist.
- Internal auditors are effective when they treat audit clients and outside auditors with respect, dignity, and humility during their interactions in audit work and nonaudit work.

In summary, effective auditors are value creators, value enhancers, change agents, team players, agile performers who are resourceful and competent, and business partners with other members of the organization while they also maintain their independence and objectivity standards.

Characteristics of Effective Audit Function

A list of characteristics that can define an internal audit function as effective is presented next. Note that the list is not all-inclusive.

- An audit function is effective only when its auditors are effective. This means auditors must be effective first.
- An effective audit function follows and encourages auditors to adhere to professional standards when conducting audit work. Any deviations from standards are explained or permissions to exceptions are obtained.
- An effective audit function:
  - Performs continuous planning of audit work.
  - Schedules audit resources for audit engagements.
  - Supervises or manages audit engagements.
  - Conducts auditors' performance appraisals.
  - Provides continuing education programs to auditors.
  - Conducts succession planning moves for senior audit management.
  - Coaches audit supervisors, senior auditors, and staff auditors about career plans and paths.

Characteristics of Effective Audit Function (continued)

- Effective audit planning focuses on:
  - Traditional assurance services (e.g., reviewing policies, procedures, and systems for compliance).
  - Consulting services (e.g., consulting auditors offer advice and insight in reviewing business processes and practices to improve their performance, productivity, and progress).
  - Value-for-money (VFM) audits (e.g., focusing on the three *E*s—economy, efficiency, and effectiveness—to ensure maximum utilization of resources and to prevent and detect fraud, abuse, and waste of resources).
  - Agile audits (e.g., small-size, short-time, target-based, and focus-based reviews with quick results on critical issues).

VFM audits require auditors to wear an industrial engineer's hat focusing on the 4*M*s: men, machines, money, and materials. Industrial engineers are often called efficiency experts. Expertise drives the three *E*s.

- An internal audit function is effective when it develops yearly audit plans with a major focus on target-based (agile), strategy-based, and risk-based audits in addition to cycle-based, operational-based, compliance-based, performance-based, and schedule-based audits (repeat/routine audits).

Characteristics of Effective Audit Function (continued)

- An effective audit function manages audit resources through budgeting, reporting, monitoring, and feedback.
- An effective audit function supports and strengthens the core business functions, such as operations, marketing, and finance through its audit work, analysis, findings, conclusions, and recommendations for improvements. It provides outside-in views and perspectives to a business function with fresh mind and new outlook as if it manages that function.
- An effective audit function acquires the required audit talent through a combination of in-sourcing, co-sourcing, and outsourcing methods as needed to complete an audit engagement. For example, some technical and complex skills (e.g., information technology, engineering, actuarial science, and statistical knowledge) are not needed in every auditor as long as the audit team as a whole possesses such skills. Audit talent is needed in cybersecurity (e.g., data breaches and ransomware attacks), emerging technologies (e.g., bitcoins), artificial intelligence (machine learning), robotics, business analytics with big data, business intelligence, and data mining).
- An effective audit function is an internal business partner with other functions of a business in terms of:
    - Focusing on value-creating tasks and separating non-value-added activities from value-adding activities.
    - Focusing on risk identification and risk mitigation efforts.

Characteristics of Effective Audit Function (continued)

  - Implementing best practices or metapractices in governance, risk management, and control.
  - Recommending implementation of cost-effective and time-sensitive continuous controls (automated and manual).

- An effective audit function obtains 360-degree feedback from audit clients or audit stakeholders, such as internal customers (e.g., audit committee members and senior and functional managers) and external customers (e.g., external auditors, bank examiners, and regulatory auditors). Kano principles can be applied to this feedback process using three rating scales, such as satisfied, neutral, and dissatisfied for measuring the effectiveness of internal audit. Each rating must give reasons and explanations. In a way, the Kano principles validate what the audit stakeholders value the most.
- The internal audit function is effective when outside auditors (e.g., external auditors, bank examiners, and regulatory auditors) and inside nonauditors (e.g., risk officer, compliance officer, quality auditor, environmental auditor, and control assessor) rely on the work performed by the internal auditors. This reliance can be achieved through coordination and cooperation efforts between these parties and due to the effect of economies of scope and size here. Reliance leads to assurance, as shown next.

Low reliance = Low assurance

High reliance = High assurance

Characteristics of Effective Audit Function (continued)

- An effective and efficient internal audit function establishes a quality assurance and improvement program to add value, improve an audit organization's internal operations, and gain credibility in the eyes of third parties and outsiders.
- The audit function is effective when it is performing value-adding audits, not doing nitpicking audits, not focusing on fault-blaming audits, and not conducting error-seeking audits. This requires conducting audits outside of typical accounting and financial areas, such as:
  - Sales and marketing
  - Human resources
  - Capital planning and budgeting projects
  - Business process improvement projects
  - Production and supply-chain operations
  - New product/service development projects
  - New systems development projects
  - New contract development projects, including outsourcing contracts
  - Mergers, acquisition, and divestitures projects

Characteristics of Effective Audit Function (continued)

- The CAE in partnership with legal counsel and the ethics, compliance, and risk officers must conduct a governance audit to ensure that the board:
  - Addresses long-term strategy with goals and objectives.
  - Reviews the compensation and benefit programs to the chief executive officer (CEO) and other officers and executives.
  - Focuses on the board's reputation.
  - Looks into succession planning for key officers and executives.
  - Identifies separation-of-duties problems between the CEO and the board chair.
  - Focuses on the board's composition (i.e., inside, outside, and shadow directors).
  - Recognizes conflict-of-interest situations (i.e., abuse of insider information and management scandals).
  - Reviews risk management, control, and compliance matters.

Characteristics of Effective Audit Function (continued)

Reputation management deals with risks and exposures facing the board resulting from the board's own practices, philosophies, operating styles, litigations, and public statements. It deals with the board's overall image in the eyes of senior management of the company, stakeholders of the company, affected regulators and bankers; and the public at large (e.g., strong board or weak board, ethical board or unethical board, effective board or ineffective board, or good reputation or bad reputation).

- Prior to making the decision to outsource the internal audit function, the audit committee and the CAE of the outsourcing organization should conduct cost-benefit, reputation risk, and T-account analyses (i.e., listing the pros on one side of T and the cons on the other side of T).
- The entire internal audit function will be effective when its internal policies, procedures, practices, processes, and operations are streamlined, simplified, and standardized to provide quick responses and faster results to management with agility to increase performance and productivity and to show progress.
- Effective audit function develops and maintains an audit test model or audit test lab for repeated use as a template to gain the benefits of economies of scale. This model contains audit test scripts, test beds, test data, test cases, and test results for use in various audit test scenarios. This model saves time, energy, and frustration from not having to repeat or start all over again for each audit (i.e., benefits). One-time audits, routine audits, ad hoc audits, special audits, continuous audits, and agile audits are the best candidates for the application of this audit test model.

Characteristics of Effective Audit Function (continued)

- An effective audit function develops and maintains an audit dashboard tool (i.e., audit reporting tool) to show various items of interest to management, including audit progress reports, actual versus budgeted spending, and actual audit plan completion versus estimated audit plan completion.
- An internal audit function is effective when it establishes escalation procedures for resolving any differences of opinion between audit staff/management and organization management (audit clients) concerning reported audit findings and recommendations.
- An internal audit function is effective when it establishes a tracking system to track and monitor all open-audit issues accompanied with aging analysis showing the number of days the audit issues are open and are not addressed or implemented.

In summary, an effective audit function always looks for continuous improvement regarding its scorecard or metrics reporting to the board and senior management (i.e., audit clients and audit stakeholders).

SARBANES-OXLEY ACT OF 2002

The SOX Act contains provisions affecting the corporate governance, auditing, and financial reporting of public companies, including provisions intended to deter and punish corporate accounting fraud and corruption. The SOX Act generally applies to those public companies required to file reports with the Securities and Exchange Commission (SEC) under the Securities Act of 1933 and the Securities Exchange Act of 1934 and registered accounting firms. Visit www.pcaobus.org or www.aicpa.org for SOX.

Specifically, the SOX Act required publicly traded companies to establish a system of internal controls over financial reporting, similar to the Foreign Corrupt Practices Act of 1997 (FCPA) and the Federal Deposit Insurance Corporation Act of 1991 (FDIC). Under the SOX Act, a company management has to establish, assess, and report on the issuer's system of internal controls over financial reporting, and auditors must report on the effectiveness of that system of internal controls. Studies show that better internal controls result in better financial reporting and more investor confidence in financial reports. The SOX Act contains 11 titles and several sections within each title. This appendix contains only the titles and sections that are of interest to internal auditors.

Title I—Public Company Accounting Oversight Board

Section 101: Public Company Accounting Oversight Board Establishment and Administrative Provisions

Establishes the Public Company Accounting Oversight Board (PCAOB) to oversee the audit of public companies that are subject to the securities laws.

Section 102: Registration with the PCAOB

Requires accounting firms that prepare or issue audit reports to public companies to register with the PCAOB.

Section 103: Auditing, Quality Control, and Independence Standards and Rules

Requires the PCAOB, by rule, to establish auditing and other professional standards to be used by registered public accounting firms in the preparation and issuance of audit reports.

Section 104: Inspections of Registered Public Accounting Firms

Requires the PCAOB to annually inspect registered public accounting firms with more than 100 issuer audit clients and to triennially inspect registered public accounting firms with 100 or fewer issuer audit clients.

Section 105: Investigations and Disciplinary Proceedings

Requires the PCAOB to establish fair procedures for investigating and disciplining registered public accounting firms and associated persons and authorizes the PCAOB to investigate and discipline such firms and persons.

Title II—Auditor Independence

Section 201: Services Outside the Scope of Practice of Auditors

Registered accounting firms cannot provide certain nonaudit services to a public company if the firm also serves as the auditor of the financial statements for the public company. Examples of prohibited nonaudit services include bookkeeping, appraisal or valuation services, internal audit outsourcing services, and management functions. Specifically, the act prohibits a public company from outsourcing its internal audit to its external auditor since doing so would lead to a potential conflict-of-interest situation for the external auditor.

Title III—Corporate Responsibility

Section 301: Public Company Audit Committees

Listed company audit committees are responsible for the appointment, compensation, and oversight of the registered accounting firm, including the resolution of disagreement between the registered accounting firm and company management regarding financial reporting. Moreover, this section establishes certain oversight, independence, and funding requirements for the audit committee. The SEC issued rules to issuers that prohibit any national securities exchange or national securities association from listing the securities of an issuer that fails to comply with these audit committee requirements.

Section 302: Corporate Responsibility for Financial Reports

For each annual and quarterly report filed with the SEC under the SEC's Exchange Act, the CEO and CFO must certify that they have reviewed the report; that, based on their knowledge, the report does not contain untrue statements or omissions of material facts resulting in a misleading report; and that, based on their knowledge, the financial information in the report is fairly presented.

Section 303: Improper Influence on Conduct of Audits

This section requires the SEC to issue rules prohibiting officers and directors, and persons acting under their direction, from fraudulently influencing, coercing, manipulating, or misleading the issuer's independent auditor for purposes of rendering the issuer's financial statements materially misleading.

Section 304: Forfeiture of Certain Bonuses and Profits

The issuer's CEO and CFO have to reimburse the issuer for any bonus or compensation and profits received from sale of securities during the 12-month period following the filing of a financial document that required an issuer to prepare an accounting restatement due to misconduct or material noncompliance. Here the compensation can be either incentive based or equity based. This reimbursement is called a clawback provision. Where material noncompliance has occurred with the SEC's securities laws, it forces the CEO and CFO to forgo compensation stemming from financial restatements made because of wrongdoing. First, a captive insurance policy, if available, can cover the wrongdoing claim. Later it can extend to compensation, bonuses, and incentives to pay for the remainder of the wrongdoing claim. This wrongdoing can create a personal reputation risk to the CEO and CFO.

Section 306: Insider Trading during Pension Fund Blackout Periods

- The SEC prohibits the directors, officers, and executives of a company from purchasing, selling, or transferring any equity security of their company during a pension plan "blackout period" for that security, which is three consecutive business days. These prohibitions apply only if the securities acquired or disposed of by the director, officer, or executive were acquired in connection with his or her service or employment with the issued company. The following transactions are exempted from the statutory trading prohibitions:
    - Acquisitions or dispositions of equity securities involving a bona fide gift or a transfer by will or the laws of descent and distribution
    - Acquisitions or dispositions of equity securities in connection with a merger, acquisition, divestiture, or similar transaction occurring by operation of law
    - Increases or decreases in equity securities holdings resulting from a stock split, stock dividend, or pro rata rights distribution

The blackout period is the period in which the company refrains from repurchasing its own shares because of insider trading concerns.

Section 308: Fair Funds for Investors

The civil penalties can be added to the disgorgement fund for the benefit of the victims of a security law violation. A disgorgement sanction requires the return of illegal profits.

Title IV—Enhanced Financial Disclosures

Section 401: Disclosures in Periodic Reports

The SEC issues rules that prohibit issuers from including misleading pro forma financial information in their filings with the SEC or in any public release. The SEC requires that issuers should not have to reconcile any pro forma financial information with the issuer's final financial statements prepared in accordance with generally accepted accounting principles (GAAP). This means that professional care and good judgment should be used when preparing pro forma financial information.

This section also requires disclosure of off-balance-sheet transactions, arrangements, and obligations (including contingent liabilities) and changes in financial condition, revenues, expenses, results of operations, liquidity capacity, capital expenditures, or capital resources.

Section 402: Enhanced Conflict-of-Interest Provisions

This section places prohibitions on personal loans to executives, directors, or officers of a company. It makes it unlawful for any issuer, either directly or indirectly, to extend, maintain, or arrange for the extension of credit in the form of a personal loan to these officers. However, this Act does not preclude any home improvement and manufactured home loans, any extension of credit under an open-end credit plan, a charge card loan, or any extension of credit by a registered broker or dealer. In addition, this Act does not apply to any loan made or maintained by an insured depository institution unless the loan is subjected to the insider lending restrictions.

Section 404: Management Assessment of Internal Controls

This section consists of two parts. First, in each annual report filed with the SEC, company management must state its responsibility for establishing and maintaining an internal control structure and procedures for financial reporting; it must also assess the effectiveness of its internal control structure, including controls over financial reporting and the results of management's assessment of the effectiveness of internal control over financial reporting.

Second, it also requires the firms that serve as external auditors for public companies to attest to the assessment made by the companies' management and report on the results of their attestation and whether they agree with management's assessment of the company's internal control over financial reporting.

This section requires the SEC to issue rules that require all annual reports filed under the SEC's Exchange Act to include certain statements and assessments related to the issuer's internal control structures and procedures for financial reporting.

Section 406: Code of Ethics for Senior Financial Officers

This section requires the SEC to issue rules about (1) disclosing whether the issuer has adopted a code of ethics for its principal executive officer (CEO), principal financial officer (CFO), principal accounting officer, or controller and, if not, the reasons why such a code has not been adopted and (2) promptly disclosing any change to, or waiver of, the issuer's code of ethics. The board of directors must approve any waivers of the code for directors, executives, or officers of the organization.

Section 406: Code of Ethics for Senior Financial Officers (continued)

The SEC rules define **codes of ethics** as written standards that are reasonably necessary to deter wrongdoing and to promote:

- Honest and ethical conduct, including the ethical handling of actual or apparent conflicts of interest between personal and professional relationships.
- Full, fair, accurate, timely, and understandable disclosure in reports and documents that a company files with, or submits to, the SEC and in other public communications made by the company.
- Compliance with applicable governmental laws, rules, and regulations.
- The prompt internal reporting of code violations to an appropriate person or persons identified in the code.
- Accountability for adherence to the code.

Section 407: Disclosure of Audit Committee Financial Expert

Public companies must disclose in periodic reports to the SEC whether the audit committee includes at least one member who is a financial expert and, if not, the reasons why the audit committee does not include such an expert. This financial expert must be independent of management.

Section 407: Disclosure of Audit Committee Financial Expert (continued)

The financial expert on the audit committee must possess the following major attributes:

- An understanding of:
  - Financial statements and GAAP, including their application to accounting for estimates, accruals, and reserves
  - Internal controls and procedures for financial reporting
  - Audit committee functions
  - Experience in preparing, auditing, analyzing, or evaluating financial statements

The financial expert can be a principal financial officer, principal accounting officer, controller, public accountant, or external auditor but not an internal auditor. The SEC rules will provide a safe harbor provision to make clear that an audit committee financial expert will not be deemed an "expert" for any other purpose; it does not impose any duties, obligations, or liabilities that are greater than those imposed on a normal audit committee member.

Major Improvements in the SOX Act

According to the PCAOB, the following is a list of major improvements made to the SOX Act in the 10 years since its inception from 2002 and until 2012.

- It restored investor confidence.
- It established the PCAOB, ending more than 100 years of self-regulation by the accounting profession.
- It dealt with the conflicts of interest in the accounting profession by prohibiting accounting firms from performing certain auditing and consulting services for the same company the firm was auditing. For example, it prohibited an accounting firm from setting up a valuation system for valuing financial assets and then auditing that system.
- It mandated independent audit committees and required issuers to disclose whether a "financial expert" is available on the audit committee. Today, an internal audit function must report functionally to an independent audit committee.
- It increased corporate accountability and dealt with tone at the top by requiring CEOs and CFOs to personally certify their companies' financial statements.
- It instituted clawback provisions, requiring CEOs and CFOs to give up bonuses or other financial incentives based on financial results that later had to be restated or were fraudulent.

Major Improvements in the SOX Act (continued)

- It essentially ended the backdating of stock options. Backdating is a misrepresentation of the dates on which stock options were granted to executives and employees during the course of their employment with a company. Through backdating, it does not appear to the outside world that the option grants were approved with a fake retroactive date when the company's stock prices were the lowest, although the actual approved date is much later, when the stock prices are higher. Backdating is a management fraud, resulting in an artificially low exercise price for stock options that could lead to financial restatements.

About the Author

S. RAO VALLABHANENI is an educator, author, publisher, consultant, and practitioner in business with more than 30 years of management and teaching experience in auditing, accounting, manufacturing, and IT consulting in both public and private sectors. He is the author of more than 60 trade books, study guides, review books, monographs, audit guides, and articles in auditing and IT, mostly to prepare for professional certification exams in business. He holds 24 professional certifications in business management in the fields of General Management, Accounting, Auditing, Finance, Information Technology, Manufacturing, Quality, and Human Resource. He taught several undergraduate and graduate courses in business administration and management programs at the university level for many years. He earned four master's degrees in Management, Accounting, Industrial Engineering, and Chemical Engineering.

Index

C

F

G

N

O

Q

R